Trance-Portation

Trance-Portation

Learning to Navigate the Inner World

Diana L. Paxson

WEISERBOOKS
San Francisco, CA / Newburyport, MA

First published in 2008 by
Red Wheel/Weiser, LLC
With offices at:
665 Third Street, Suite 400
San Francisco, CA 94107
www.redwheelweiser.com

ISBN: 978-1-57863-405-7

Library of Congress Cataloging-in-Publication Data available upon request.

Cover design by Maija Tollefson
Typeset in Eidetic Neo, Scala Sans, and Priori Serif
Cover photograph © Spectral-Design/iStockphoto

Printed in the United States of America

10 9 8 7 6 5 4 3 2

Acknowledgments

This book could not have been written without the contributions, insights, and support of many members of my community. I am especially grateful to Lorrie Wood and to Dr. George Hersh for suggestions and comments throughout the text, and to all those who shared their experiences in the training.

Contents

Introduction

When I was in college, many of my friends were involved in the charismatic Christian movement. I used to go with them to services, sitting in envious silence as they babbled away. Clearly they were having an ecstatic experience, but no matter how I strained, I found it impossible to let go. When I met Marion Zimmer Bradley, I joined the Aquarian Order of the Restoration, a Ceremonial Lodge that she and her husband had founded in the sixties. I loved the rituals, but when other members spoke of their past lives, their possessed trances, and their prophetic dreams I was silent, convinced that the only role I could fill in the Order would be to keep an eye on the candles and guard the door.

It was not until I took a course in self-induced hypnosis from Harvey Foreman that I began to suspect I might not be hopeless at trancework after all. I had assumed I was learning nothing because I was not taking notes, and I seemed to fall asleep whenever he began to narrate a meditation. But one afternoon when my niece got a leg cramp and started to go into hysterics, I found myself launching into a hypnotic induction to calm her. Apparently some part of my mind had been listening, and if that could happen, it might be worthwhile seeing what else I could learn.

And so I began a process of chipping away at my mental blocks that has continued for more than thirty years. Eventually I realized that this slow progress was actually an advantage, as it gave me the time to observe the process and identify the stages by which one gains the ability to work in trance. Understanding the steps, I have been able not only to teach those who, like me, find their spirits too well armored, but to slow down the process for people who are shaken by every psychic breeze.

Today, every city has a metaphysical bookstore, and "New Age" is a publishing category. In the sixties, when researchers such as Charles Tart were just beginning to explore consciousness, books imported from England, the already venerable Weiser Books, and the newly founded Llewellyn were the only sources for material on the esoteric. Those who wanted to learn trance work haunted used bookstores, hoping that some dusty volume by Dion Fortune or W. E. Butler would turn up in the bin. But the times were changing, and from the sixties to the present an ever-increasing flood of material from a wide variety of traditions (and varying widely in value) has filled booksellers' shelves.

Just as the writings that came out of the Western Mystery Tradition from the thirties through the fifties tried to incorporate into their explanations of occult phenomena the new theories of psychology that were becoming popular, in the sixties, Timothy Leary's experiments with LSD inspired research (with or without drugs) into what scientists like Tart called "Altered State of Consciousness," or ASCs. This was a term for all those states of mind in which one feels not merely a *quantitative* change or shift in degree of alertness or other awareness, but also ". . . that some quality or qualities of his mental process are *different.* Mental functions operate that do not operate at all ordinarily, perceptual qualities appear that have no normal counterparts, and so forth" (Tart, 1969). As he observed, Western culture has tended to view non-ordinary states as undesirable, if not downright pathological. However the research into ASC that began in the sixties opened up the field, and the spread of meditation techniques from Asia made such practices popular.

This is nothing new. Interest in ways of transcending ordinary consciousness, whether we call it trance work, occultism, parapsychology or the latest neo-shamanic teaching, has ebbed and flowed since the nineteenth century, which saw the emergence of the Spiritualist Movement, Christian Science, and the Western Mystery Tradition, exemplified by the short-lived but highly influential Order of the Golden Dawn. All three traditions taught that there is more to reality than the physical world, and that with practice one could learn to experience and transform it. In the thirties, inheritors of the Golden Dawn tradition such as Dion Fortune and her Society of the Inner Light sought to interpret and teach psychic skills in the light of new scientific concepts. Fortune's work, which lays out the principles of occultism, has been in and out of print ever since. In the fifties and sixties, W. E. Butler, who had been her student, wrote a series of little books discussing training methods for esoteric skills appropriate for people living in a Western (i.e., First World) culture. This approach is the foundation for the exercises presented in this book.

These books were written with the assumption that the reader is interested in ceremonial magic, and is, if not still a practicing Christian, then still Christian by affiliation. Today's community of practicing pagans would have filled Mr. Butler with amazement. Nonetheless, these books by Fortune and Butler are based on a great deal of hard experience, and if you can find copies, well worth reading as an amplification of the material in this book. Unlike earlier works, which confined themselves to esoteric theory, the material that came out of Fortune's tradition embedded instructions for training one's psychic abilities in the text. What was missing from the published work was an organized sequence of training exercises.

After having worked with the Western Mystery Tradition in general and the (Western Esoteric) Kabbalah for many years, I felt the need for a magical practice that would be more solidly based in Earth spirituality. *The Way of the Shaman* by Michael Harner had just appeared, followed by a number of other books on shamanism. I found that my previous training in guiding meditation enabled me to lead "shamanic" journeys.

As traditions that seek a more culturally focused and authentic practice have emerged on the neo-pagan scene there has been a certain amount of debate regarding the value of Harner's work. From his later writings, it is clear that Harner and his students are aware that what they are teaching is not traditional shamanism–nor was it ever intended to be. Instead, he has done a brilliant job of extracting from the shamanic practices of many cultures the core elements they have in common, and adapting these for use by contemporary Western practitioners in much the same way that the earlier Occultists developed the Western Mystery Tradition.

Since then, my research has included a deeper exploration of traditional shamanism, and I have ranged widely over the esoteric teachings of many cultures. The focus of my own spiritual practice began with Goddess spirituality, and has continued with intensive work in Northern European (Ásatrú) and Afro-Diasporic spiritual practices, including oracular and possessory trance. For the past twenty years I have taught classes and led rituals on the average of two or three times a month, adapting and refining the basic trance skills to help others seek spiritual guidance and increase the effectiveness of our work. These skills, which have empowered all my spiritual practice, are presented here.

I originally began teaching trance techniques as preparation for oracular *seidh,* the Norse tradition of oracle work described in the Viking sagas. For a weekend workshop, the exercises had to be pared down to a bare minimum, and it soon became apparent that the students who were most likely to be able to build on the workshop material and develop their own oracular practice were those who were already trained in shamanism or other spiritual disciplines. Clearly there was a need for a more extended form of the training. More recently, deity possession (also known as aspecting or drawing down) has become more prevalent as well as more popular–especially in the pagan traditions which seek to reconstruct the religions of specific cultures–and we have found that developing good trance discipline makes this kind of work safer and easier as well. In my opinion, basic trance skills are a prerequisite to success in any of the more specialized kinds of spiritual and magical work. Once this book is available I hope it will serve as a foundation for additional books on oracle work and deity possession.

In 2002 I announced the first trance class and worked with a talented and enthusiastic group of people to practice and revise and expand the exercises. As I wrote the handouts, we also experimented with distance learning, e-mailing the material to various people all over the country, who then participated in discussion with those in the live-action class between meetings via the class e-list. In 2003 two graduates of the first class, Lorrie Wood and Bella Crow, conducted the beta-test of the materials to see how they worked when taught by someone other than me. This class also generated many ideas that have been incorporated into the system. In 2007, a gamma-test was conducted by Ember Leo, Hilary Ayer, and Dave Schultz, to whom I am indebted for additional notes and suggestions.

This book is designed for use in solo study, but as I have noted above, the exercises were originally written for use with a class. The student comments quoted at various points in the text will give you an idea of the insights that can come out of group discussions, in person or online. Every learner is different, and despite my best efforts, this book does not cover every possible way of addressing the material. When someone was having trouble dealing with one of the exercises, very often another student would come up with an idea that helped with the problem. Some found that the shared energy of a group makes it easier to move into an altered state. It is certainly easier to keep working when you realize that you are not the only one who finds some of the skills hard to learn. Even if you are not able to join or lead a class, you may find it useful to recruit a "trance buddy" as a companion on the road. If you do wish to form a group for study, you will find "Notes for the Tour Guide" in appendix I.

The goal of this book is to teach skills that underlie the spiritual practices of a variety of traditions, from the ceremonial to the shamanic. But acquiring the "gifts of the spirit" cannot be an end in itself.

They have to be used. Eastern spiritual traditions teach that the purpose of spiritual transformation is to free the soul from the Wheel of Karma so that it can escape the world. Those few who, like Kuan Yin, refuse to accept permanent union with the Divine until all living creatures can share it are considered boddhisattvas. As Evelyn Underhill points out in her classic work *Mysticism,* in the West even contemplatives have found in their ecstatic union a mandate to turn around and try to transform the world.

We are all born with the potential to use our inner senses as well as our outer ones, to transcend the limitations of the selves we thought we knew. This is the Way of Power, but rather than seeking *power over* others, through this training we seek the *power to* help others do the same, and in doing so, to nourish, rather than stunt, our own souls.

Chapter One

Travel Planning

A journey of a thousand miles must begin with
a single step.

Lao Tzu, *Tao Te Ching*

We are about to begin a journey. Some parts of it will be easy, filled with the delight of discovery. You will speed along and wonder why you never found this road before. At other times, you may hit roadblocks or detours and wonder if you will ever get where you want to go. Do not lose heart. As Robert Louis Stevenson once put it: “To travel hopefully is a better thing than to arrive, and the true success is to labor” (1881). With time and patience, you will find that the road itself is as interesting as its end, and the things that you learn along the way are as rewarding as those you hoped to gain when you began.

The road may lead ever on and on, but, unlike Bilbo, a sensible traveler does not dash out the door with no more than a pocket handkerchief. Before you can range freely through all the worlds, you must have at least a basic understanding of the geography. As you set out to explore, you must have a realistic understanding of your resources and abilities.

To make progress, you will need to work through all the chapters and exercises of this book in order. Even, or especially, if you already have a given skill, you must practice it regularly–several times a week–for about a month, or until you feel ready to go on. Those with more experience may actually find some of the early lessons harder, as they may have old habits to unlearn. However, you will find that these skills, once mastered, are useful in themselves and may provide a foundation that can support the practice of more esoteric skills like oracular and possessory work.

As you work your way through the exercises, you will be offered options. Most occult and spiritual traditions require those they train to master their own methods for meditation and trance work. The approach to trance work presented here requires a systematic mastery of skills, but leaves the means by which you accomplish this up to you. No single approach works for everybody. The motto of Mills College, where I spent four very happy years, is *Una destinatio, viae diversae*–"One destination, many roads." This has always seemed to me to be good advice for the spiritual, as well as the physical, traveler.

As anyone who has taken music lessons knows, there are sequences of fingering that seem difficult at first, but are necessary if you want to get past the easy pieces. Continual practice helps you develop a sequence of responses that automatically come into play when needed. Learning this sequence is like learning to shift gears on a car. At first, you need to look at the diagram; but with practice, you automatically move the knob in the correct pattern while your conscious mind focuses on avoiding the accident that has just occurred up the road.

Consciousness

Dion Fortune described magic as "the art of causing changes in consciousness at will" (Butler, 1952). On his Web site, Isaac Bonewits expands on this by calling magic "a general term for arts, sciences, philosophies and technologies concerned with (a) understanding and using various altered states of consciousness within which it is possible to have access to and control over one's psychic talents, and (b) the uses and abuses of those psychic talents to change interior and/or exterior realities. . . ."

What do we mean by "consciousness"? The word ordinarily refers to a particular level of brain activity at which we can intentionally respond to stimuli, communicate, and understand what is going on around us. "He's regaining consciousness . . ." in a medical setting indicates the moment when a patient opens his eyes and rejoins the world.

But neurologists chart many different kinds of brain activity. Clearly, the mind is doing something even when it is not communicating. Some of this activity involves thought; some may not. In sleep, for instance, we dream in the REM state. For most people, dreams come and go at their own will, and if we are lucky (or in some cases unlucky), we remember them. However, some people have developed skill in "lucid dreaming"–moving into a dream state while retaining some awareness that they are doing so, and exercising some control over the experience. I realized the connection between that ability and those we can use while awake when, some years after I became a professional writer, I found myself editing my own dreams. Some people simply train themselves to remember their dreams by articulating a firm intention to do so before falling asleep, and keeping a notebook or recording device handy to capture their memories when they wake.

The kinds of consciousness experienced at various stages of sleep are well known and considered normal. Also within the "normal" range are a variety of states in which we focus on one activity to the exclusion of other awareness. This kind of hyper-focus is particularly familiar to people with a talent for working with computers–"programmer's trance" has enabled many a programmer to transcend normal needs for sleep and food in order to meet a deadline. For a novelist, the moment may come when the work stops feeling like pulling teeth and becomes an exhilarating and rewarding ride in which the story carries you along. In its more extreme forms, the compulsion to hyper-focus can become a master rather than a servant, and may be a result of Asperger's syndrome. People with this tendency may have an easier time with some aspects of trance work, but may have difficulty developing flexibility and control.

Anyone who has driven from one point to another without any memory of the journey has been in an altered state. In these instances, your conscious mind is concerned with its own affairs while some other part directs your body. When you are absorbed in a movie or a good book, time passes without your awareness. You exist in the world of your imagination, and the demands of your body are suppressed. Only when you finish the book, or when some stimulus jerks you back to "reality," do you realize that your neck hurts or that a visit to the bathroom is long overdue. Runners strive for their own kind of altered state, in which there is no reality but the smooth flex of muscle that carries them over the ground. Training for other sports induces its own kind of trance state, in which action and being are one.

In ordinary conversation, the word "consciousness" is used to mean the beta-wave state in which we spend much of our waking hours. In this state, our awareness is outward-directed; we react, communicate, and understand what is going on in the physical world. Psychology and philosophy, on the other hand, do a pretty good job of complicating what we think of as the simplest and most accessible state of consciousness. As Ned Block puts it: "the Hard Problem of consciousness is how to explain a phenomenon in terms of its neurological basis. If neural state N is the basis of the sensation of red, why is N the basis of that sensation rather than some other experience or none at all?" (Block, 2003).

Neuroscience continues to explore what goes on in the brain when we act, think, and feel, without conclusively answering this question. It is more practical, perhaps, to define ordinary consciousness as the state in which we not only process external stimuli, but are sufficiently aware of our own bodies to respond to our environment and be aware of that awareness. In this state, you not only can go about your daily activities; you can contemplate aspects of yourself perceptible to others, like your appearance, and those that are purely personal, like your feelings. "Meta-self-awareness" is the state in which you not only have a feeling, but know that you are feeling it (Norin, 2004). From the literature, it is apparent that even what Michael Harner calls "consensus reality" is capable of extensive subdivision and analysis.

Trance

The limitation of consciousness, powerful focus, and the liberation of the unconscious are all part of normal human experience. How, then, do we define the altered states that we call trance? We encounter this term, not only in discussions of religion or magic, but in areas such as music and psychology as well. Historically, however, the context in which people are most likely to seek an alternative way of experiencing reality is spiritual—what my friend Ember has dubbed "altared" consciousness. The literature of all religions includes techniques for prayer and meditation whose purpose is to bring peace or put people in contact with their gods. The training methods developed in Asia for yoga and the *Spiritual Exercises* of St. Ignatius Loyola are two examples of highly developed spiritual training systems. In magical practice, trance states are used for a variety of purposes, from enabling people to perceive beings or energies that are not noticed (as opposed to not *present*) in ordinary consciousness, to creating or journeying in "inner" worlds, to setting the human personality aside and allowing another to move in. When we engage in trance work, we intentionally alter the way we experience the world.

Fortunately, or unfortunately, what we will be referring to in this book as "trance" includes a variety of states of consciousness about which science has had relatively little to say. The phrase "altered state of consciousness" used by Charles Tart for those mental states in which people feel that the quality of the way in which they experience the world is different from ordinary awareness comes closest to describing what I mean here.

Altered states of consciousness include a wide variety of experiences, many of which most readers will already have encountered without seeing any necessity to give them a name. In addition to the state of mind in which you know you are aware, you may, on any given day, experience a variety of levels involving the limitation of consciousness through focus on other things–reading, working on a computer, running, or driving a car. When you are enthralled by a book or a movie, you feel the emotions and thoughts of the characters rather than your own. Many activities require a mental focus so complete that you lose awareness of yourself and your body as well.

We perceive all these activities as ordinary. Everyone engages in them. Dreaming, for instance, is an altered state that we all experience spontaneously. For some people, the boundaries between the waking world and the inner realities are thin. Others have difficulty remembering even those visions that occur while they are sleeping. But everyone dreams, whether or not they remember it. I contend that anyone who can enter the world of dreams can, with training, access altered states at will and exercise control over what happens while they are in them.

When our minds are anchored in our bodies, physical factors play a role in how they behave. Any traveler contemplating a strenuous journey will take his or her physical condition into account when planning. Factors like blood sugar, hormones, sleep, biorhythms, and general physical condition can affect your ability to go into (or stay out of) trance. However, we must remember that, although we are all the same in many ways, we each have distinct characteristics that affect how we will respond to the exercises. In other words, at any point in the lessons, your mileage may vary. This is to be expected, and does not imply a value judgment regarding your ability.

Who goes into trance? Everybody. As we have seen above, everyone experiences some altered states spontaneously. The ability to shift from one level of consciousness to another is wired into the human brain. But if we define trance as those states that are *not* part of most people's experience, we begin to find a broader spectrum of abilities. Virtually all humans can use their hands to make marks with a pencil and their voices to make sounds. But some have a "natural" ability to draw recognizable pictures or to sing on key. For them, becoming an artist or a singer is easy. With the right kind of training, however, almost anyone can learn to draw or sing.

We find the same range of abilities in trance work. For some people, getting beyond what Michael Harner calls "consensus reality" is very difficult, whereas others seem to have trouble staying connected to the ordinary world. Some call those for whom trance is so easy as to sometimes become a problem "trance sluts" and those who are so firmly grounded they feel stuck to the floor "cement heads." We find "open-heads" and "closed-heads" a more friendly way to indicate the ends of this continuum. In fact, most people fall somewhere in the middle, depending on a variety of factors–including everything from body mass to psychological history, and such physical variations as blood-sugar levels, physical condition, and biological cycles. Age may also have an influence–children are often more open than those who are older.

Those who believe their heads are "closed" should not envy those whose heads are naturally "open," and the latter should not wish their feet were nailed to the ground. Those whose dominant mode of perception is aural or kinesthetic are no less talented than those who work primarily with visual imagery. With experience, we learn to identify levels of consciousness and what we can do with them. By developing those skills that do not come easily, we learn to travel in all terrains and all weathers.

Crazy Wisdom

Those of us who feel the call to practice magic or walk a spiritual path are moving out of the safe world of consensus reality. Although the curriculum at Hogwarts bears little resemblance to any kind of real magic, the psychological divide between the Muggle and Wizard cultures is something that most of us have experienced. We must accept the fact that many consider those who intentionally loosen their grip on ordinary reality crazed. For many years, ethnographers studying shamanic practice assumed that the shamans were crazy. And sometimes they were right. A case in point is the story of the anthropologist who went looking for a shaman and ended up interviewing the village idiot.

Of course there are times when the idiot is the wisest man in the room.

Don't let these messages from the dominant culture deter you, but rather use them as a signal for healthy self-examination. A runner pays attention to odd twinges that may signal a problem; you should do the same. You must distinguish the problems caused by psychic work from those stemming from physiology or personal history. "Mind over matter" does not mean that matter can be ignored. The purpose of self-evaluation is to make you aware of the kinds of things that can have an effect on spiritual work. "Know thyself" is not only the goal of philosophy; it is also the foundation of magic.

Given that caveat, we'll take a practical approach to psychic experience. Rather than asking whether something is "real," let's ask whether it is *useful*. The bottom line in distinguishing a functional from a dysfunctional experience is to learn whether it helps you live and work productively. A problem in the work is a signal for some serious consideration. Is this a wake-up call? A symptom of spiritual emergence? Does this mean that you've just found one of your psychological "buttons"? Or did you forget to eat lunch today? Even a traumatic experience can be helpful if it is caused by a "thwop" of the Divine "clue-by-four." As you explore the practices in this book, you will be remodeling your mind. As is common in such projects, the process may make a bigger mess than you expect before you begin to see improvement. Keep a record of your progress and your process. When in doubt, get regular "reality checks" from people who know you well and wish you well, and whose judgment you respect.

Cumulative Learning

The key to controlling trance work is to use cues and conditioning. When you are conditioned to go into trance in response to a certain stimulus, you move into that state *only* when that cue is given. Conditioning helps you control your state of consciousness. It also gives an inexperienced or blocked individual the sense of security needed to "let go." Because our minds manifest through our physical bodies, the outside world provides us with stimuli and images that can be used in the world within. The worlds of trance are a symbolic reality.

This book will help you condition yourself to respond to specific cues so you can reach a specific state of consciousness if and when you want to–*and return*. This is the equivalent of a physical-fitness program, in which you develop specific muscle groups in a certain order so they will respond correctly. A disciplined body can dance or climb a mountain because the muscles obey the will. A disciplined mind can travel between the worlds.

You understand the physical world pretty well, or at least you are sufficiently accustomed to it to navigate it safely. For most people, however, the contents of the unconscious are a mystery. Carl Jung's voluminous writings describe his explorations of the collective unconscious–a treasure house of symbols and patterns that are apparently part of the inherited human "software." Another source of awareness comes from the culture and environment in which we live.

Each individual also has a personal store of significant images, however. As Paul Edwin Zimmer puts it (Zimmer, 1979):

> The womb in the head waxes and blooms,
> Begotten by every book bedded down by,
> Dwelling in darkness, dreaming, swelling,
> By some stranger's seed in the soul kindled . . .

You are the sum of all that you have met, and all that you are becomes accessible to you, for good or for ill, when you journey into non-ordinary reality.

To do this successfully, you must understand how to manipulate that reality. You must also understand the physical, psychological, and social factors that can affect your ability to do spiritual work. I call this "evaluating flight status." When you seek to dissociate from "ordinary consciousness" safely, self-knowledge is as important as conditioning.

The first step in planning your trip is to take stock of your resources by filling out the self-evaluation questionnaire below.

Practice: Self-evaluation Questionnaire

Answer these questions thoughtfully and thoroughly. When you have completed the work and finished the book, review your answers and consider whether any of them has changed. The commentary that follows each question is intended to explain why the question is being asked, and may help you find an answer.

Support Systems

1. **What is your living situation? Do your family or housemates support your spiritual practice? Will they allow you the privacy in which to practice the exercises? If you are in doubt, negotiate, or find somewhere else to work.**
   There is a reason so many religious traditions provide monasteries or retreats for those with a calling to become mystics or adepts. It's hard to focus on spiritual practices while fulfilling the demands of the working world. "Opening up" can be difficult when you need shields against other personalities, even, or especially, when they are people you love. Trance work requires practice. In order to do the work, you need a time and place where you can be free from demands and distractions. This usually means somewhere that is reasonably soundproof and where you can lock the door. Your nearest and dearest need to understand that you are not rejecting them.
2. **Do you belong to a prayer circle, kindred or coven, or other spiritual group? Does it practice trance work or meditation? If so, what kinds? How often? For what purposes? Are any other group members working with this book? Will your group support your efforts to master these skills?**
   Working on spiritual practices with others can be a blessing or a curse. Ideally, this work will increase your ability to contribute to any group with which you work. If the group already has its own system, however, you must adapt the cues suggested here. In some cases, you may have to skip certain practices to avoid confusion.

3. **Do you already have a power animal or totem? How did you acquire it? How often do you contact it, or how does it contact you?**
   If you already have "invisible friends," you have a head start. Call on them to help you with the early exercises. If you don't, you will have the opportunity to find some as you work through this book.
4. **Do you have a strong affinity with/devotion to specific god/desses? How did you acquire them? How often do you contact them, or how do they contact you?**
   What is true for "invisible friends" is true for deities. Involve them in the process, but don't be surprised if, in the course of your study, you find yourself encountering them in new and surprising ways.

Background

1. **How do you make a living? What states of consciousness or mental skills do you use in your job, and how did you learn to attain them?**
   The answer to this question can be very helpful to those who think they spend all their time in one state of consciousness. "Programmer's trance," for instance, is a well-known phenomenon. The changed mind-set that goes with putting on a suit or uniform is also a shift in consciousness.
2. **What other work or hobbies occupy your time? What states of consciousness do you use? How did you learn to attain them?**
   Again, computers come to mind. The adventures in another world provided by interactive role-playing games are good training for inner adventuring. Specific states of consciousness are associated with different sports. Make a list of the ways you spend your leisure time, and consider how the way you feel and think changes for each.
3. **What is your academic training? What kind of thinking did your department teach?**
   Each academic discipline has its own "culture." To enter a profession, you must master not only its knowledge and skills, but its

jargon and ways of thinking. Were you taught to analyze? To look at the facts? To be sensitive to style and modes of expression? To see shapes and patterns?

4. **What strengths or skills do you already have that can help you in trance work? What do you think will be hardest to learn?**
   Those who have studied magical or spiritual practices will have a list, but don't limit yourself to the obvious answers. As for the rest of you, you know more than you think you do. By the time you have answered the preceding questions, you should have some idea what the answer to this one is. Those who are experienced should also consider what habits they may need to unlearn in order to reorganize their thinking.

Physiology and Psychology

1. **What is your general state of health?**
   You should ask yourself this question when starting any new activity. In this case, however, physical strength is important mainly as it affects your ability to sit and concentrate for long periods. Some conditions may also affect your ability to work on skills like counted breathing.
2. **How do you rate your temperament in the following areas? Consider the column on the left to be 1 and the column on the right to be 5. Where do you fall on the continuum?**

calm	lively
forceful	responsive
robust	sensitive

   Your answers here may indicate whether you are an "open" or a "closed" head, but do not worry too much about being typecast. Knowing where you fit on the continuum is more important as a clue to how you should approach some of the exercises.
3. **How do you react to stress?**
   You will be opening a lot of doors, and you may be surprised by what you find behind them. Just as you learn to recognize the

symptoms of an allergic reaction, learn to identify your signs of stress. They can be a signal that you need to ease up, or to look more closely at what you are feeling and why.

4. **Do you have any chronic or cyclical problems or conditions (especially heart, blood-pressure, diabetic, menstrual or menopausal symptoms) that affect your mood, energy, or focus? Are you on any medications?**
   You must be able to distinguish between psychological or psychic and physical symptoms. For instance, if you have any condition that may be affected by changes in heartbeat or blood pressure, you may have to be careful how you work with the breathing exercises. Medications that alter your focus and state of consciousness may affect your ability to concentrate and meditate. Learn to work with your body, rather than fighting it.
5. **How do you react to alcohol or drugs?**
   Mind-altering substances have introduced many to the existence of altered states of consciousness, but they tend to be debilitating and, in some cases, illegal. Nonetheless, having had such experiences may help you recognize the states you are working to achieve through training.
6. **How much and what kind of exercise do you get? And are you eating your vegetables?**
   This may sound snarky, but, for some years, these were among the first questions every spirit or ally I contacted asked. A sound mind functions best in a sound body. Although there are many traditions that require austerities as a path to enlightenment, if you are going to practice trance work while living in the world, you need strength and energy. Eating right and getting exercise improves your ability to do the work.
7. **Have you ever had a life-threatening accident or illness? Did you have any weird experiences during the crisis? Did it change your attitude toward life?**
   Stories about people who suffered ill-health or near-death before discovering (or admitting) their calling are a staple of the literature of shamanism. While most of us have not had visions of

being dismembered and devoured by power animals or the ancestors, life-threatening events change our lives, even when they do not take them.

8. **Have you been in counseling? What kind and for what? How did you respond to it?**
   The occultist Israel Regardie recommended that anyone who intended the serious study of magic should first go through a course of therapy. For most people, learning to open and close access to the unconscious makes it possible to live a more productive, and certainly a more interesting, life. However, this work is very likely to uncover any buried issues you may have. If you have reason to believe this may be the case, I recommend that you also work with a sympathetic therapist.

Skills and Knowledge

How would you rate yourself on the following topics? Excellent? Adequate? Willing to learn?

relaxation
breath control
visualization
lucid dreaming
self-hypnosis
shamanic journeying
sensing and moving energy
divination
folk magic
mythology
shamanism
Jungian psychology

Some of these skills are addressed in this book; others are related skills or areas of knowledge. This list will help you identify what knowledge you have and what you need to know.

Purpose

What are your goals in beginning this training. Why do you want to learn how to do trance work? Once you have learned it, what do you want to be and do?

Write down your own answer to this question, then think about William Butler's statement in the first chapter of *Apprenticed to Magic:*

> You have asked me to train you in High Magic's Way. Why do you wish to be trained? What is your real motive? Do not make the mistake of thinking that this can be answered without a good deal of careful thought. . . . There are, of course, quite good motives for the study and practice of magic, quite apart from the question of vocation. It is a worthy motive to search for truth, *if the results of that search are going to be used in service.* "I desire to know in order to serve," is the motive which admits to the Mysteries (Butler, 1962).

Half a century later, we are still exploring the worlds of the spirit and learning to realize our own potential. If there is a difference between those who first read Butler's book and those who seek this knowledge today, it is that altered states of consciousness are no longer relegated to the realm of the "occult." A community of people who are comfortable with alternative lifestyles and philosophies has emerged. This means that many now believe these experiences are possible and desirable, and also have an immediate and practical need to control and use them. People want to learn trance work for many reasons. Some of my students have had awareness of the unseen thrust upon them, while others are struggling to achieve it. Some found themselves counseling or teaching others, and wanted a better "bag of tools."

The goal of the mystic is to *know*, but the priest or priestess seeks to serve God (or the Goddess, or the gods), and his or her community. This work is healthiest and most productive when you seek "power" to realize your full potential and help others to do the same.

As Lorrie Wood has observed, there are two conditions to this service that you must keep in mind:

Not to serve others at the expense of yourself.
Not to serve yourself at the expense of others.

With these as our watchwords, let us begin.

Chapter Two

Crossing the Threshold

> Most of my treasured memories of travel are recollections of sitting.
>
> Robert Thomas Allen

In earlier times, people often traveled on foot; today, we begin most trips by wedging ourselves into the seat of a car or train or plane. Yet, whether you are traveling in the body or the spirit, you must make certain preparations before the vehicle will move. Most trance work succeeds best when done in a position in which your body feels secure so that your spirit can fly free—the psychic equivalent of fastening a seat-belt. On these journeys, you will not actually leave your body, but you will leave your awareness of it behind. So you need to do your work in a place that is protected both physically and psychically. You must "plug in" to that place, so that you can be sure of returning safely. And you must be relaxed enough that discomfort will not jerk you back to physical awareness.

Some find it useful to protect their space psychically as well as physically by casting a circle and consecrating the area to the work at hand. This is rather like shutting the door and making sure that the car is ready. Just remember that the road you are taking runs at right angles to the rest of your reality.

Altering Consciousness

The first step in trance work is to learn how to move from one level of consciousness to another at will, without making it so easy that you do so involuntarily. The best way to control this is to condition yourself to shift only in response to verbal or kinesthetic "cues."

Shielding

You will find it easier to "open up" if you feel protected. Before you practice these exercises, make sure you will not be interrupted physically. The writer and magician Randall Garrett once observed that the best symbol for a sharp sword is a sharp sword. By the same reasoning, the best symbol for a safe place is a room with a locked door. With practice, you will find that you can enter various trance states while riding the bus or sitting in the dentist's waiting room—indeed, the latter may be one of the *most* useful places to alter your consciousness. As you begin, however, the security of knowing that you will not be disturbed from the outside will make it easier to relax and concentrate on what is going on within. Following the same reasoning, try to work in a room that is as close to soundproof as you can manage. Put a "Do Not Disturb" sign on your door. Turn off the ringer on the phone and turn off your cell phone.

If the room is messy enough to distract you, clean it up. If distracting or destructive energies have been left there, clean it up psychically as well. You usually perceive these energies as a kind of "atmosphere." Some places simply feel depressing or make you nervous. If people have had a bitter argument in a room, you can sometimes feel the leftover anger. Most of the time, however, you won't perceive that energy unless or until you manage to open yourself up to trance. So you have to take it on faith. These energies are like germs–you can't see them, but they can mess you up if they get inside you.

This habit of psychic housecleaning, known in esoteric traditions as the "Labor of Preparation," can be useful. You can help prepare your space by doing some physical housecleaning while affirming that you are also bringing peace and order into the room, even if you do nothing else. The European tradition recommends moving around the space counterclockwise, saying something like: "May all that is negative be gone from this space." Moving counterclockwise, or "widdershins," helps banish that which is evil or unwelcome (except in the Hellenic tradition, in which counterclockwise is the direction used in ritual). To communicate this more clearly to your unconscious, you can actually sweep in a counterclockwise motion with a broom. Other methods involve sprinkling with water or smudging with incense. Voodoo tradition features drawing crosses in the four directions, above and below. This kind of action can also help you make a distinction between the state of consciousness you are trying to enter and your ordinary reality.

Now you need to protect your space psychically as well. You can ward the entire working space, or simply create a personal shield. There are a number of ways to achieve this. Wiccans may cast a circle in a way customary to their coven. Heathens may do a quick Hammer Rite, or chant a rune circle. One simple and basic method that can be used by anyone is to turn clockwise, arm extended, and visualize a circle of light surrounding your working space. Define it as a protective sphere that admits air, light, and positive energy, and keeps out anything that might disturb you. Practice doing this until you can "snap" it into place. People who do magical work on a regular basis may already have their homes so well warded that doing so for meditation seems superfluous. Nonetheless, I recommend at least a token warding to establish the habit.

Some may doubt the existence of malicious spirits, and wonder why all this abracadabra is necessary, or ask how mere visualization can be an effective protection if something is actually there. One answer is that warding has, at the very least, a placebo effect, because it affects your mind and your mind is what you are working with here. However, it is also true that there's no such thing as "mere" visualization–visualization is one of your most important tools. It is not so much a matter of "believing" as "affirming" the reality you want to work with. This is how your conscious mind sends messages to your unconscious. As for malicious spirits, deal with them as you deal with germs. Either they are there and you have not perceived them (yet), or they're not, but protection is a good habit anyway.

Personal warding in a group setting can present some special problems. When everyone is listening to the same guided meditation, their energies are usually in harmony. If you open yourself up completely near others who are doing their own work, however, you may pick up their energies or emotions. One solution is to sit near people with whom you feel comfortable. Another is to create your own personal protective warding within the larger circle. You can adapt the Anglo-Saxon journey charm in exercise 1 for this purpose, or you can simply draw your own personal circle within the larger space.

To develop your skill in personal warding in a group, practice in some public place, like a subway station or shopping mall. Choose a time when the spot is not too crowded and work up to rush hour. Define your circle as a semipermeable barrier that lets images, sound, air, and positive energy in, but repels anything negative. Some find it useful to visualize this shield as an opalescent sphere. Draw your circle and "see" the shield rising to enclose you. Work on this until you feel your awareness of your surroundings muted and dulled, but you are still able to hear things like your train being announced. Eventually, you will be able to do deep meditation while riding the train, cueing yourself to return to ordinary awareness swiftly and safely as you approach your stop, or if there is some emergency.

Exercise 1. The Journey Charm

This *galdor*, or incantation, known as the "Sith Galdor," is adapted from an eleventh-century manuscript (Storms, 1974, no. 16). It was used to protect travelers at the beginning of a journey. Stand in a relaxed, balanced position. You can draw the circle with a staff, a wand, or your finger. "Sig-" is the Old English word for victory; it is associated with the rune "Sigil," which looks like an angular "S" tipped back–ᛋ. With practice, you can do this silently as you turn around.

> With this sphere I gird me round
> *(turn clockwise, drawing a circle around yourself with your finger, wand, or staff)*
> By God's grace may I be bound,
> *(Here you can substitute "Goddess" or the deity of your choice.)*
> Against sore stitch, against sore bite,
> Against all horrors that haunt the night;
> 'Gainst dread that folk fear everywhere,
> And loathly things that here would fare,
> Sig-galdor I chant, a sig-rod is my stay,
> *(Draw a Sigil rune in each direction)*
> Word-sig and work-sig ward today.
> No nightmare do my spirit harm,
> No foe oppress, no fear alarm.
> Nor wight nor weather threaten me,
> From danger defended I will be.
> I bid the good God victory give,
> Guarded so, safe shall I live.

If you begin this work as a "closed-head," you may not be able to perceive any difference in the atmosphere, and will simply have to take it on faith that your warding procedure is doing something useful. In this case, try making a visible, physical difference by sweeping or cleaning up the room. Usually, there will not, in fact, be any negative energy around. However, if you get into the habit of psychically cleansing and warding your space, you will be protected if there ever is any trouble. Think of it as the equivalent of a pilot's preflight check.

Even if you view warding as a placebo, the effect is certainly important. By establishing a good habit, you begin to create your own set of cues. At this stage, it does not matter if you actually make a psychic difference in the space. What is important is that you teach yourself to shift gears.

Grounding and Centering

The next step in preparing for trance work is to ground and center yourself. Relaxation is a part of this process, and some find that they need to pay attention to that first. There are instructions for releasing tension from the body a little farther along in this chapter. Try it both ways—with grounding and centering followed by relaxation, and then by going through the relaxation process as soon as you are seated comfortably, followed by grounding and centering.

As one student put it: "I think grounding and centering is about preparing oneself for the work that one is about to undertake, quieting the mind and body so that it can pick up on other things going on around us that we normally are not aware of. All of existence is alive, constantly moving, creating and destroying, whispering to us the names of our own Gods and Ancestors. We have simply over time become numb to the more subtle parts of existence, more subtle parts of ourselves. Grounding and centering moves us away from the mundane, secular world and tells our mind that we are getting ready to do something that is not normal but, supernatural, it tells us that we need to listen and pay attention 'cause we are in the company of the spirits and of course they have something to say. It is about truly being in the moment and finding who you really are so you can go forth with a clear head and understand what it is that is going on." (Patrick)

Sitting

Before you begin, decide on a position for meditation. Obviously, relaxation is easiest if you are lying down, but for most of us, lying down is already the cue to go to sleep. Since the only time many people have for practice is late at night, when they are already tired, lying down may be a poor idea. In fact, the "sleep training" prescribed for insomniacs requires that the bed be used only for sleeping and sex.

In the Eastern traditions, the standard position for meditation is sitting with your legs crossed. If you are limber enough to do this, it works well. Bodily pain, however, can be a constant distraction and, thus, counterproductive. The Western Esoteric Tradition recommends the seated position seen in statues of Egyptian kings—with your back supported, your feet on the floor, and your arms resting along the tops of your thighs. This is a position that almost anyone can assume easily. The position of your arms transforms it from ordinary sitting to a specific posture, and keeping your feet on the floor helps with grounding.

Balancing

Many people also find that it helps to orient themselves to the four directions. Position your chair so that you are facing one specific direction. If you work in one of the Wiccan or ceremonial traditions, face east. For the Norse traditions, face north. If you are familiar with the principles of *feng shui*, you can use them to set up your meditation space. Or you can simply position your chair in whatever you find to be the most harmonious position in relation to the room.

Sit in your chair, relax, and count your breathing. When you have achieved a slow, steady rhythm, focus your awareness on the movement of your chest as you breathe. Pay special attention to your solar plexus, where your diaphragm expands and contracts with each breath. This is your power center. Take a few moments to sense how the energy pulses with each breath.

Western esoteric traditions usually begin with a salutation to the east, then move clockwise to the south, west, north, and east again. If you work with the four elements, honor each one in turn (you can also do this along with a circle-casting before beginning the meditation).

Exercise 2. Two Simple Forms of Balancing

North and south *(point)*
East and west *(point)*
I am the center, grant me rest. . . .

Another form goes like this:

Before me,
Beside me,
Behind me,
Beside me,
Over me,
Below me
Within me,
Around me . . .

Of course, there are more than four directions. Some people find it useful to balance in relation to "Above" and "Below" as well as the cardinal points of the compass. This has the effect of orienting you in space instead of simply in relation to the ground.

Extending Awareness

Simply put, "awareness" means "what you are paying attention to at the moment." The best analogue I can think of is physical vision. Think of awareness as the psychic equivalent of focus. When you focus on something close at hand, things farther away are blurred, and vice versa (at least until you pass forty, when what's close at hand is blurred until you put on your glasses). You can do something similar with your eyes closed, using all your other senses to give you information about one direction or another. Practice extending your awareness in each direction in turn.

Exercise 3. Extending Awareness

Look in a specific direction, then close your eyes. Imagine you are still looking in that direction, but try to get information with your other senses. What can you hear? Smell? What's the temperature? Is there air movement? When your mental focus is more there than here, your awareness has shifted. If you still have problems "seeing" with your eyes closed, ask yourself what you would be seeing if you could, and imagine that it's there.

Grounding

Our definition of "grounding" is not exactly the same as the definition used in electrical engineering, but the latter can give you some insight into how it works. In engineering, the essential idea is that excess energy is attracted to a conductor, which leads it safely from its source into the earth or some other neutral location. This keeps the energy from frying either you or any of your equipment, such as your computer, that touches its source. In radio communications, the "ground" is a metal object driven or buried in the earth that serves as a reference for radio-frequency antenna signals. This principle also governs the use of the radio antenna or lightning rod, in which the ground conductor transfers the energy from a lightning strike into the earth.

In metaphysics, you can also use "grounding" to discharge excess energy, usually by setting the palms of your hands on the floor at the end of a ritual. You can also use this connection to set up a power circuit between the earth and your body that draws up energies and equalizes their flow. The metaphor also suggests the ground cord that tethers a balloon to the earth, an image that is especially useful for those who are reluctant to "let go" in meditation for fear of floating away. Grounding puts you on a firm foundation.

Exercise 4. A Simple Grounding Technique

Take a deep breath and, as you exhale, let your awareness and your energy sink downward to your solar plexus. As you breathe, take a few moments to sense the movement of your diaphragm. Your solar plexus is just beneath your lower ribs. Pay attention to that area. Each time you exhale, feel heat growing in your solar plexus. Visualize that heat as a ball of light that leaves a glowing ribbon behind it. Hold that heat there as you breathe in and out a time or two. When you are certain of the sensation, with the next exhalation, allow it to sink to your belly, and from there to your buttocks. Focus your attention on the boundary between your flesh and the chair; feel how gravity holds you securely down. When you are ready, let subsequent exhalations carry your awareness further, first to the floor and then beneath it, down through the foundations of the house and deep into the earth below.

Spend a few moments breathing in and out, noting how it feels to have this umbilical energy connecting you to the earth. When you feel yourself firmly rooted, with each inhalation slowly draw your awareness back up again. When you are finished, quicken your breathing and restore sensation to your limbs. Thank whatever powers you have invoked to keep you balanced.

For obvious reasons, this exercise works best if you are sitting or standing. If you are working lying down, move your awareness to the base of your spine and extend it downward from there. The sensation will be a little different, as more of your body will be anchored, but it will stop you from feeling that you are sinking into the earth.

In most locations, this exercise will help you feel extremely steady and secure. You can use this technique to "plug in" to the earth energies of any place you go, and learn to identify the differences. In places where the water table is high, like the Netherlands, grounding on land feels like trying to ground on a boat—the depths beneath you are fluid, and all you can do is throw down an anchor. In a region that is seismically active, like the rift at Thingvellir in Iceland, grounding plugs you into an energy flow that is so active you have to pull your awareness back to the surface and set up some filters in order to do any work at all. Trying to ground at 30,000 feet in an airplane just leaves you floating. In situations like these, forget about grounding; center and balance your energy instead.

You can remain grounded while you do other work, or you can release the connection and reel it back into your center. In some traditions, an exercise of this kind is used to align the body, the intellect, and the spirit in a straight line from earth to heaven before any other work begins.

A quick method for grounding is to focus on the pull of gravity. Allow yourself to feel the weight of your body anchoring you to the earth. You can do this standing or sitting in a chair. Or you can try sitting upright and balancing a book on your head, which will hold you in a balanced position. Feel the weight pressing down the axis of your body to the chair. That's your center.

As one student put it: "There's a common Windows screensaver that's a ball that explodes into lots of little shiny squares, and they spin out, and then come back together into the shape of the ball, only to explode again. . . . To ground and center is to pull myself into that ball, from all those little pieces, only to change direction and push back out again, this time in a different color. When I ground, method aside, I feel that my When and Where are firmly rooted. Wherever else my brain may have been, it is *here, now.* When I Center myself, I am calling all my pieces together, any bits that may have been floating about (perhaps keeping tabs on a relationship, or a task I was performing, for example. . . .). So, now that I am entirely *here*, in the *now*, and *myself*, I can choose to go elsewhere, or be something else. When I am done, before going back out into the mundane world, I need to collect all those parts again (not that I leave them lying around, but perhaps I'm thinking three things at once again), and put them back in the time and place where I belong." (Ember)

If you have trouble mastering the concept of moving the energy up and down from your body to the earth, try the Tree Meditation in exercise 5. This is also a very useful way to calm and reenergize yourself when you are upset or discouraged.

Exercise 5. The Tree Meditation

Find a friendly tree. If you have none in your yard (or live in an apartment with no yard at all), locate a park where you can walk on the grass. Look for a tree that is reasonably straight and healthy. Say hello, and thank the tree for its work in exchanging oxygen for carbon dioxide. Ask its permission to share its strength and energy and wait a few moments, extending your awareness to see if it feels welcoming. If the energy doesn't feel right, move on to another tree.[1]

Depending on the weather and the shape of the tree, sit on the ground with your back supported by it or stand leaning against it. Take a few moments to get comfortable, and draw your protective circle around you and the tree. Focus your awareness on the places where your back touches the tree. Feel the texture of the bark and the pressure on your flesh. If there is a wind, note the slight flexing as the tree responds. Then move your awareness back through your body and into the tree.

When you have finished, slowly bring awareness back into your body, flexing your muscles and increasing the rate of your breathing before you try to stand. Thank the tree for sharing. Depending on the setting, offer it a little water or food.

Though a tree seems still, its internal processes are in constant, if slow, motion, drawing water and nutrients upward from the soil through the trunk to the leaves, and drawing in power from the Sun through the leaves to photosynthesize nourishment. Imagine yourself a part of that process, reaching down into the earth and raising energy, exchanging it above and bringing it down again. Feel the strength of the tree's roots, its joy in the sunlight and wind. Trees are very good at doing their job; they bear witness to the principle of order in the world. They stay put, and can teach inner stillness. Trees take the long view and can help you gain perspective. But it may be wise to set a time limit for your meditation before you begin–it can be very seductive, being a tree.

Some may find other imagery more useful for centering. Try imagining yourself sitting within an egg and pull all your awareness inward until it is contained within the egg's shell. Or begin by remembering

---

1. This may sound fanciful, but folklore has a lot to say about tree spirits. Reread the part about Old Man Willow in the chapter called "The Old Forest" in *The Fellowship of the Ring* to refresh your memory regarding what a negative tree spirit can do. Fortunately, most trees that you encounter will be pleased, if rather surprised, to find that you have noticed them.

someplace where you felt absolutely safe and secure. Note the sensory characteristics of the setting—the temperature, scents, and textures. Build them into a sequence in which the evocation of each sense puts you increasingly at ease. Make a note of how you do this; the information can help you build your "base camp" later. The point of the practice is to achieve focus and balance.

Relaxation

Relaxation is the next important skill. It is very difficult to let your mind float free when your body is tense. Simply telling yourself to relax may, in fact, have the opposite effect, causing you to focus on your tension. Soaking in a hot bath or having a massage can be effective, but neither is particularly practical as a regular prelude to meditation—although, when you have the opportunity to do this, take careful note of your sensations so you can try to reproduce them later in your imagination. Here are some relaxation exercises that many have found useful.

Exercise 6. The Tense-and-Release Method

Most of us carry so much tension in our muscles all the time that the simple instruction to "relax" reaches only the most obvious areas. One way to learn where your muscle groups are is to identify, contract, and release each muscle group in turn. This is the method taught by the Western Mystery Tradition.

You may find this easiest to learn lying down, although you will eventually be doing trance work in a sitting position as well. Lie down on (on top of, not in) your bed or on a mat that is soft enough to be comfortable, but not too yielding. You can use a pillow or neck support for your head. If the temperature is cool, wear socks, but not shoes, and cover yourself with a light blanket. Close your eyes.

Begin by focusing attention on your feet. Curl your toes and arch your feet, holding them in tension for a moment. Then release all control so they feel like dead weights at the end of your legs. Now contract the muscles of your calves, and then your thighs. Hold them that way for a few seconds, then release and let your legs sink into the surface. Now everything from the hips down is gone—you can feel that your limbs are there, but you couldn't move them if you tried.

Now, move awareness to your hands. Make a fist, hold it, then let your fingers relax into a loose curl. Tighten the muscles of your forearms, and then your upper arms. Hold the tension, then let it go.

Now your only volition is in your torso. Lie still for a little while, paying attention to how that feels. Focus next on your back and buttocks, tensing them until you are lifted from the bed. Let them go and sink down once more. Clench the muscles of your belly, then let them go. This is one of the most important muscle groups to identify, since, when your stomach muscles are relaxed, it is almost impossible to retain tension elsewhere.

Now your only volition is in your head, but even here there are muscles that you can release. Tighten your neck muscles to tip your head back. Scrunch up all your facial muscles. Try to feel the muscles of your scalp, and then let everything go. Now the only things moving should be your heart and lungs. Lie still for a little while, paying attention to how it feels to be totally relaxed.

Now take a deep breath and blink. Twitch the muscles of your face and open your eyes. Move your head and then your shoulders, twist your torso a little. Move your hands and feet.

When you feel completely reconnected to your body, you can sit up again.

You can practice this exercise daily. If you do it when you go to bed, it can help you sleep, but you should also practice it when you are wide awake. Gradually, speed up the sequence, so that, with merely a thought, you can relax each area in turn and, with another, restore awareness.

A variation on this technique was taught to Dana Kramer-Rolls by her mother. "What you do is just go into those muscles, work at isolating them mentally, and let go quietly and gently, and then let go deeper, and sometimes (I discovered on my own) you have to backtrack and let go of a lower back or hand or neck or jaw or wherever you express tenseness when you are trying to do something." The gradualness of this technique has advantages, because it involves you with your body in very subtle ways and makes you aware of little tensions you experience in normal space and time.

Another student commented that your sense of touch can help you to focus on a given part of your body. Notice the feeling of skin against skin where one toe touches another; notice the texture of clothing, the touch of air, sensations of heat and cold. Follow that awareness inward and relax.

Still another method starts at the top of the head and lets tension flow away and downward limb by limb. Let the muscles of your face sag, your shoulders sink, and let energy flow down through your arms until your hands lie limp on your thighs. Feel your back settling and release the muscles of your belly, leaving only enough tension to stay upright. Let your legs become very heavy, held in place by the chair. Let everything go slack until you feel it would take a conscious effort to make any part of your body move. This approach works well in conjunction with the grounding technique in exercise 4.

Exercise 7. Stretching

Some people find that tensing their muscles causes them to cramp. If tensing and releasing your muscles does not prove helpful, or you have trouble identifying and isolating your muscle groups, stretching may be a useful alternative. Stretching may also be easier to do in a group or public situation. You can find instructions for safe and effective muscle stretches in any book on fitness. At its most advanced level, stretching becomes yoga. However, as a preliminary to meditation, some very simple stretches will do.

Stand up and reach for the sky, feeling the stretch through your back and abdomen and shoulders. Slowly bend and reach for your toes. You may keep your knees a little bent while you do this. Straighten up, put your hands on your hips, and twist to one side and then to the other. Tip your head back and rotate it (carefully, if you have neck problems).

You can also stretch while sitting in a chair, holding onto the seat or back to help yourself twist and leaning toward the floor to stretch your back.

Many have gotten excellent results by building up the sensations of being in a warm bath, or imagining being at the beach being carried away by a warm, gentle tide. Those inexperienced in visualization (or "kinesthetization") may find this method easier after they have worked through some of the exercises in chapter 4. For more information on relaxation exercises, try texts on method acting, which teach the same kinds of preparation as a way of moving from ordinary consciousness into a role.

Practice

1. **Review and evaluate:** Reread the questionnaire you filled out before beginning. Given what you now know, estimate which skills will likely be easiest for you, and which will be difficult. Are there any changes in diet, etc. that you should address? Any areas in which you need to know more about yourself?
2. **Record and journal:** Get a notebook in which to record dates, times, and results of the exercises you practice. If you have a blog, you can keep your journal there. Write up interesting dreams and other experiences that may be relevant. It is very important to practice regularly, even, or especially, if this is a skill you have learned before, because you will be connecting it to new cues that are the foundation for the later work.
3. **Warding:** The first week, use the exercises in this chapter to develop your own procedure for warding, grounding, and centering. Practice until you can do it in a few moments. Then reverse the process, and practice until you can cue yourself fully back into ordinary consciousness. Practice the journey charm in exercise 1 or your own personal warding procedure.

4. **Relaxation:** The second week, add relaxation. Build the four steps–warding, centering, grounding, and relaxing–into a sequence and practice until you can do it smoothly. Don't forget to reverse and return when you are done.

Chapter Three
Getting Started

The only language for some things is experience.
You have to go, to know.

Tom Brown, Jr.

Now you are all packed up, settled into the driver's seat, seat-belt fastened, key in the ignition, and ready to go. It's time to turn the key and get into gear. Those whose heads are too open may find themselves on the road without really knowing how they got there. Many of us have had the experience of realizing we are already halfway to work without any memory of the first part of the journey. However, we can, if necessary, remember what the steps in starting the car and leaving home were, and make ourselves slow down and pay attention to the process.

The goal is to "drive" your psyche as well as you drive your car—with understanding, direction, and control. To do so, you intentionally change the pattern of your breathing, and use sensory stimuli like sound, rhythm, or scent to cue a shift in gears. The last step before turning onto the highway is always to make sure that the pathway through the mind is clear.

Modes of Perception

How do we experience trance? We experience the world through our senses, and our senses give us a "language" with which to manipulate the virtual reality of trance. The language of the unconscious is symbol, and in order for your (ordinary) conscious mind to communicate with the rich world of the un-(or other-)conscious, you must develop a symbolic vocabulary. Those who have repetitive or sequential dreams, or the occasional single dream that is immediately recognized as "significant," will find that they already have a symbolic language, though it may take time and guidance to decode it.

Humans respond differently to different kinds of sensory stimuli. The wealth of visual terminology in English demonstrates the primacy of visual sensitivity in our culture. Second in frequency are the words for different sounds, followed by terms for scent, texture, and movement. Educational theory identifies many kinds of intelligence, though it has become common to focus primarily on visual, aural, and kinesthetic learning. What this tells us is that, if you are trying to communicate with a group of people, you must use many kinds of imagery. Interestingly enough, however, a person whose ordinary mode of perception is focused on one sense—for instance, the visual—may be powerfully affected by an appeal to one of the other senses.

This is true for learning as well as trancing. Some learners may find it easier to absorb the material in this book aurally. Whether you prefer to hear or read the text, if you are working alone, it may help you to read the instructions aloud, or record them and listen to them, so you don't have to keep looking at the book.

Shifting Gears

With experience, you will learn to identify levels of trance, ways to reach them, and what you can do with them. You control trance by developing a system of cues and conditioning. Even the states of consciousness that everyone experiences are controlled by cues. When my first child was born, it took less than a week to condition myself to awaken at the first gasp that preceded the full-throated cry. In this case, the trauma of dealing with a screaming infant acted as a powerful motivator to respond before the child started to yell his head off. No doubt sleep deprivation and hormone changes played their part as well.

When you drive on cruise control, you still (hopefully) stop for red lights. Even when you are engrossed in a book, you may be recalled by the ringing of the telephone. The basic and essential principle is that, when you are conditioned to go into trance in response to a certain stimulus, you move into that state "only" when that cue has been given. Conditioning helps sensitive people control their state of consciousness. It also gives inexperienced or blocked individuals the sense of security they need to "let go." Cues can be physical and/or symbolic, but they have their impact in "non-ordinary" reality.

The purpose of this book is to teach you how to condition yourself to respond to specific cues, so you can move from one level of consciousness to another safely, predictably, and easily.

We understand the physical world pretty well. But most of us do not know much about what is buried in our minds. Some of it is part of the collective unconscious–symbols and reactions that we share with other humans; some is cultural; and some is specific to each individual. When you move into a symbolic reality, you must understand how to manipulate these elements. You also have to understand all the physical, psychological, and social factors that can affect your ability to do spiritual work. Self-knowledge is as important as conditioning in safely dissociating from "ordinary consciousness."

Breathing

For a normal healthy person, breathing is a function of the autonomic nervous system. Your breathing gets faster when you exercise and slows when you relax, but you don't have to think about it to make it happen. Because the rate and depth of your breathing so often reflect your physical or emotional states, consciously altering the way you breathe is a powerful way to change from one mode to another. A specific pattern of breathing that you only adopt when you want to achieve a trance state can be a very useful cue. As a side effect, breath work can also improve your singing.

For trance work, it is most effective to breathe very slowly and regularly. It may take some practice, but eventually you should be able to breathe in for four slow counts, hold for four counts, let out your breath for four counts, then hold it for four counts more. I find that I take about five complete respirations (in and out) a minute, but the most comfortable and effective rates for different people vary.

Count silently as you breathe in and out. If you have trouble focusing, try using a loudly ticking clock or a metronome to set your pace. Mentally count as you inhale and exhale, keeping your attention on your counting, until all other awareness falls away. If you time your breathing to a clock that ticks once per second, and draw in for three seconds and out for three, you will inhale and exhale five times a minute. This practice will provide you with a helpful cue for trance work; it can also begin to teach you about conscious concentration. Combined with relaxation, counted breathing is also very useful for lowering your blood pressure.

Students who have worked with this system have had some interesting experiences. Meredith reported that, "After a week of sinking the first chapter in and working with the breathing, I realized that the ticking clock helped me to Alpha out. It's mentioned in the materials—but this happened quite by accident with one of those electric clocks that—for some reason—tick out every second. (No second hand—only a soft tick—a conundrum for sure!) Anyway—being the Celt that I am—the number three seemed more comfortable than four, so I slowed my counting and used a three. Then it hit me—three times four is twelve. Twelve times five is SIXTY. Five circuits in a minute!"

I assured Meredith that, for the most part, as long as an adaptation of the practice works, she should use whatever version meets her needs and fits her tradition. This may only be a problem when meditating with a group, when the narration has to get everyone moving at the same pace. In that case, you may need to train yourself to work in both ways.

Sensory Cues

We go through life surrounded by sensory cues. Many of them are visual. When you are driving, a green light stimulates you to step on the gas, and a red one, the brake. Even before you read the word "Stop," you recognize the shape and color of the hexagonal red sign. An ambulance siren sends you to the side of the road, and a policeman's whistle stops you. Your sense of smell attracts you to food or mates. Since you are already conditioned to these stimuli, you can intentionally use all of your senses to create cues that will help you change consciousness when you want to go into trance.

Your sense of smell is one of the most powerful emotional triggers known. Everyone has had the experience of unexpectedly encountering a scent that releases a cascade of memories—the smell of newly cut grass on a summer day, the scent of old books in the stacks of a library, the smell of oil paints, or of horses. In the Orphic hymns, the kind of incense to be used in a rite is listed along with the prayers to the Greek gods. The tables of correspondences in the material developed by the Order of the Golden Dawn include the incense appropriate to rituals in each *sephiroth* on the Tree of Life. Crowley lists perfumes for all thirty-two paths on the Tree.

Whether or not a particular incense is related to a given set of symbols by nature, it can become so by association. These days, smoke alarms and allergies often prohibit the burning of incense, but you can carry a small flask of essential oil anywhere. Choose a scent that is attractive to you, but unusual enough that you are unlikely to encounter it in, for example, someone's room freshener. A dab on your upper lip before you begin meditation will speed you on your way.

Another sensory cue is texture. The luxurious softness of silk or fur can put you into one kind of mood; the stiffness of canvas into another. Putting on a specific garment or an accessory like a pendant or a veil when preparing to meditate can signal your unconscious that it is time to begin.

Sound

Melody, tone, and rhythm are powerful cues for inducing altered states of consciousness. As Joscelyn Godwin observes in the preface to *Music, Mysticism and Magic* (1986):

> At the higher levels of music little changes: it is always the same vehicle for voyages to the other world, the same revelation of divine and cosmic laws, the same powerful tool for self-transformation, as it was in ancient and even prehistoric times.

Music works by association; a particular piece or style of music can produce particular moods or evoke certain memories. Music can soothe rage or inspire a frenzy. Film scores are specifically created to intensify the effect of the visions on the screen. Culturally appropriate music like the playing of a Celtic harp can, by itself, carry us to Tir n'an Og. In the Afro-diasporic traditions, specific rhythms and songs call in the *orishas*. Music that is soft, slow, and sweet, like the vibrations of Asian temple bells, induces contemplation; loud and highly rhythmic music can stimulate a state of excitement and ecstasy. When we address trance journeying in later chapters, we will explore these possibilities further. For now, we'll concentrate on the use of tone and rhythm in producing trance.

In the Western Mystery Tradition, sound production focuses on the use of Words of Power. According to Butler (1959):

> There are four kinds of vibration which we may use for our Words of Power. They are rhythm, pitch, vowel sounds and consonantal sounds. The first two can be produced on musical instruments, the other two by the voice. To induce emotional states, rhythm is the greatest of them all, and this rhythm can be regular or irregular. Syncopation is an example of rhythm-and-break which has an enormous value in the evocation of certain emotional states. There are sounds which affect the sub-consciousness, even though the conscious mind may not like them at all. They are the mental analogues to the condiments of the dinner-table acting as

emotional irritants and stimulants. It is evident, however, that like the condiments, they should only be taken in small doses.

Chanting

The stereotypical image of chanting is a roomful of monks—black-robed Cistercians singing Gregorian chant or saffron-robed Buddhists chanting AUM. Gregorian chant is written without bars and is intended to flow freely. Eastern mantras consist of single syllables or phrases endlessly repeated. Unlike most European music, mantric chanting, whether Eastern or Western, is pitched lower and shifts in quarter tones. The tonal quality can be irritating until you are used to it, and the repetition can be boring until it becomes a springboard to an altered state of mind.

As generations of monks have found, chanting is a good way to breathe and focus. The simpler the vocalization, the better. Of course, when the sounds have meaning, the practice becomes more intense. But even the focused effort necessary to produce a sustained tone can help you center. The better your breath control, the longer you can hold a note. You can intone AUM, a rune, or simple vowels. Toning by yourself can help you focus. Toning with others increases rapport. It also does wonders for your breath control for other kinds of singing.

In Eastern traditions, the chanting of mantras is a mainstay of spiritual practice. Chanting the same phrase for hours while thinking about its meaning occupies the body while freeing the spirit to contemplate the divine. According to Alain Daniélou, in Hindu religion, a *mantram* is a word or phrase composed of the root words of the primeval language (1985). The word itself means "thought-form." By understanding its inner significance, you can reach beyond the limits of your perception and apprehend the true nature of the power the mantra represents. The chanting of mantras can accomplish everything from attaining liberation to communicating with spirits or increasing your spiritual powers.

The root word AUM means "I accept," implying acceptance of the active force of Brahma, which is signified by the A. The concentrating force of Vishnu is signified by the U, and the destructive force of Shiva is represented by the M. AUM is discussed in most of the Hindu holy texts, for instance, the *Chandogya Upanishad* and the *Tantra Tattvaprakasha.* This account only scratches the surface of the symbolism and implications of this syllable, which begins all Hindu rituals, and which is said, when repeated faithfully, to lead to self-realization, liberation from bondage, and the attainment of Supreme Reality.

AUM should not be chanted unless you recognize that, by doing so, you are making a commitment to seek the realization of your full spiritual potential. On the other hand, that goal is presumably compatible with the reasons you are studying trance work. Take a deep breath and let it out slowly as you intone "AAAAUUUMMM." How often do you have to breathe? Practice until you can hold the tone steady for a count of twenty-four beats. For one week, every day after you do your grounding, centering, and relaxing exercise, count your breathing until you feel awareness shift, and then chant the mantram for five to ten minutes. When your mind wanders, return it to the sounds. Don't try to think about anything, or to *not* think about anything. Simply be. . . .

If you prefer to focus on a goddess, you can instead chant AIM, the mantram of the goddess Sarasvati. This syllable is the "Seed of Consciousness" or "Seed of Speech." Its purpose is to acquire knowledge and wisdom, mastery over words, and the power of speech.

Or you can try the same practice with a name or term from whatever tradition you follow. If you follow a Celtic path, chant one of the words from the Ogham tree alphabet. There are two accounts of its origin. The eleventh-century *Lebor Gábala Érenn* tells how the scholars of the Scythian king Fenius Farsa created a sacred language from the tongues scattered after the fall of the Tower of Babel. He created the ogham signs with which to write it and gave the signs their names. In *In Lebor Ogaim*, however, we are told that the god Ogma created the system for use by the learned, naming the signs after trees.

For chanting, I recommend one of the signs that begins with a vowel—for instance, *ailm*, given in the tree alphabet as a pine or fir tree. According to Erynn Laurie, Ailm means "inception." "Ailm is the cry of both birth and death. It is the *fid* of initiation . . . Ailm is the beginning in its purest form: origins and creation" (2007). This makes it a particularly useful chant to use as you begin your training in trance work. Another possibility is *onn*, the ash tree or the furze. Laurie gives its meaning as "foundation-wheel," that which carries you on your journey. "It concerns direction or intention in our decisions. It is also anything that makes the journey quicker and easier." This one is even more appropriate to the imagery we're using in this book.

If you are Ásatrú, you can get good results by chanting the runes, which, according to the Old Norse *Havamál*, were "taken up" by the god Odin during his nine-day ordeal hanging on the World Tree. The rune ᚩ, *Os*, means "mouth" and communication in the Anglo-Saxon *futhork*, and ᚨ, *Ansuz*, means communication and a god, especially Odin, in the Elder and Younger rune rows, may be especially appropriate. Since Ansuz has two syllables, you have to ration your breath to get both out. Because of the syllable shift, this takes a little more breath. Try to allow at least eight beats per syllable: "AAAHN-SUUUZ." Another choice is *önd*, the breath of life and spirit that Odin gave at the creation of humankind.

For those who work with the Greek pantheon, I recommend a word like "Arete" (UH-REH-TEE), which means excellence, "to be all you can be," and expresses the Hellenic quest for self-realization. Distribute your breath through the three syllables as indicated above. Call on Hermes, who is both the messenger of the gods and the conductor of souls, to help you. Here is an exercise in vowel toning that can be a good way to open up your chest. It also shifts your energy focus somewhat with each vowel. Done in a group, it can build rapport; as the tones spontaneously alter, harmonies develop to create a truly beautiful sound.

Exercise 8. Vowel Toning

Take a deep breath and intone– "AH . . . EE . . . AI . . . OH . . . OOH . . ." Allow four slow beats per vowel, and try not to breathe in the middle.

Now vowel tone free-form, letting the sounds change as they will. Take an occasional quick breath to keep them going. Try to maintain the same volume.

Practice this with a friend and see how your voices blend. How long does it take you to synchronize? Experiment until you find the tone that resonates in your skull. Lower it to resonate in your throat, your chest, your belly. Alter the degree to which your throat is closed or open to change the sounds. Vibrate the sounds in different parts of your body to activate and energize them.

A student who had studied singing pointed out: "A good visual tip for sustaining sound is to consider the upper half of your body a vacuum after your initial deep breath. No air in or out. (The voice works on vibration–not breath. It's not a wind instrument.) If one would like to work toward longer sustained sound, be very aware of escaping air–especially at the first moment of sound. . . . Pay really close attention to the initial moment of sound. Then, if you hear/feel breath escaping, play about until you can 'put a cap on the leak.'" (Meredith)

Many people find that listening to New Age or Trance Techno music can help them relax and focus. Look for an unstructured piece that is recorded at a fairly even sound level, without strong rhythms or recognizable melodies–a piece on which you can simply "float away." Songs and program music can be powerful aids to trance work that has a specific goal, such as getting in touch with a deity or journeying to a specific place. Because of this, however, you should avoid these types of music when you are learning how to clear your mind for meditation.

Sonic Cues

Drumming is a sonic cue often used in trance work. Drumbeats and other repetitive sounds, known as sonic drivers, can produce changes in the central nervous system. Drumming is particularly effective because the beat can include many sound frequencies and thus affect many nerve pathways. The low-frequency sounds of most drums are also very easy to hear. A drumbeat at four to seven cycles per second induces a theta wave in the brain that seems especially conducive to trance states. Not only does the shaman who uses a drum associate its beat with the work so strongly that hearing it will move him toward the Shamanic State of Consciousness, the regular beat acts as a carrier wave, bearing him, like the horse with which traditional shamans compare it, on his journey.

Different rhythms can become powerful cues for particular states of trance. For focused inner work like journeying, I favor a regular, even beat at medium speed. Experiment until you find the tempo that works best for you. Drumming has the added advantage of drowning out any other sounds that may distract you and giving you something on which to focus if your mind begins to wander. Earphones let you listen to recorded drumming without disturbing others in the house—an important consideration if you are working late at night. You can find drumming selections at many metaphysical stores, or you can record your own.[2] When you use a CD or drumming, you have an automatic timing device for your meditation. In core shamanism, a sequence of three sets of four beats followed by a very rapid beat is the signal to end the meditation.

Eventually, you may learn to drum for yourself, as the physical act of drumming gives you an additional anchor and helps you split your consciousness between the physical and spiritual worlds. This is particularly useful if you plan to lead groups in meditation. One of the advantages of drumming (either for yourself or by listening to a recording with earphones) is that it blocks out distracting sounds and gives the top layer of your mind something on which to focus. The disadvantage of learning to meditate to a drumbeat is that you may find it difficult to meditate without the drumming. This goes for other sound cues as well. Eventually, you will learn to "auralize" a drumbeat or music from memory, and use it as a cue without needing an external source for the sound. Ideally, you should be able to shift gears anytime,

---

2. A CD called the *Shamanic Journey Solo* is available from the Foundation for Shamanic Studies (P.O. Box 1939, Mill Valley, CA 94942, or via their website, *www.shamanism.org*).

anywhere, through mental cues alone. However, sound is an extremely useful stimulus and, if it helps, especially when you are learning, use it.

Clearing Your Mind

Later chapters will include exercises for improving your ability to perceive and hold an image. But just as you clear your desk when beginning a new project, you must be able to clear your mind before you can receive images. This is by no means easy. Infants may experience life as a succession of sensations, but from the time we learn words, we produce a perpetual internal monologue that continues as long as we are conscious of being conscious.

So how do you stop that internal monologue? Strength of will is of no use here. The more you will yourself *not* to think about a blue monkey, the more vividly its image will appear. Instead, you have to use a kind of mental judo, leveraging your opponent's own strength to defeat him. You can avoid thinking about the blue monkey temporarily by imagining a pink elephant instead. Your goal, however, is to reach a state in which you don't see anything at all. There are a number of ways in which you can accomplish this. Exercise 9 may help you develop the skill of clearing your mind.

Exercise 9. Clearing Your Mind

Use the skills you developed in the earlier exercises to relax and focus. When your breathing is steady, imagine you are looking at a darkly flowing river. Other thoughts and images will interfere. As each one comes to mind, recognize it, then let it slip into the water and flow away. Gradually, as you focus on the water, the images will come more and more slowly, until there is only the moving water. And presently, it too will flow away.

If visualization does not work well for you, "auralize" the process using toning. Imagine you can hear one of the sounds you used in the last exercise, and keep "hearing" it when other thoughts intrude. At first, the moments during which you are thinking of nothing will be brief, but gradually you will find that you are able to maintain this state for longer periods. If you are inhibited by a fear of being lost in the meditation, set your mental alarm clock for a specific period—say five or ten minutes—with the affirmation that, at this time, you will return to ordinary consciousness. If you are really anxious, get a timer and set the alarm, but this is rarely necessary, or should not be needed for long.

Sometimes people wonder whether emptying their minds in this way may create a vacuum that will attract any nearby nasty spirits. If you have set up your wards properly—which by this time should have become automatic—this should not be a problem. A more reasonable fear is that this kind of meditation may open the door to monsters from your own unconscious. In fact, clearing your mind can not only serve as a transition to spirit journeying, it can also provide a transition to other states, such as the open, neutral state of consciousness in which you can do oracular work or receive spiritual guidance, or even lead the way to the experience of union with the divine discussed in chapter 12.

For now, just fill your mind with an image or sensation that you have internalized and can summon up at will. If you are visually oriented, try an image like sunlight glittering on waves, moving tree shadows, or grasses rippling in the wind. Watch a DVD of images from nature until you have internalized the images. If your focus is aural, try a vibration or tone, or play a CD of ocean sounds or New Age music. Other soothing sensations include floating in warm water, stroking fur, or tasting your favorite food.

If you intend to pursue this path, however, you must confront the problem of intrusive images one way or another. As I mentioned earlier, trance work stirs up the unconscious, and the practices taught in this book are likely to give you a first-class tour of your issues, whatever they may be.

Returning to the World

When you travel, organizing your return trip can be as important as getting started. This is also true when you do trance work. Whether you are simply practicing grounding and centering, or have added breathing, toning, and clearing your mind, or have made a full-scale spirit journey, take the time to reorganize your psyche before returning to the mundane world.

In the Harry Potter books, the train ride to Hogwarts serves as a transition from the Muggle to the Wizarding worlds. The trip back reverses the process. Fortunately, most of our homes are more welcoming than #4 Privet Drive, but the principle is the same. As you explore practices for grounding, centering, relaxing, or clearing, note how you can reverse these procedures. Write down the sequence in both directions and, when your work is finished, draw up and internalize the energy that kept you grounded. Quicken your breathing, and extend your awareness into each limb. When you have control over all your muscles, move around a little and open your eyes. Feel your alignment with the energies in the room. If you have put up a magical barrier, visualize it coming down. You may find it helpful to drink a little water or eat something with a strong taste, like salt, to complete your return.

Practice

1. **Counted breathing**: Add counted breathing to your grounding and centering practice. Work on this for several days, or until you consistently feel a shift in the focus of your awareness when you change the pattern of your breathing. Do this for several minutes, paying attention to how you feel, then deliberately increase the tempo of your breathing until you return to your usual rate. Restore movement to your body and pull your awareness back to its normal limits.
2. **Smell**: Choose an essential oil to dab under your nose when you begin practice. After you have been doing this for a week, do it without the scent. Is it harder to shift mental gears? Sniff the

scent without doing the exercise. Do you find your consciousness changing?

3. **Touch:** Get a veil or piece of jewelry with which you have no previous strong associations and put it on as you begin the grounding/centering/breathing/mind-clearing sequence.
4. **Sound:** Practice doing the sequence with and without sound cues. Experiment with toning, music, and drumming while you do exercise 9. Once you have tried several methods, settle on one set of cues and practice with them. A month of steady practice should imprint the cues pretty well. Then go on to the exercises in the next chapter. As you continue to go through the basic steps (breathing before journeying, for instance), you may notice changes when you compare current experiences with notes made earlier.
5. **Clearing the mind:** Working from exercise 9, or using the induction in exercise 10 below, practice clearing your mind each day as the culmination of your preparatory sequence. You may find it useful to read the induction onto a tape and play it. When you are finished, record your experience. Note any physical sensations, such as a feeling of falling or rising, or a shift in the apparent locus of consciousness within.

Exercise 10. Induction for Clearing Your Mind

Ward your space and assume your meditation position. Balance, ground, and center according to the process you have developed.

Sit in balance upon the earth . . .
Let each limb relax . . .
Here you are safe and secure.
If there is need, you will be able to easily awaken and return.
You hear sounds, but they mean nothing,
all that does not concern you fades away.
Anything you hear will only make it easier to look within.
Let your eyes close.
Breathe in . . . hold. . . .

and out . . . hold. . . .
Breathe in . . . hold. . . .
and out . . . hold. . . .

Allow a minute or two to pass as you count your breaths.

Now let the image of the place around you come to mind. . . .
Note the texture of the floor, then let that memory slip away. . . .
See the colors of the walls, and as you do so, watch them fade.
Remember the placement of the furniture,
then let shadow erase it all.
Feel the temperature of the air,
then withdraw awareness so that you feel nothing at all.
All images and sensations begin to ripple and flow.
All that you see, or hear, or feel dissolves and flows away,
A thought comes to you–recognize it, then let it go. . . .
Again and again, all is carried away. . . .
It all goes. . . .
You are open and empty. . . .
You need nothing. . . .
You want nothing. . . .
You have only to BE. . . .

Allow two to five minutes of silence.

Reality is flowing around you.
You see light flickering on water,
You hear the ripple of a stream.
Gradually it gives way to an image of the room around you,
Feel your weight in the chair.
Twitch your fingers and toes.
Breathe in . . . and out . . . in . . . and out. . . .
Let the air of that place become the air of this place.
Sigh and stretch, open your eyes
And return.

When you have finished working, reverse the procedures by which you warded the room.

Chapter Four

Trance-Perceptions

We live in a wonderful world that is full of beauty, charm and adventure. There is no end to the adventures we can have if only we seek them with our eyes open.

Jawaharlal Nehru

When we travel, we use our vehicle's instruments to gather information on temperature and direction, speed and fuel. Inward journeying requires that you use your own instrumentation—your senses—even if you apply them in a kind of virtual reality. If the purpose of trance training is to learn how to "know what we know," then one of your most useful tools is the ability to focus your attention and remember what you have perceived. If you cannot learn to do this, the things you encounter in your trance work will vanish as swiftly as the knowledge that comes to you in dreams.

A good technique for learning focus is to sharpen and develop sensory memory. To make detailed observations, remember accurately what you have perceived, and use cues to move from one state to another require the ability to remember sensory perceptions. Our minds are the tools we use to explore inner reality, and they must be tuned and calibrated in the same way you prepare your equipment when you journey through unknown lands.

Multiple Intelligences

By the time you reach this point you will have realized that "your mileage may vary," especially if you are working with a group. Don't let anyone persuade you that there is One Right, True, and Only Way to learn trance work. It is very important to approach the work in a disciplined and methodical way, building each skill on the ones that precede it, and there are some hazards that everyone must learn to avoid. But at each stage in the process, you must make adjustments and adapt the practices to your own context and learning style.

Earlier, we discussed the three primary ways of learning. It may be more accurate to say that these are the three best-known learning styles identified by the scientists who developed the field of neuro-linguistic programming. This field has been recognized, to some extent, by the educational establishment, and I suppose we should be grateful that academics have acknowledged even this much variation in how people learn. A more sophisticated approach was introduced by Dr. Howard Gardner in the early 1980s when he proposed the theory of "multiple intelligences." Gardner identified different gifts and learning styles for those who are good with words, logic, and numbers, visual-spatial relations, body awareness, music, working with others, understanding themselves, and responding to nature.

George Hersh, another student, evokes the variations more poetically:

> The people who do visual patterns, color memory, jigsaw
> puzzle zip finishers.
> The people of rhythm and movement, dancers, drummers,
> marchers, whirlers,
> tolerant of disturbances of the inner ear, the waltz
> drunkards.

The word smiths.
The ritual junkies and artifact collectors, the complicators of space,
the compulsively messy,
The abstractors of the quintessence
The tactile clay and stone people and their cousins who delight in the properties of metals.
The runners and walkers.
The drunks and druggies, the ones who slot in on a particular chemical and
are lost for a long time, the ones who take it or let it alone.
The emotion geniuses
The autistic animal empath and her ilk
Who else?

For each life-organizing theme a different realm of power and a different way to work magic?

In most people, these types of intelligence are mixed, but some abilities are more dominant than others. I, for instance, am strongest in the linguistic and visual/spatial areas. If you are curious about your own abilities, you can take a simple online test.[3]

Educators are still working out this theory's implications for teaching, but it seems to boil down to the idea that, in addition to focusing on words and numbers, we need to offer images, music, and the opportunity to make things and use our bodies as ways to learn. In teaching trance work, it means there may be more than one way to address any of the component skills. When I first taught the class, this quickly became apparent in the online discussions that occurred between class meetings, as students compared notes and offered solutions to each others' learning problems. In teaching, instructors often learn as much from their students as their students learn from them—and this was certainly the case for me.

3. www.bgfl.org/bgfl/custom/resources_ftp/client_ftp/ks3/ict/multiple_int/index.htm

Visualizing and Vision

The literature of meditation and trance work makes it apparent that traditional teaching has placed a strong emphasis on vision. The fact that the English language has more adjectives describing the way things look than it does for the way things sound, taste, smell, or feel supports this idea. Hence, a spirit journey is often referred to as a visualization. We say "visualize" or "see with the mind's eye," rather than "imagine," because it is a more concrete instruction. In visualization, you create an inner image—that of something remembered or an image built up from remembered elements. Visualization is one of our most powerful psychic tools. Patricia Norris, who works with cancer patients, defines it like this:

> Visualization is the consciously chosen, intentional instruction to the body. Imagery is the spontaneously occurring "answer," qualifier and modifier from the unconscious. Thus, a two-way communication is set up by the interplay of visualization and imagery.
>
> The relationship between visualization and imagery can be thought of as a metaphor, as the relationship between a transmitter and a receiver. The visualization acts as a message to the unconscious, including the subcortical parts of the brain and particularly the limbic system, hypothalamus, and pituitary. The images are messages from the unconscious to consciousness, much as dreams are (1985).

Most people, however, go through much of their lives without really *seeing* what they are looking at. To some extent, this reflects a necessary triage that keeps us from being overwhelmed by sensory input. But when you are *trying* to remember what something looks like, it helps if you have trained your powers of observation. This is as true when viewing the inner world as it is when looking at the outer. Only the fortunate few who have an eidetic memory can call to mind a page of text and reread it rather than having to remember its content, but most of us can learn to take a mental "photograph" to preserve some particularly important scene in memory. I always pack a camera when I travel, but I have found that the things I wanted to photograph when the camera was out of film are the ones that remain most vividly in my memory.

Exercise 11. Observing, Remembering, and Visualizing

Start with an actual physical object. Select something with plenty of detail that you can hold in your hand–an interesting rock, a flower, a statuette, or something similar.

Relax, breathe, and clear your mind. Then look at your object. Consider every aspect of its appearance–color, shape, decoration, texture. Take a mental photograph. Then close your eyes and try to "see" the object with inner vision. Open your eyes and look at your object again– what did you miss? Contemplate the object and then close your eyes and try again. Do this until you have memorized your first object, then practice again with a second. Try this with a number of objects, both familiar and unfamiliar, until you can remember most of the details on your first or second try.

Some people have come up with mental tricks to help with visualization. My student Lorrie reported,

> I also admit with only slight embarrassment that when asked to focus and visualise objects with Startling Amounts of Detail, yes, I may well start with a 'wireframe' like you see in computer-generated special effects things. However, I *don't* then proceed by filling in with progressively finer-detailed polygons. . . . usually I just, er, "spray-paint the wireframe," if you will. On a random note: I first started visualization exercises some years ago by working thus, "See a fruit. Okay, now spin it. Now see two. Spin them both. Okay . . . now spin them both in *different directions*." . . . ow.

Exercise 12. Creative Visualization

Here, Alice Karlsdottir offers another useful exercise from her experience in the theater.

Place your attention within a small circle around you, on yourself and immediate objects; then within a medium circle, including several people and groups of furniture or objects; finally within a large circle, encompassing everything within your hearing or field of vision (if your attention wanders, return it to one single object to regain your concentration).

You can do the same thing, of course, with the other senses. Prepare yourself, play a phrase of recorded music or a line of poetry, then turn off the recording and try to repeat the music or poem until you can "hear" it echoing in your mind. Record your version, then play both and compare them. Try texture next, then scent, then taste. There are fewer words to describe smells and tastes. Do you find it harder to remember things for which you have no words, or can you reproduce sensations without them?

Having studied art, I know a great many terms for different colors. I find this very useful when I am trying to select fabric to match something I have at home and have forgotten to bring the item or a sample. Knowing the terms "aqua," "turquoise," "teal," "spruce," and "forest green" helps me differentiate between shades and fix the exact one I want in my memory. If you like to draw, spend some time in life drawing, as if you were a naturalist recording a new species. Though you may strive for accuracy, you will find that you also interpret what you see. Look at Audubon's portraits of birds and compare them to photographs. What does the artist's eye "see" that the camera does not?

Accuracy of observation can also be affected by what the observer knows. A friend who had served in the Israeli army once went to a Midwestern psychic reader. After a little while, the seer shook her head in confusion. What she had "seen" was a group of men in bathrobes throwing balls at her client. My friend, of course, recognized them as robed Arabs throwing grenades.

One of the most memorable scenes in Rudyard Kipling's *Kim* has become known as "the Jewel Game." In the story, Kim is sent to stay with Lurgan Sahib, a dealer in jewels and antiques, who tests the boy's abilities, including his powers of observation, in a number of unusual ways.

> "Play the Play of the Jewels against him. I will keep tally."
>
> The child dried his tears at once, and dashed to the back of the shop, whence he returned with a copper tray.
>
> "Give me!" he said to Lurgan Sahib. "Let them come from thy hand, for he may say that I knew them before."
>
> "Gently–gently," the man replied, and from a drawer under the table dealt a half-handful of clattering trifles into the tray.
>
> "Now," said the child, waving an old newspaper. "Look on them as long as thou wilt, stranger. Count and, if need be, handle. One look is enough for me." He turned his back proudly.
>
> "But what is the game?"
>
> "When thou hast counted and handled and art sure that thou canst remember them all, I cover them with this paper, and thou must tell over the tally to Lurgan Sahib. I will write mine."
>
> "Oah!" The instinct of competition waked in his breast. He bent over the tray. There were but fifteen stones on it. "That is easy," he said after a minute. The child slipped the paper over the winking jewels and scribbled in a native account-book.
>
> "There are under that paper five blue stones–one big, one smaller, and three small," said Kim, all in haste. "There are four green stones, and one with a hole in it; there is one yellow stone that I can see through, and one like a pipe-stem. There are two red stones, and–and–I made the count fifteen, but two I have forgotten. No! Give me time. One was of ivory, little and brownish; and–and–give me time . . . "
>
> "One–two," Lurgan Sahib counted him out up to ten. Kim shook his head.
>
> "Hear my count!" the child burst in, trilling with laughter. "First, are two flawed sapphires–one of two ruttees and one of four as I should judge. The four-ruttee sapphire is chipped at the

edge. There is one Turkestan turquoise, plain with black veins, and there are two inscribed–one with a Name of God in gilt, and the other being cracked across, for it came out of an old ring, I cannot read. We have now all five blue stones. Four flawed emeralds there are, but one is drilled in two places, and one is a little carven–"

"Their weights?" said Lurgan Sahib impassively.

"Three–five–five–and four ruttees as I judge it. There is one piece of old greenish pipe amber, and a cut topaz from Europe. There is one ruby of Burma, of two ruttees, without a flaw, and there is a balas-ruby, flawed, of two ruttees. There is a carved ivory from China representing a rat sucking an egg; and there is last–ah ha!–a ball of crystal as big as a bean set on a gold leaf."

He clapped his hands at the close.

"He is thy master," said Lurgan Sahib, smiling.

"Huh! He knew the names of the stones," said Kim, flushing. "Try again! With common things such as he and I both know."

Try this for yourself. Have a friend arrange a dozen small knick-knacks on a tray and let you look at them for a few minutes. Try first with things that are familiar, like kitchen items or jewelry. Then experiment with unfamiliar tools or other objects. How many can you get right? Do you find it helps if you know the correct words to describe things?

Many find that it helps to begin by counting and classifying the objects. Even those who are visually oriented may find it easier if they can handle the items. Some are able to list what they have seen, while others find it easier to draw a diagram showing the positions of the items on the tray. One class member developed another way to remember–by placing the items in the context of a story: "I was walking down the street and in a shop window I saw a BRASS ELEPHANT. I went into a café and the waitress had a PINK BOW in her hair. I picked up the SALT SHAKER to season my food . . . "

In Kipling's book, Kim is made to practice observation until he can do it swiftly and accurately, although the Hindu boy is still better.

When you can remember what you *see*, practice with a random selection of words or other sounds, a series of scents, or textured items that you touch. The sounds will have to be presented sequentially, but you can bind your eyes before touching the textured items or smelling the odors.

Sound and Sense

Like vision, speech has a respected place among those who have trained trance workers. Traditions in cultures that did not use writing, like the Native Americans, or that considered their religion too holy to put into writing, like the Ancient Celts, taught their students to memorize quantities of sacred lore. Few today have developed their memories to the same extent, but many people respond best to stimuli that are aural (or oral)—that is, they learn best when the material they are learning is spoken or heard.

The aural equivalent of an eidetic memory is the ability to replay words or music in memory as if you were playing back a mental recording. This ability is highly developed in musicians—especially composers, who can listen to entire compositions in their heads. Thus, Beethoven was able to continue composing even after he became deaf, because he could "hear" the notes he was writing down, in the "voice" of the proper instrument, both singly and in conjunction with what he had written for the rest of the orchestra.

In the work from the previous chapter, you found that you could use unstructured toning to relax and detach your mind from its usual preoccupations. As you continue to practice, you will discover which sounds and rhythms work best to move you into a state of trance. Intoning a mantram can block out all other awareness and allow your mind to float free. You can also use runes or the names of deities in this way. Just intone the name and let its vibrations resonate through your body while you focus on its meaning.

Perhaps the most widely used cue for moving into trance states is song. For those who are completely nonmusical, a repeated phrase can also help, but in most cultures, the words are accompanied by a tune to create a "power song." In Asia, a mantram is chanted on one note—"Om mani padme hum." Sometimes these songs can be wordless, like the Inuit song that protects against attack by bears—"Ai ya, ya, ya; ai ya, ya, ya. . . ." It may be a phrase taken from a visionary experience:

> The Great Sea has set me in motion, set me adrift, moving me as the weed moves in a river.
>
> The arch of sky and mightiness of storms have moved the spirit within me, 'till I am carried away, trembling with joy (Eliade, 1964).

The song may be an affirmation—"Ai, ai, ai, ai, a warrior am I!" Or a prayer—"Raven, raven, dark and bright, guide my journeying tonight." Singing the song not only keeps the top layer of your consciousness busy, it also, through repetition, becomes a cue for you to move into an altered state. You may find that, over time, you will develop a number of different songs you can use to attain various types of trance.

Those who have never studied music may find it hard to believe that they can write a song. Start by creating something simple that you can use as an inner signal to move into a trance state. It can be based on a familiar tune, but you should alter it until it no longer sounds like something you are likely to hear in any other context. You can even intone it on a single note. The words can be equally simple. Try an affirmation of one or two lines—"Like a feather in the wind, like a leaf upon the stream, I float away, away, away . . . ," or something even simpler—"Around and around my soul's unbound. . . ."

To reach an even more subliminal level, experiment with nonsense sounds. These can be very powerful—"babble" is the tongue of glossolalia, the first song a baby sings. Such syllables are often found in the power songs of traditional peoples. George Hersh wrote:

> I am adopting a trance induction chant used by the Cahuilla Indians to create a mood of calm and unity with the surrounding world. I was told by the person who taught me that a proper use of the chant on a still day could call a dragonfly to sit on a proffered finger. I was also told that it was not secret or exclusive to tribal members. The chant sounds almost infantile to my untu-

> tored ear, but it works just fine for me: *Oosh Kana Oosh - Ooo Ooo,* [repeat.]

Rather than constructing your song formally, let it evolve naturally. Play with different tunes and let random words emerge from your subconscious. You can refine it later, but let the song create itself. At first, you may find it hard to hang on to the tune. Melissa reported,

> A particular song of my youth has arisen as jumping off point. . . . It has a haunting, lyrical melody that I've always loved. Once I'd settled on that, I've been letting myself improvise and play with the melody, not using the words, and trying to keep concious control out of it as much as possible. And now, a question: I never get the same song twice. Instead, what I find MOST trance inducing is the improvising, getting lost in the theme and variations of the original melody, finally devolving to something simplified and more or less repeatable but retaining enough room for variation to keep it engaging. Later on, though, I won't remember the distilled tune.

Although a familiar song or the first line of a known melody is a good place to start, these tend to have their own associations. As Melissa found, improvising on a theme in the unstructured style of New Age music can be very hypnotic. This works well as a transition into trance, but not so well as a quick cue. Keep working with the words and, eventually, you will find that they attach themselves to a consistent strand of melody.

For some, rhythm may be more powerful than melody. A two- or three-note sequence with a strong beat can be very powerful. Songs may arise spontaneously as you are engaged in some repetitive activity. However, I counsel against trying to develop your trance song while driving, tempting though that may be. If you succeed, the act of driving may be associated with the song, and sitting behind the wheel may become a cue, not only for the music, but for moving into trance. This can be less than productive, especially if you want to reach your destination safely on the physical plane.

Touch and Movement

Movement is another way to access your inner music. Sway as you sit, or stand up and move around as you sing. Jan Fries has some interesting theories about the relationship of shaking and trembling to trance, which he describes as a kind of psychogenic pseudo-epilepsy that changes your vibrational rate and moves you into an altered state. He sees this phenomenon in the practices of a number of traditional cultures, from the "davening" of Hasidic Jews to the shaking trance of the Kalahari Bushmen (Fries, 1996). Intense rhythmic movement should be handled with care, however, as the kind of trance it is most likely to cue is both active and ecstatic.

Kinesthetic memory is cultivated to its highest degree by athletes and dancers. Through practice, muscles learn to coordinate in a sequence of motions that bypasses consciousness. Many people find a dance step or a move in sports impossible to explain, although, once they start it, they know what to do. There have been some interesting experiments in combining physical and mental training. It was found that, although those who practice do better in sports than those who don't, athletes who also spend some time *imagining* themselves making perfect baskets or passes or goals do better than those who engage in physical practice alone.

Many people use physical movement to key different states of consciousness. My brother-in-law used to pace constantly when he was working on his novels, sitting briefly to type another sentence or two, then roaming around again. I find that going for a walk often helps if I am having trouble getting the words to flow, but I have to remember to take a notebook with me or I am tormented by unexpressed words.

Some people find that moving around helps them recapture straying memories, or that shaping the air with their hands as if opening an invisible box gives them access to what's within. In the Eastern traditions, hand positions called *mudras* symbolize various concepts, and are used in iconography to indicate the powers of the various goddesses and gods. The *asanas*, or body positions, of yoga can be used to invoke or channel different kinds of power. In nineteenth-century Germany, rune magicians like Kummer and Marby adapted this concept to create a system of runic gestures and postures called *stadhagaldr*. You can use the same idea to develop a hand movement or position to cue meditation. My favorite pose is one in which my hands rest, palms upward and gently curved, on my thighs.

Some find that appealing to a sense other than their dominant one can deepen trance more effectively than focusing on the sense they usually use. Just because you use one sense—for instance, vision—for most other purposes, doesn't mean that aural or kinesthetic stimuli may not bypass your conscious mind more easily. I myself am primarily visual, but, if someone leads me in a pathworking describing only sound, scent, or touch, I sink into a very deep state immediately. This may be because I associate my dominant sense, vision, with ordinary consciousness. Working with a different sense is a cue to me to shift into a deeper state.

Experiment to find the best way to work with your memory. For some people, one dominant sense acts as a stimulus to bring back memories of the other senses. Some people associate colors with tones, and vice versa. A person who remembers the texture of a garment may be able to use that memory to access recollection of its color and shape as well.

The Taste of Memory

Taste and smell may have the most powerful impact as cues for trance work. Almost everyone has had the experience of catching an unexpected scent and receiving along with it an entire associated memory. A particular perfume may bring with it a sense of the presence of the person who wore it. The scents of newly cut grass, sea air, or a turkey just out of the oven are just a few of the odors that can bypass our conscious control. For this reason, some magical traditions have developed an elaborate array of incenses used to put the magus in touch with different beings or spheres. In the same way, memories can be evoked or consciousness directed in particular directions through the taste of particular foods or drink.

All of the senses can provide cues for psychic or magical work. By repetition, we condition ourselves to move into a particular state when we experience a specific stimulus. As the Christians say: "Put yourself in an attitude of prayer and you will find that you are praying." This is why many find that lighting their favorite incense, putting on a veil or special garment, playing a certain piece of music, or lowering the lights makes it easier to shift consciousness. Compare this to the steps you might take to "get into the mood" for a romantic encounter.

As I suggested in the previous chapter, carrying a small vial of perfume and putting it on just before beginning work can be a less obtrusive way of triggering a trance state than lighting incense that can affect everyone in the room and may be against fire laws. Choose a scent that is uncommon enough that you are unlikely to encounter it by chance, but common enough so that you can always replace it.

There is a long tradition of using striking tastes and smells as a cue for bringing someone *out* of trance as well. In some Siberian shamanic practices, yak hair is burned under the nose of shamans to jerk them back to ordinary reality. The same principle was behind the use of smelling salts to revive fainting Victorian ladies. Salt, as a specific flavor that is easily available, also works well as a cue. Rock or sea salt are even more distinctive, and are easy to carry. However, someone who works closely with a deity associated with the marshes or the sea may find that the taste of salt puts them more deeply *into* trance. In this case, another option, such as sour salt (crystals of citric acid) works just fine. Strong flavors, though useful, are not essential. Any experience that activates the senses or draws attention to bodily functions, like drinking water, can help bring someone back to consensus reality.

Sensing Energy

Your senses can also provide information about "energy." The phenomenon we refer to in spiritual work as "energy" is most frequently likened to an electrical current produced by a human body (Becker,

1998). For more information on this, see *The Body Electric,* by Robert Becker and Gary Selden. Some fortunate people may "see" energy as a shift of color in the aura.

It is more common to be able to feel energy as heat or pressure. If you rub your palms together for a few moments and then hold them facing each other, you may be able to feel your body's energy field. Your palms will tingle; move them closer and farther apart until you find the distance at which you feel a difference. This is not the same as body heat, because it often becomes more apparent when your palms are farther apart. The tingling tells you that energy is present. If you take time to experiment, you will become more sensitive to its presence. Ember reports success at feeling this tingling sensation and making energy flow even without moving her hands. "I can distinguish more details," she says, "like direction of flow. It helps that others whom I trust to be honest with me have confirmed that they can also feel the energy flowing, however they perceive it. It may not be scientific proof, but a little confirmation never hurts."

Another student, Jessica, suggested the technique described in exercise 13. Her approach has the benefit of eliciting feedback.

Exercise 13. Sensing Energy with a Partner

If you have a partner or a willing volunteer, you can try touching them, paying particular attention to any spots that are unusually warm (indicating irritation) or cold (indicating tension and reduced circulation).

Once you are able to sense these changes with your hands lightly touching your partner, try moving your hands gradually farther from the surface of their skin. It's possible that you, like my partner, will learn to sense the less physical energy that accompanies physical distress just as you could sense the tangible thermal variances. Also, it makes your partner feel all warm and squishy after hours of massage-y practice.

If you don't have a partner, you can do this with your own body.

Start by feeling the places where you're tense or hurting, deliberately tense and then relax those muscles. You can feel the way energy moves in them, experienced as temperature shifts and changing states of tension, and the way energy seems to increase in areas you're focusing on.

I think of greater tension as condensed energy, and less tension as more diffused energy. Cold spots often feel stuck and still, hot spots stuck and jittery, warm all nice and flowy.

After physically relaxing your muscles, try doing it by thinking about the area, visualize or imagine colored light or warm honey or increased blood flow filling that area.

If you sense a physical change, or an increased feeling of relaxation, or a sense of well-being, you're successfully sensing and moving energy. Go you!

Sensory and Emotional Memory

When we begin to journey within, we are explorers. Our purpose, however, is not only to observe, but to understand and to feel. To recreate an experience in imagination so fully that you feel you are there requires that you recapitulate what happened and what it felt like in every detail. You can do this through sense memory. In the theater, this technique is used to help actors get inside a role by activating their emotions through their senses. Alice Karlsdottir describes the process like this (2007, ch. 9):

> Emotional memory is based on the peculiar fact that if you use sense memory to relive some highly emotional experience, you will re-experience the emotions you felt then. A very imaginative person can even make himself feel emotions by reliving an imaginary incident he never actually experienced.

Sound weird? Did you ever cry over a movie or a book? It does work.

Exercise 14. Building Your Emotional Memory

Pick an emotional experience from your past (but not one so traumatic and deeply buried that you'll require a therapist to get you through it). Start fairly early in the experience, before the important events take place. Try to visualize all the sights, sounds, smells, etc., as vividly as possible as you proceed through the actions in your mind. By the time you get to the climax, you should be feeling some of the same emotions you felt in the past. If you don't, don't be concerned; just try another incident. Again, the goal here is not to force yourself to deal with forgotten past experiences; it's to find those experiences which you can use to stimulate your emotional responses. Any event that does that, even if it's small and stupid (my personal favorite for grief is the time I broke my very favorite water-gun) is valid. In fact, it's better to use smaller events, because you can control the emotional responses more easily and not get lost in your own angst.

Once you have tuned up your senses through practice, try coordinating them with a meditation in which you re-experience an incident that affected you strongly in the past, or participate in a scene from a book or film that moved you strongly. This is the principle behind the *Spiritual Exercises* of St. Ignatius Loyola, in which Jesuit novices are instructed to contemplate an incident from the life of Jesus in such detail and intensity that they feel they are experiencing it. In extreme cases, this kind of contemplation can result in sympathetic physical symptoms like the stigmata.

Checksums

By now you have practiced your meditation sequence (warding, grounding, centering, and clearing your mind) often enough that the process is becoming automatic. You should be able to move more quickly through the sequence. If you have been keeping up with your journal, you also have records of the effects of the different exercises and suggestions for how to change them so they work well for you.

Trance work is intended to be transformative. Thus, you must have a good sense of who you are and how you react to things that you can use as a basis for comparison as you develop new awareness and skills. Change can be either useful or problematic. To decide the kind of change you are experiencing, you have to be aware of what has changed. Lorrie Wood, returning to a computer-based analogy, explains this as "checksums."

> Data runs around the Internet in packets. You can compare this to a post office, where packages, letters, and bulk mail advertisements are all flitting hither and yon, being routed to their destinations. However, unlike those letters, a packet of data on the Internet also has a value at the end that reflects the contents of the foregoing data. Should the data inside the packet be corrupted, this ending value, this checksum, will no longer match the stuff inside, so you know something is wrong. To cut back to the post office analogy, this is as if someone wrote on the back of an envelope, "This letter has seven sheets of cream-colored parchment paper inside, with handwriting on both sides of each one." If you get seven sheets of handwritten letter out, then this checksum is correct. If a sheet is missing, if it's typed, if it doesn't match that description . . . then that checksum is incorrect, and you'd better get hold of Aunt Sadie and get her to resend that letter, as a packet on the Internet would then be resent. A proper algorithm would complain if so much as one letter of your letter from Aunt Sadie had been muffed up, but the basic idea is here. So where does this hook into woowoo stuff? If you know what you normally feel like, and current feeling doesn't match, it may be time to go looking to see if there's extra stuff, missing stuff . . . see why your checksum failed.

Use exercise 15 to run a "checksum" on your own preparation sequence.

Exercise 15. Running a Checksum on Your Trance Work

Start with the self-evaluation questionnaire with which you began and run a self-check after completing the work in each chapter. Whenever you feel one of the exercises has affected you especially strongly, or you find your equilibrium upset in some other way, make a notation in your journal. Watch for symptoms like disturbed sleep or disturbing dreams, difficulty focusing on work or school, depression, emotional hypersensitivity, or illness. Identify and evaluate any other factors that may affect the way you function—health, diet, and stress from other sources. If external disturbances are unavoidable (you are under a deadline at work, or you or someone close to you is ill), ease up on the trance work. If the trance work seems to be *causing* the problem, take a short vacation from the work, or drop practices from your list until you get back to a sequence with which you feel comfortable. When you feel stabilized, begin moving forward again, at a slower and more careful pace than before.

Practice

Here are five simple exercises you can use to evaluate your readiness for trance work. Exercise 16 will help you improve your ability to observe and remember, thereby making objects a doorway to contemplation of concepts for which the object itself is only a symbol. Exercise 17 will help you hone your reactions to sound cues. Exercise 18 gives techniques for developing your tactile sense. Exercise 19 will help you enable your emotional memory. Exercise 20 helps you track and validate your trance work.

Exercise 16. Developing Your Vision and Focus

Choose a familiar object—a piece of jewelry you often wear or a tool you work with—and contemplate it using the techniques in exercise 11. Close your eyes, building up the image, and look again to compare.

Write down a description of the object, and/or try to draw a picture of it. Wait a day and try to bring up the image again. How well did you remember? Do the same thing with an unfamiliar object.

The purpose of the first level of this exercise is to improve your ability to observe and remember. However once you can do this easily, contemplation can trigger a different kind of consciousness, in which an object becomes a doorway to contemplation of concepts for which the object itself is only a symbol.

Play the "Jewel Game" with a friend, first using familiar, and then unfamiliar objects. The first time, use only your sight to identify the objects. Then try again, touching and handling each item. Draw or diagram their positions. If you are still having trouble, try making up a story around them.

Exercise 17. Closing Your Eyes and Paying Attention

Choose a tape or CD of someone reading poetry in a style you like, but with which you are not familiar, or record a friend with a good voice doing a reading. Listen to the recording with your eyes closed, paying attention to the timbre, accent, and resonance of the voice. Play a line, then pause the recording and try to repeat it, striving to reproduce the voice as well as the words.

When you can do this, repeat the process with a paragraph of prose. Which did you find easier? Which was most enjoyable?

Create a chant to use as a cue for moving into a state of receptivity. Start with an affirmation of your purpose, such as, "I am seeking the world within . . . " Play with suggestive words: "down," "in," "deep," "slide," "rest," etc. Note the emotions each one brings up and work with those that seem most effective and comfortable. Explore and experiment with tones until you can repeat the chant with reasonable consistency. Add the chant to your meditation sequence before doing the mind clearing exercise 9.

Exercise 18. Developing Your Tactile Sense

Study the Hindu and Buddhist *mudra* traditions and choose one of the traditional gestures to work with as a cue for meditation, or develop a hand position of your own. Add it to the position in which you meditate. When you finish your meditation, flex your fingers as part of your procedure for returning to ordinary consciousness.

Instead of following your preparatory practice by clearing your mind, sway rhythmically while intoning your chant. Decide beforehand how long you want to spend on this practice and set your internal timer. Does adding movement change the effect of your chanting?

Choose a sensory cue, such as tasting a pinch of salt, to bring yourself out of trance, and add it to the end of your meditation sequence.

Rub your hands together for a moment to sensitize them and then hold your palms facing each other. Move them back and forth until you find the position in which you feel the greatest pressure. Now try the same thing with a partner. Cup your hands around an invisible sphere of energy and pass it back and forth. Have your partner lie down and move your hands through the air above his or her body. At what distance are you the most sensitive to changes in pressure or temperature? Do the places where you notice differences correspond to your partner's perceptions of pain, stiffness, or other symptoms in those areas?

Exercise 19. Enabling Your Emotional Memory

Choose an incident from fiction or memory that affects you strongly, but not traumatically. Contemplate the incident, paying specific attention to sensory details. What can you see? What is the temperature of the air? What sounds can you hear around you? If you are in the scene, what are you wearing? Notice weight and texture. When the scene has played to its conclusion, return to ordinary consciousness and write down everything you can remember. If you are working with an episode from a book, reread the passage and note where your experience was the same or different, and in particular, what sensory impressions you remember that were not explicitly stated.

Exercise 20. Validating Your Trance Work

Analyze your physical and emotional well-being. Note any changes since you began your trance training, and evaluate their impact on the way you function in daily life and in spiritual work. Look for evidence of stress or increased well-being, and any changes in your health, emotions, and relationships not attributable to other causes. If it seems necessary, find someone to whom you can go for a reality-check or counseling.

Chapter Five

There and Back Again

And so today I build in space my own roadways from there to there and back, where I enjoy the advantage of living in two worlds at once—the mundane world and the world "out-there" where the sun never sets and adventure lurks in every breath, where destiny and free-will meet, and like past and future are irrevocably wedded.

Eileen Garrett

Think about journeying. The earlier chapters have covered ways to get ready, but how do you plan your trip? How do you know where to go? If you are preoccupied and driving on autopilot, you may end up at the place you go most often instead of where you actually wanted to go. Even when you are going the right way, changing traffic conditions may require you to alter your route.

When you travel somewhere unfamiliar, you prepare more carefully. You want directions, or a road map. If you have no map, you are even more careful to note landmarks and directions so you can find your way home again. You consult AAA or Mapquest and ask about milestones or road names. If the trip is a long one, you allow for fatigue, rest stops, and food. If you are lucky, your sources are accurate and you interpret them correctly. Sometimes, you seek advice from someone who has been there before.

The same is true when you journey through inner space, with the added complication that, here, you not only choose your destination, but to some extent you also design the landscape you are traveling through. The terrain through which you travel in the outer world is created by natural forces and human activity. But what about your inner landscape? Although you are capable of imagining settings, you can never completely invent them. As Tolkien points out in "On Fairy Stories," we cannot visualize a green Sun unless we already have the concepts "Sun" and "green" (1986).

Both our conscious and unconscious minds create landscapes out of familiar materials. Jung's theory of the collective unconscious is one way to explain how people who have never studied mythology can come up with traditional figures in visions and dreams. Are these archetypes programmed into our psyches, or do they exist in some kind of cosmic data file to which altered states of consciousness can give us access? For all practical purposes, it doesn't matter–so long as the images are there.

Navigating Inner Space

Many cultures have developed "maps" of inner space to aid those who journey there. We'll discuss this in more detail in chapter 8. The Norse diagram of the Nine Worlds arranged on Yggdrasil, the Kabbalistic Tree of Life, and a Buddhist mandala are all examples of "glyphs," or maps, evolved by specific cultures to serve as aids to meditation. Where a map takes you depends on the culture that produced it. The important point here is that some kind of map be available.

When you journey without a physical body, you have to rely on mental analogues to your sense of direction. You keep your inner explorations under control by developing your sense of structure. Each journey has a beginning, in which you move from consensus reality to the Otherworld; a middle, in which you travel (hopefully toward a goal); and a conclusion, in which you make your way back, bringing with you what you have learned. Whether you travel on the inner or outer planes of existence, you can only afford to take shortcuts when the route becomes familiar. When you no longer have to pay attention to each turning, you can move directly from your starting point to your destination.

For some people, "teleportation" is their favorite way to get into the Otherworld. Moving with the speed of thought to the place you want to go has the advantage of being swift and efficient. However, it offers less adaptability and control than a more intentional and gradual journey. Just as you move along streets and through intersections during physical travel, in the inner world, you travel through a series of passages. Sometimes they are immediate and obvious; sometimes you have to seek them, or even create them.

The opening scenes of *Alice in Wonderland* or the *Oz* books or the Narnia novels of C. S. Lewis are excellent examples of passage imagery. In depicting travel, you need two images—an opening and a passage. A classic example is the German fairy tale about a girl whose wicked stepmother makes her spin night and day. One evening she is sitting on the edge of the well spinning flax, which must be wetted regularly in order to be spun. She drops her spindle down the well, and afraid of being punished for losing it, leaps in after it. The well leads to the Otherworld. She emerges in a country where it is summer and, after several adventures, comes to the house of Frau Hölle (the goddess Holda). After serving the goddess well for some time, she becomes homesick. Because she has been such a good housekeeper, when she goes through the door (which now leads directly to our world), she is showered with gold.

Passages

There are many doorways to the Otherworld. They include gateways, doors, curtains, and other openings. When you visualize going through a barrier, it sends a powerful message to your subconscious. Passages, on the other hand, can be more varied—from roads, paths, tunnels, and staircases, to rivers down which you float, trees you climb, and bridges you cross. Whatever gets you from one place to another in physical life works in the Otherworld as well. Depending on the terrain, you walk, ride, swim, or climb. You may even fly, which makes some things simpler, but requires more careful attention to the terrain below. Having a mental map of the Otherworld helps you retain a sense of direction. "Up," "down," "north," "south" may all be mental constructs, but they can be very useful. To further fine-tune your journeying, choose images that relate directly to the purpose at hand. If you want to contact a deity from a particular mythology, use images from that culture.

Back Again

To journey safely in the Otherworld, you must remember not only what you see, but the order in which you see it. This is essentially the same thing you do when you find your way home from a new place or try to remember where you parked your car. Coming back to ordinary consciousness will be much more comfortable if you make the return journey in exact reverse order. With practice, you can remember backward as well as forward, so that, even when you are under stress, you will automatically return the way you came. This is also useful, by the way, when you are trying to remember where you left your car keys.

The guidelines offered for planning your outward journey are applicable to your journey back as well. In fact, one of the reasons for observing landmarks and planning your trip so carefully is so you will be able to find your way home. If the route is charted, in an emergency, someone else can help you retrace your steps. The more profound your trance experience, the more important it is that you go back the way you came without leaving any pieces of your psyche behind. I am sure that one reason I coped so well with my first "interesting" visionary encounter with Odin was that my years of disciplined journeying enabled me to pull all my pieces together and get myself home.

One hazard of a speedy teleportation or an emergency ejection is soul loss. Physical symptoms include dizziness, nausea, or headache. You may feel generally out of sorts, or suddenly be deficient in some skill at which you were formerly proficient. My friend Lorrie once came out of trance too fast after an oracle ritual and lost her sense of direction.

"I was out of sorts for most of the next week," she recounts. "Eventually, as I went to bed, I flipped Elseworld, grabbed Otter, and we tromped down to the Well. He dove in, swam down, and came back up with a small, nickel-sized compass in his hand, symbolic of my sense of direction, and I took it back and felt better." A young woman attending one of my workshops had had a rough week and, as I later learned, a disorienting experience on the morning of the workshop. On the way back from the last trance journey, she left several pieces of herself along the way. Fortunately, I had guided the journey and knew where we had gone, so I was able to take her back along the route to gather up the missing soul parts and put them back.

This is, in fact, the recommended method for dealing with the effects of returning to ordinary consciousness too quickly, whether from a trance journey or a dream. Go back into trance and retrace your steps exactly as you would if you were trying to figure out where you parked your car. Repeat your return journey slowly, opening your awareness to any parts of yourself that may have been left behind. If you are still having problems, find someone with experience in soul retrieval to work with you. The Harner Foundation may be able to recommend a shamanic therapist who has learned the technique for Soul Retrieval taught by Sandra Ingerman. An experienced trance worker may also be able to apply the technique by studying her book, *Soul Retrieval* (1991).

When you return from a trance journey, take a few moments to make sure you have reconnected. Review the "Checksum" exercise given in the previous chapter. In the first lesson, we worked on the progressive relaxation of muscles. This technique can work as an exercise in body awareness as well. It can give you a sense of how you feel when you're more or less together, and how each *part* of you should feel.

This makes it easier to know if something is missing when you return from a journey. If you discover that something is missing, retrace your steps to get it back.

Organizing Memories

Retracing your steps in trance is much easier if you practice "reverse memory." Exercise 21 will help you develop this skill.

Exercise 21. Developing Reverse Memory

Before you fall asleep, relax, breathe, and clear your mind.

Starting with the time you spent preparing for bed, try to move your memory back through your day. Do this every night until you can recapitulate most of the events of the day in reverse order.

When you can do that, try remembering back through the week. You can also search your memory to identify the places you have lived during the past ten years, visualizing each of them as completely as possible.

Vary this exercise by remembering specific kinds of events–a birthday party, a trip, or a given period in your life. Begin with whatever event you can remember, and extend your memory forward and back until you can recapture all the high points.

Some people find this practice interesting and easy; to others, it can be quite annoying. Those who have to rise early for work may begrudge the extra half-hour spent in meditation. Others may feel that they are already remembering what they need to bring back from meditation and, in a kind of mental triage, forgetting the things they don't need to know. When this issue came up in the class, it provoked a lively debate, as others pointed out the dangers of the "forget and fester" technique of managing trance memories.

It's an interesting question. Not everything that burbles up from the unconscious is important. Practicing reverse memory can improve your ability to remember your dreams, but many of those dreams may be no more significant than many of the events of your waking life. Trying to remember every detail can lead to sensory overload. Processing traumatic memories is important, but can be dealt with more productively when your unconscious is ready to release them, when you feel ready to deal with them, or they are causing you enough problems that you *have* to deal with them. In the case of serious problems, you should seek the support of a therapist. For the purposes of this exercise, the important thing is not to remember everything, but to recall enough landmarks, in the right order, to find your way home again wherever you may roam.

Articulation

Once you have mastered the techniques for journeying to a chosen destination and dealing with what you find there, you must work on remembering what you learned. This is one reason why dreaming can be such a frustrating experience. Improving your "reverse memory" not only makes it easier to find your way back, it increases the amount of information you can carry, because you don't have to waste energy trying to figure out the way home. Learning to focus on and remember sensory input improves your ability to bring back information from a trance journey. This is what you will practice as you work through this chapter.

I call the skill that enables us to "know what we know" *articulation.* Articulation is the ability to analyze and distinguish parts of an experience, or the ability to put what you have learned into words. Through the words of your internal monologue, you interpret your experiences and translate them into memories. Many things happened to you before you learned how to talk, but what were they? Without words, very few of us can remember. After a profound mystical experience, Pascal wrote, "From half-past ten to half-past twelve. Fire!" (Underhill, 1961). The phrase was, presumably, enough to revive the essence of the experience, for he wore a scrap of paper with these words over his heart until he died. Without a way to describe what happened, however, could he ever recapture the whole? Experiences like Pascal's may seem of overwhelming importance to us while we are having them, but if we cannot put them into words, they dissolve like dreams in the dawn.

When you clear your mind at the beginning of meditation, try to still your internal monologue–not because words have no place in trance work, but so you can focus your attention on other things. The state of "no-mind" is useful for rest and restoration, but if you want to remember and learn from your trance states, you need disciplined perception, multisensory imagery, and the ability to put your perceptions into words.

Compare this practice with accounts of dream processing in the Icelandic sagas. In *Viga-Glum's saga*, the protagonist dreams he sees a gigantic woman walking toward his farm. He goes out and invites her in. He then processes the vision in a series of kennings:

> I saw her walk with her island (her wrist, the hawk's small island)
> Like Earth, in the fjord of islands,
> Wrist-spanned with icy silver, that guardian spirit.
> So the goddess who ends the battle
> Seemed in my awesome dream,
> (She who fells you, troubler of armies)
> Helmeted between the fells to stand.

Turville-Petre decodes this as follows:

> I saw a woman spirit of towering stature, a goddess of the head-dress, walk hither to Eyjafjordhr, with a helmet on her head. So that in my dream the battle-goddess seemed to stand beside the hills, warrior (McKinnell, 1972).

Typically, a character in the saga has a dream that, fortunately, is described. Otherwise we would never be able to interpret the next step, which is for the dreamer to translate the experience into a stave of poetry as soon as he wakes up. In the processing, all the facts of the dream are turned into kennings. Once he has got that far, he sits down with a friend and tries to analyze and interpret the dream. In this case, Glum interprets the dream as meaning that his grandfather, Vigfus, has died and his *hamingja* (personal guardian spirit) is coming to become Glum's protector.

In the movie *Contact*, Jody Foster's character, an astronomer, babbles, "They should have sent a poet" as she journeys through space and time. In fact, after making their Moon voyages, several of the Apollo astronauts started writing poetry. Poetry can give us a language with which to articulate our experiences. Describing them enables us to remember them.

Poetry also gives us tools to use during our journeys. Spells are commonly cast in rhyme, and a journey can be viewed as a kind of extended metaphor. The practice of writing poetry, especially poetry that depends heavily on symbolism and simile, can limber up your mental muscles and make it easier for you to come up with useful images for defense or direction. Sensory imagery that invokes vision, sound, smell, and texture improves your ability to make your experiences "real." If you are not already a poet, by the time you have finished with this chapter, you will be. Dig out one of your old English textbooks or the *Oxford Book of English Verse*, or pick up a poetry handbook like the classic *Sound and Sense* (my personal favorite) or *The Science Fiction Poetry Handbook* by Suzette Hayden Elgin to refresh your memory on poetic forms and tools like metaphor and simile.

Put a notebook in your pocket and take a Sunday afternoon "poetry hike." As you stroll along (marching is good for getting ideas to flow, but stroll if you actually want to notice what's around you), keep an eye out for arresting images. This will exercise your body as well as your spirit. Your goal is to come home with a collection of verbal snapshots and sound bytes that will evoke the events of the day. Haiku are good for capturing the moment:

> Plum blossoms falling
> scatter snow upon the grass–
> winter changed to spring.

Or a glimpse can turn into fantasy, as in this piece I wrote a long time ago:

> Noon . . .
> Beneath the thorn,
> A hot breath whispers in the sighing grass.
> Basking, ochre hills
> Hump, maned with light, against a blazing sky.
> The undefended ground
> Trembles to the heavy padding tread.
> The lion comes.

If you cannot get outdoors, look for inspiring images in a coffee-table nature book, or even a Sierra Club calendar.

Once you have had some fun turning images into words, reverse the process and turn words back into images. (For the purpose of this exercise, "image" includes sound, smell, texture, and the rest of the senses.) Some writers describe things more vividly than others. J.R.R. Tolkien in particular has the ability to capture a scene in words. Have someone read you a passage like the one that begins "Frodo ran to the eastern window . . . " in the chapter in which he stays with Tom Bombadil (1956). Close your eyes and, from the description, build up the image in your mind.

Another interesting exercise is to work with words chosen at random. You can do this by using bibliomancy on a dictionary, or by some even more arcane method, like the one chosen by George below. Keep looking until you have a variety of parts of speech, especially a good selection of nouns and adjectives. If they suggest a being or object, try to visualize it, or find a way to use them all in a poem or a narrative.

The results can be . . . interesting . . .

> I split the digits of "pi" into pairs and took each pair as a page number. Then I took a stack of books and copied the first noun on the indicated page, a new book on a different subject for each page choice. Some of the nouns can be read as other parts of speech, but they were all nouns in the contexts where I found them. Then I duplicated the process for the adjectives.

NOUNS	ADJECTIVES
publisher	single
understanding	great
unconscious	gloomy
stones	severe
sea	young
church	peaceful
needle	poor

The first level of processing produced the following combinations:

Single needle
Great understanding
Gloomy unconscious
Severe church
Young publisher
Peaceful sea
Poor stones

Developing the material further, George came up with the following piece:

A young publisher,
although uniformed in a single-needle tailored shirt,
shows no great understanding.
His severe church has given him a gloomy unconscious.
Looking at the peaceful sea shore, he sees only poor stones.

Hilary took six of the words and got:

Unconscious as a bone upon the severe sea,
A single tuning is all the direction I can find,
Pulled to the north as a needle is.
A gloomy church, this grey ocean proposes
Understanding as clear as sea on stones.
Where once largesse of choices overwhelmed me,

> This poor narrow arch enfolds me as the sea
> Drives home into the land rocks, takes possession.
> I struggle, joyed as dolphins, splashing foam.

Electra took a different tack:

> Single young female publisher seeking that needle in a haystack, a peaceful understanding man. I like walks by the sea, Wednesdays at church and am great in bed. You are a stone that has gathered no moss. Together we will explore our unconscious. No gloomy, severe or poor men please.

As you can see, this exercise can lead in directions as varied as the people who pursue them.

The Base Camp

You will find it much easier to journey if you first create a "power place" in the Otherworld to serve as your home base for journeying. This can be a point of departure for you, and a place where you can keep magical garb and tools. Michael Harner starts journeys by instructing students to imagine a place outdoors that they know well. By beginning with a real place, you can use all your senses to recreate its image. Neo-shamanic journeys generally involve an analogue of the natural world; beginning in a natural place provides for an easy transition.

However, your home base can be more than a jumping-off point. The more personal and fully realized you make it, the more powerful it will be as a homing beacon. If you envision it as a place where things can be stored, you can create a whole wardrobe, tool kit, and arsenal for spirit journeying (rather like the amazing trunk of Rufus in Robert Heinlein's *Glory Road*). Exercise 22 will help you build and flesh out your base camp.

Exercise 22. Building a Base Camp

Begin by moving into a reflective, open state. Wait to see what images come up by themselves.

Remember a place you know and improve upon it, or design your home base from scratch. The landscape can be a real place or imagined. Choose a spot you remember fondly from childhood, or from more recent experiences.

Whether you arrive at your images through vision or imagination, once you have the basic picture, write a description of how you got there and what it looks like. Be sure to include doorways! Work on the description–polish it and add to it. Put in as much sensory detail as you can. Memorize your description, then pay your base camp a visit. Are there things you forgot? Add them to your written description.

If you are having difficulty choosing a location, or have trouble staying focused, record your description and play it for yourself. When you can see, feel, and sense your place, give yourself five minutes of silence to explore it before directing yourself to return to ordinary consciousness.

To help you along, here is an example from my first class. Rather than inventing an imaginary place, George envisioned his basement as he would like it to be. Notice the careful use of directional and sensory cues.

My Beginning Place
Go out the door, headed south
turn left and down three stair steps to the west.
(turn right to the garden and be lost)
Turn left and down six stair steps to the north.
Turn east, enter the door in the wall,
Turn right, pass in through the inner door to the north.
Cross the tiny antechamber.
Greet the Medusa and the Head of Glory who stand guard.
Open the innermost door to the north,

Step down the last step and into the chamber through its south wall.

The chamber is not large and it appears yet smaller because it is packed and crammed and overfilled with the implements of magic. The temperature tends toward constant, warm in winter, cool in summer. The air holds faint scents of herbs, oils, smudges, the ghosts of past rituals and workings. The beige neutral walls are hung with masks and pictures: demons, guardians, animal powers, deities, and grotesques. Electric and candle light and darkness can be chosen at need.

North

The North wall, partially obscured by freestanding shelves and cabinets, is hinged and can swing up to open out into enormous spaces. A floor-to-ceiling map displays the geography of California. The shelves are filled with boxes of various sizes, materials, and shapes. One of the smaller cabinets, glass-doored, is crowded with figures, idols, deities, and the effigies of the powerful. A fire extinguisher stands in the northeast corner.

East

The east wall holds, from north to south, a workbench full of tools and materials, the place of the keeper, who sits awaiting need, four feet tall, bald and white-bearded, lynx-eyed, robed in strength and perched on a high wooden stool, a large, old, dark, wooden altar table before the curtained window, and another jumble of shelves and boxes and containers.

South

The south wall, from east to west, holds the entrance door, more bookcases with statues of Diana of Ephesus and Oshun (they seem to coexist amicably in this space), a collection of staves, sticks, wands, and weapons.

West

The west wall, from south to north, holds a small curious door, and a row of cabinets and bookcases. Here are the talismans, fetishes, beads, rings, and amber, the carriers of enchantment. The oils and incenses, the colors and forms that play upon the imagination to guide and shape its products. The small door can open to many places: a robing room, a rough worktable, a book vault, a fabric stash, a gateway to elsewhere. It is guarded by a small but sincerely toothy dragon skull.

Zenith

The ceiling is not high. A few figures dangle from its fittings: a flying cat, a fetish.

Nadir

A large wool rug, patterned with lightning zigzags, covers the concrete floor. It is overlain and obscured by many smaller rugs.

The chamber holds many chairs, too many chairs until a group meets here to work. A great chair of state, a soft chair with a footstool, a captain's chair, an office chair, a faldstool, four folding chairs, another office chair; who holds this space loves company. A mobile altar, its top inlaid with a carpenter's star, waits in one corner. A set of black and white large plastic cylinders wait to be assembled as the pillars of Joachim and Boaz.

This is my refuge, my work space of delight, my armory, my safe and certain portal to The Wood Beyond the World. I once knew every inch of this space and all its contents, but the insatiable urge to acquire has long drowned my memory in details and clutter.

Now I must root for what I need, but it is here.

As you become more experienced in journeying, you may discover variations in your inner landscape. Some scenes will appear only once, while others will become a permanent part of your internal map. Some things will clearly be invented, while others will have the air of discoveries, each with unique energy and significance. An inner landscape may have its own energy fields and sacred sites.

Although we have discussed experiences in terms of visual detail and poetic description, don't forget the power of the other senses.

The description of your base camp may be more powerful if it evokes sounds and smells, as in this example by Melissa:

> My actual inner perspective of the hobbit home is: the swell of the grassy hill which smells green and rich. The feel of lying in the tall, soft grass. The deep soil beneath that forms the hill and surrounds me when I'm inside, dark and loamy and cool. The smell of the earth. The warmth of the Sun outside, the scent of my favorite flowers and herbs. Inside, it's the sound of my feet moving from silky wooden flooring that smells like lemon polish to plush throw rugs that have all the colors of gemstones. The many textured paneling made of redwood and beech and oak and other woods for which I have no name.

Those who work in a specific tradition may find that their home base draws on its mythology, as in this example by Swanhild, which also shows how the base camp itself can become a passage, as well as a place for doing work:

> I always start out with a tree. Usually it's the tree in my yard where I Blot—a wild cherry—because I'm so familiar with all its details, but it doesn't have to be. Whichever tree I use, I ask it to be Yggdrasil for me. If the answer is no, I try again later, or with another tree. If the answer is yes, I can go down through a hole at the base of one of the tree's roots, or I can simply relax against the trunk and let my etheric body sink into it and meld with it, or I can climb the tree, find a place to sit among its branches, and let myself meld with it. Whichever route I use—the branches, the roots, or simply becoming one with the substance of the tree—in a few moments, I find myself relaxing against Yggdrasil in Otherworld. Usually from here I can see the shrouded figures of the Norns and the dark depths of the Well of Wyrd, with a white swan and a black swan gliding silently across its surface.
>
> I also have a home I can go to Over There, but I'm not yet clear on the details of how I get there from the Tree. I do know

that where I go is high on a lush green mountainside overlooking a vast valley, with thick forests to one side and a gleaming river winding away to the other. The room I spend most of my time in here is made of white stone and pale wood elaborately carved with designs and runes. The ceiling is high, and crisscrossed with beams in which the shapes of several runes are also discernable. There is a huge stone fireplace with a fire always roaring in it, and a huge bed covered with large white animal skins. White animal skins also cover the floor. Against one wall is a silver basin that magically fills with water whenever I want it. The entire room is bright and gleaming, although there is no other apparent source of light other than the fire.

There are carved doorways leading out of this room to various places, but I haven't fully explored all of them yet. One door leads to a workroom, where I have magical tools, drinking horns, various weapons, and other paraphernalia, plus tools for carving runes, a large worktable, and an indoor garden with growing herbs. Adjoining the workroom is a vast library. Another door leads to a bathroom with a big silver tub, large enough to swim in, and an adjoining dressing room, where I know I can find, among other things, a cloak made of white swan feathers and one of white wolf's skin. Another leads away from my suite of rooms into the rest of the building, which is enormous. And another leads out onto a balcony overlooking the mountainside and the valley far below it. This place is so high up that mist clings to the side of the mountain below me as I look down, but if I focus my attention I can see through it, and can seem to see whatever I want to see, in any direction. Raptors wheel through the air here, and ravens call out constantly. The air is crisp and clean, with a slight bite of chill to it and a crystalline clarity. There is a faint scent of evergreen and snow.

Often there are others present when I go to my place, but that's another story. . . .

Practice

1. ***Reverse Memory:*** For a week, each night before you go to sleep, remember the events of your day in reverse order from the point at which you got into bed back to when you got out of it that morning. When you have practiced remembering backward often enough for it to come easily, reconstruct a sequence of events forward, such as the journey from your home to work or school, and write it down. Put in as much detail as you can, noting each transition from one road to another, and describing what you see, hear, smell, etc. You may have the best results with a journey you do not repeat too often. If the route is so familiar you can follow it without thinking, many of the details will be buried in your unconscious and hard to bring to mind. When you are done, take a new piece of paper and write a description of the return journey without referring to the first account. When finished, compare them. Were there things you remembered about the outward journey that you missed on the return, or vice versa? What differences did the change in perspective coming and going make in what you noticed and how you described it?
2. ***Building a Base Camp:*** Build a base camp, either by articulating your need, then clearing your mind and waiting to see what your unconscious creates for you, or by intentionally designing (or transforming) a place that will meet your needs. Your base camp should be a place where you feel safe and relaxed, yet energized enough to work. It can be a house, cave, temple, garden, or place in nature, or you can add grounds and have all of the above. Furnish it with anything you think you will need. Create a magical closet or a trunk to hold your gear. Design the gear, or include a workshop where you can make it. In addition to the door or gate by which you enter, make sure it has one or more exits through which you can go to places you may want to explore. Once you have created it, add a visit as part of your regular meditation practice, which you should still be doing several times a week. Write a description or draw a picture.

3. ***Articulation:*** Look at a scene, a picture, or an object and write a few lines of poetry about it. Experiment with forms—haiku, Anglo-Saxon alliterative verse, etc. Read poetry, with particular attention to the use of images. Take verbal "snapshots" to help you to articulate the images you encounter in vision and dream. Once you can remember physical items that you have perceived with your senses accurately, practice putting these elements together to improve your ability to build up new images. Start by reading (or having someone read to you) a vivid description of a place from a book or poem. Try to build up an image from the description. Write down or draw what you have perceived. Then work with random elements. On slips of paper, write a number of nouns and adjectives. Draw several at once and read (or have someone read) them. Close your eyes and build up in your mind's eye an image of what a thing of that description would look like—for instance a "one-eyed, one-horned, flying purple people-eater," a blue and green galloping giraffe, a grey eight-legged horse. . . .
4. ***Passages:*** Practice working with journey structures by reading fairy tales (Grimms', Andersen's, Lang's, etc.), the journey to Hades in the *Odyssey*, or classic fantasy literature (especially nineteenth-century fantasy and fairy tales for children like George MacDonald's and James Barrie's). Choose one and retell it in your own words, paying special attention to how the characters get from one place to another and deal with challenges.

Chapter Six

Native Guides

Once I was young and went alone,
and wandering lost my way;
when I found a friend I felt myself rich . . .
Hávamál: 47

The vehicle is moving and is carrying everything you need, from a camera to record what you see to a butterfly net to capture memories. You have a home base. You are all set to go. Now you must learn to travel safely. Who are you likely to meet on this journey, and will you need protection? How can you find your way to unknown locations? Can you call 911 in the Otherworld?

With the skills you have already, you can decide on a goal and begin your journey. You can reach the worlds within and return—but think how much easier it will be if you have "a local" as a companion. It is not necessary to have company when you are journeying, but it can be extremely useful. A wise traveler studies what is known about his destination before leaving, and, on arrival, seeks out a native guide.

The Source and Nature of Inner Guides

Guides—allies, helpers, "invisible friends"—are found in the visionary literature of almost every culture. Who are they? What are they? Is the Raven who advises and leads me actually a separate entity? Is she, as she once informed me, Huginn and Muninn's mother? Perhaps. Certainly, the more I know about her, the more vividly she appears to me. The more time I spend with her, the easier it becomes to interact with her, to hear her clearly. Many people who begin to work with a particular animal in the spirit world find that its real-world kindred starts turning up everywhere in the world of everyday experience. Ravens move into the neighborhood; someone gives you a cat; a stag appears in your headlights and then leaps away.

On the other hand, sometimes the form of your guide may alter—as if it were only a disguise for something, or someone, else. In a shared meditation, one woman saw my raven as a black airplane large enough to carry the entire group. From this, we concluded that Raven had decided to adopt the kindred. And, in fact, she continues to watch over those who make the journey to the Underworld with us when we perform oracular *seidh*. My friend Ember feels that the rabbit form taken by her ally doesn't bound him, but that her need for a helper of that type has determined the shape in which he appears. Spirit guides, like the figures we meet in dreams, can be polymorphic, shifting from one form to another as the situation requires. Of course, in vision, we ourselves may also change form without losing our essential identities.

An alternate hypothesis is that the form we perceive is simply a shape our guide takes to meet the needs of the moment—just as we dress in robes, or running clothes, or a business suit, depending on the task at hand. At the beginning of Book IV of *Masks of God (Creative Mythology)*, Joseph Campbell speaks of "... the historical transformations of those imagined forms that I am calling the 'masks' of God, through which men everywhere have sought to relate themselves to the wonder of existence . . . " (1991). He assumes that the masks are created by humankind. My feeling is that, although their forms may come from our minds, it is the Otherworld beings who choose which shapes to wear.

In that case, my ally would "really" be a spirit who "dresses" as a raven because the shape is convenient and the traditional personality is compatible with its nature. I will say, however, that the raven did not come to me because I was interested in Norse culture. Rather, I became involved in Germanic religion because Raven came to me.

In August 1987, I finally had the opportunity to attend one of the Foundation for Shamanic Studies Basic Workshops, conducted by Michael Harner. I had been using the instructions from Harner's book with some success, both to work on my own and to lead journeys for others. Following those instructions, I had made a good connection with a stag, who usually counseled me to eat more vegetables and get more exercise. I had also contacted Coyote, who seemed to feel that I needed to lighten up and occasionally tried to cop a feel, but was also quite happy to guide me around the Otherworld. So when Mr. Harner explained that the journey for the first day would be to the Lower World to find an ally, I figured that I was well-supplied already, and could simply take advantage of the opportunity to go down and hang out with my friends.

The first part of the journey went according to plan, and my old buddies showed up as expected. However, we hardly had time to exchange greetings before a large raven lit on a branch over my head and announced that she had come to be my guide.

"But I already have an ally—several, in fact." I explained.

"You need me. I know the way to places you need to go."

"You are a raven . . . " I considered her. In European, as in Native American, mythology, ravens are heavy medicine. In Greece, they are the companions of Apollo; in the British Isles, heralds of the Morrigan; in Scandinavia, the allies of Odin, ruler of Asgard, bestower of the mead of poetry and lord of the slain. If I had been inventing an ally for a character in one of my novels, I might have chosen a raven. But not for myself. And there was another problem.

"Do you know how many people in the pagan community have raven totems? Are *called* Raven? You are a stereotype, a cliché," I informed her. "I'm not going to be just another raven-groupie, thank you. Now go away, I want to spend some time with my friends." I started walking. Coyote was laughing at me; the stag snorted disdainfully and snatched a mouthful of grass. The raven spread her wings in a long glide to the next tree.

"You analyze things too much, you know," she said. "You should stop thinking and just open up to what's happening. You people are so stupid, sometimes I wonder why we bother with you."

That is a question I have often asked myself. Inner allies seem to view us as rather backward children with whom they are nonetheless required to deal.

"Look, will you just sit still for a minute and listen to me? Stupid human . . . " she muttered, settling on another tree. "You were supposed to look for an ally, and here I am. I'm the one who can help you with what you need to do now, what you came here to learn."

Well, these were probably not her exact words, but the emotional tone was clear. She yammered at me along these lines until Harner started drumming the signal to return.

"All right, already," I finally said. "If you're going to be like that about it, I'll take you on—at least for this workshop. See you tomorrow!" I retraced my steps back to the here-and-now.

The result of this encounter was that Raven has been my principal inner guide ever since. In 1982, when I wrote *Brisingamen*, a contemporary novel featuring Norse mythology, there were no ravens in Berkeley. In the nineties I began to notice them. In the years since then, they have become numerous around here. My conscious mind tells me this population explosion was probably made possible by the ban on DDT. But my unconscious mind snickers and alerts my ears to a distant raven call.

I have studied the natural history of ravens and spent many hours watching them. On every birthday, someone gives me a raven picture or a piece of jewelry. My grandchildren like to come up and count the number of raven images in my room. At last count it was twenty-four, but sometimes the numbers change. Although not everyone ends up with such a visible connection, my life has certainly been enriched by this one.

A third theory put forward to explain our inner guides is that they are actually projections from our own psyches—personae that we split off to do specific jobs. In its extreme form, this is the mechanism that produces multiple personalities that take over in the waking world in order to protect the ego from unbearable pain. In more ordinary circumstances, we only change our clothing and sometimes our way of speaking when we move between home, work, and visits to conservative relatives. But we know that our minds *can* create these beings. The figures in your dreams are created by your psyche. In books and films, you find characters that become more real to you than many people you know. A small child in need of a playmate, or sometimes a scapegoat, creates an invisible companion. Dramatic play, whether with a costume box or a chest full of toys, is a natural and healthy way for children to work out tensions and explore new modes of being in the world.

If your conscious mind is uncertain about its ability to function in trance, or unable to access the contents and power of the unconscious on demand, a powerful magical helper who can reach into the collective or personal unconscious and manifest whatever is needed can be an extremely useful invention. In that case, creating such a figure intentionally, instead of involuntarily, would be a very sensible move.

The Viking Age magical term *seidh* is often translated as "playing with minds." In my experience, the minds we play with most often in such work are our own. A great deal of trance work consists of creating ways for the conscious and the unconscious to talk to each other. We intentionally condition ourselves to alter our states of consciousness through posture, breathing, and imagery, thus decreasing the likelihood that such a shift will happen involuntarily. So why not intentionally invent our inner guides?

The main problem with talking to the unconscious is getting it to believe what you say. When we call upon legendary figures or gods, the weight of tradition (or the fact that they do indeed exist on another plane) may make it easier to believe in them. But how do you get your mind to believe that a red fox or an otter is advising you?

Shifting your state of consciousness to a level where the voice of your conscious mind weakens or even fades away moves you into a state in which it is natural to communicate in images. In this state, your helpers, whether they are projections of your own mind or forces from the spirit world, can assume a shape in which you will believe.

Ever since the time of Plato and Aristotle, philosophers have debated whether objects have their own inherent existence or are a manifestation of archetypal models. In practice, we continue to sit on chairs without worrying about the nature of their reality. Thus, in my opinion, the question is not where the chair comes from, but whether it will support me when I sit down. Likewise, the spiritual question is not whether my inner guides really exist, but whether they can help me get around in the Otherworld. Do they give me good advice? Can they keep me out of trouble?

Native guides can appear in many ways. In shamanic traditions and fairy tales, they often take animal form. In medieval Europe, they were seen as saints or figures from legend. Unless a culture has a taboo against such contact, helpers may be spirits of the dead. Elemental spirits and the folk of faerie may appear in sacred places; plant spirits can be very useful advisors when you are seeking healing.

The Way of the Animal Powers

In shamanic cultures, spirit guides commonly take the form of animals. In some cultures, everyone has some kind of animal totem or helper. Shamans or medicine people may have a whole menagerie of different animals that come to them at different times, or help with different types of work. Some may disappear when their work is done, to be replaced by new ones; others remain for a lifetime. Animal allies can include mammals, birds, reptiles, aquatic species, and legendary creatures. Michael Harner teaches that we should avoid using insects as guides, but I know people who have worked productively with certain insects that have a cultural significance for them, such as spiders and butterflies. Currently, a number of people are beginning to work with the bee.

Why, you may ask, are spirit guides so often encountered in animal form? The world of the unconscious is a place of primal power, so it should be no surprise if we instinctively identify it with the world of nature. When humans first began to speculate about the world around them, they found it populated by a variety of animals, all of whom seemed much more powerful than they were. Hunter-gatherer societies, which have legends of the days in which the animal kindred were people too, still see their culture heroes in animal form. Coyote steals fire and scatters the stars. Raven pecks open the clamshell to release humanity. Spider Grandmother leads the people from world to world.

Even when gods and goddesses in human shape took over those roles, beast fables remained popular—from Aesop, to the medieval *fabliaux*, to the cartoons watched by children today. Bugs Bunny and Mickey Mouse are the heirs of Br'er Rabbit and Anansi. We give our children toy ducks to protect them in the bath, and Teddy Bears to ward their sleep. When small, my grandchildren were guarded by a tattered toy in the shape of a bear that belonged to their great-grandmother when she was a girl.

I have vivid memories of an afternoon in the Cornish town of Padstow, when a friend and I watched the procession of the Padstow "Hobby Horse." This is a stylized horse-shaped construction that has been carried through the streets to bless the town every May 1 for centuries. We listened to a young man from the procession explain very seriously to his young son why the "'Oss" was more powerful than Spiderman. We have been conditioned to believe in and trust our animal helpers since we were very small.

In animals, we see the wisdom that comes from an unbroken connection with nature and the innocence of beings uncorrupted by the human world. We relate to them in a visceral and preverbal way that bypasses conscious inhibitions. By developing your connections with the animal powers, you expand your capacities without losing the advantages of living in the human world. For more information on these beliefs, see Joseph Campbell's *The Way of the Animal Powers* (1988).

In medieval tradition, witches have familiars that are animal allies in physical form who provide advice and power. They may serve as steeds for astral journeys or lend their shapes for journeying. Animal allies connect you to the power of nature–your own as well as that of the world.

Some people acquire a totem animal spontaneously. They may always have felt close to or identified with a certain animal; friends may give them pictures of it; it may even show up to keep an eye on them. It takes very little additional effort for them to contact the animal on the inner planes and develop a relationship. Others can use the method described below.

Journeying to Find an Animal Ally

If you are working in a culturally based tradition and looking for a helper for your work, you should use the imagery and environment of that culture for your journey. If you are heathen, for instance, go to Yggdrasil and the plain of Midgard that lies within. For Wicca or Celtic reconstruction traditions, seek the faerie realms; in the Hellenic (Greek) tradition, try Arcadia. You will find pathworkings for a journey in each of these traditions in Appendix III.

The instructions for a non-culturally specific journey to find a power animal in the Practice section of this chapter are inspired by those given in Michael Harner's *The Way of the Shaman* (1990). These pathworkings take you into the "middle world" that lies within, and provide instructions for connecting with an ally and then returning. As suggested in previous exercises, you can memorize the directions or record them, leaving five or ten minutes of "free time" in the middle in which to do your own work. Or you can find a site outdoors for an "out-sitting," in which you contact your animal ally. To build on the work described here, however, I advise you to begin with an inner journey to the personal power place you have created or found and continue on from there.

Once you have found a promising place, stand still long enough for an ally to find you. Relax. Watch for movement. Wait until something appears several times and finally comes close enough for you to ask whether it is interested in working with you. From there on (whether you are talking to an animal or another spirit), the contact can resemble the social negotiations that go on at a cocktail party. You see someone who looks like a possible business or romantic partner. You make eye contact, smile, begin to talk; if things go well, you end up by trading names and e-dresses, and making plans to get together again. Sometimes the new ally will take you on a tour of the area; sometimes it will lay down conditions for further interaction. Or it may just want to play.

In some cases the animal, or animals, may seem threatening at first. It is natural when faced with an apparently hungry bear or a pack of wolves to flee or fight them. Stories in which a new shaman is carried off by the spirits and dismembered or eaten are staples of the literature. Terrifying as the experience may be, it is followed by a sequence in which the successful shaman is reconstituted and given a magical body and powers. So if you are looking for a spirit helper and it tries to eat you, traditional wisdom would be to let it do so. Being devoured is the ultimate means of "opening up" to the spiritual world and becoming receptive to what the spirits want to teach you.

Some years ago, a member of my group encountered a pack of wolves on his journey to find an ally. He, being a warrior-type, fought them off. When everyone returned and shared their experiences, he was rather surprised to hear that sometimes you are supposed to let the monster eat you! Naturally, we were all highly amused when we saw the episode of *Star Trek* in which the part-Klingon crew member is described as ". . . the only person I ever met who tried to kill her power animal." Of course, there are other perspectives. Another class member protested that any ally or pack that couldn't get past her guard wasn't worthy to eat her.

Unless the attacking being feels really nasty and negative (as opposed to being simply fierce and dangerous), the traditional response is to let yourself be devoured. However you may, before submitting to this, ask if its purpose is destruction or transformation. Just remember that, although the shape a spirit animal wears expresses its nature, the fact that you have, say, a bear spirit as an ally doesn't mean that any bear you meet in nature is automatically your friend. Wild animals are wild. Treat them with caution.

Spirit Guides

In the Western Mystery and New Age traditions, inner guides are more likely to take human than animal form. These spirits can be anything from demigods, to angels, to ascended masters or other legendary teachers, to your grandmother. The Channeling movement of the eighties produced volumes of good advice from figures like "Michael," who was, I am told, originally the author's invention, until "he" began turning up independently for other people. Madame Blavatsky channeled reams of material from the Ascended Masters. Pagans tend to move directly to relationships with gods or goddesses, but the "Mighty Dead," who are less likely to have their own agendas and are more understanding of the human condition, can establish an intermediate, and sometimes very useful, relationship.

The Spiritualist movement of the nineteenth century demonstrated the willingness of the dead to give counsel to the living. Ancestors, or dead relatives, are traditionally sympathetic to the needs of their descendents, as the many stories of grandmothers who became guardian angels suggest. In *Grandmother Moon*, Z. Budapest tells the story of how her dead grandmother protected her when she was a teenager during the Hungarian Revolution.

> I was going to attend another demonstration against the Russian occupation of Hungary that was to be held on the Pest side in a medium-sized plaza. . . . I got dressed and walked as fast as I could, but somehow it wasn't fast enough. My body felt like lead. I was all legs at this time; such exercise should not have strained my body, yet I could not move, could not make it to the opening of the gathering. . . . When I was about to enter the plaza, I realized that instead of the rumbling of the voices and cheers and songs, there was a silence. I turned the corner. And then I saw. There

> were thousands of people in the plaza—men, women, and kids, all shot to death, lying freshly killed on the ground.
>
> Had I been on time as I planned, I would have been gunned down with the rest. . . . I think my grandmother has protected me all through my life, and here again, she displayed her powers of protection, making my body heavy, slowing me down, saving my life (1989).

In many cultures, the dead who consistently answer prayers gradually assume the status of demigods. The heroes of Greece whose tombs became places of pilgrimage eventually were believed to be the sons of gods. The names of Danish kings who continued to bless the land after their death were said to be names of the god Freyr. (Freyr was also considered a deified mortal king—it seems to have gone both ways.) Maya Deren describes the Haitian ceremony of recalling a spirit from beneath the waters. This brings back the *ti-bon-ange* of a dead relative, which is then contained in a pot on the altar and given offerings. If the spirit is consistently helpful, it will continue to receive worship, and may eventually be assimilated to the *loa* to whom it belonged in life, or become an independent entity (1970).

In *The Divine Comedy*, Dante is guided first by the poet Virgil. But when he nears the summit of Purgatory, the pagan Virgil may no longer accompany him. As he is now approaching heavenly realms, he needs a figure that has already transcended humanity.

> Over her snow-white veil with olive cinct
> Appeared a lady under a green mantle,
> Vested in colour of the living flame.
>
> And my own spirit, that already now
> So long a time had been, that in her presence
> Trembling with awe it had not stood abashed,
>
> Without more knowledge having by mine eyes,
> Through occult virtue that from her proceeded
> Of ancient love the mighty influence felt.

As soon as on my vision smote the power
Sublime, that had already pierced me through
Ere from my boyhood I had yet come forth
(*Purgatorio* xxx: 31-42)

Trembling, Dante recognizes the woman who became his Muse and, in a wonderful moment of revelation, she replies, "Look at me well; in sooth, I'm Beatrice" (xxx: 73).

The Elder Edda includes a poem called "Svipdagsmál," in which a young man seeks wisdom by sleeping on his mother's grave mound after his step-mother has fated him to love the mysterious maiden Mengloth, who lives in the Otherworld. Coming to the mound, he summons her:

"Awake, Gróa, good woman wake up!
At the door of the grave I awaken you,
Do you remember how you bade your son
To come to your grave-mound?"

And his mother's spirit replies,

"What is it that ails my only son?
What makes so heavy your heart,
That you call your mother who lies under the mould,
And has left the living lands?" (Svipdagsmál: 1-2)

The folklore of the British Isles is full of stories in which the dead speak to the living. Faerie sightings describe a host composed of a motley mix of nature spirits, devolved gods, and the dead, usually dressed in the high fashion of the previous generation. In classical literature, the dead are also a source of wisdom. In the *Odyssey*, Odysseus dares the dangers of Hades to get information from Tiresias; in the *Aeneid*, Aeneas does the same to speak with his father.

Some people receive valuable guidance from relatives. Those who prefer to leave their blood relations alone can sometimes make a good contact with an unrelated (or very distantly related) spirit who shares their interests. I once led a meditation in which I visualized the "Mound of the Ancestors" on the Plain of Midgard and asked if there was a spirit who would like to work with me. The person who came forth was a Frisian called Helga who said she would be happy to watch over me and my family—but not until I did something to improve my kitchen. She also appeared to another woman in the group and promised to teach her how to make strudel.

In structure, the journey to connect with a teacher is much the same as the journey to find your power animal. In the Practice section at the end of this chapter, there is a text you can use to journey. Work with your inner guide in much the same way you do with your animal ally. The intensity and usefulness of your encounter will depend on how faithfully you follow your teacher's instructions. Follow the steps in the Practice section to make the most of the journey. If you are able to do automatic writing, it will be easier to keep a record of your teacher's communications.

Exercise 23. Journey to Find a Spirit Guide

Center, relax, and breathe as usual, then visualize the journey from your real-world starting point to the Otherworld. Call on your ally and ask it to lead you to the being that is willing to teach you trance work. When you find him or her, negotiate the terms of the relationship. What will the ally do for you? What are you expected to do in return? Discuss the type of work you will be doing and the frequency of visits; or leave this for another encounter. Just be sure to agree on the kind of commitment expected and decide whether you are willing to make it. Call on your ally to help you return, and write down as much as you can remember.

Another method is to articulate your question and write it down or type it in on your computer, then close your eyes. Use mind-clearing exercise 9 to open your awareness. Wait for the words of an answer to precipitate and write them down. This is easiest when done on a computer, because you do not have to worry about running off the edge of the page. Just make sure your fingers are in the correct position on the keyboard, or you will end up with a coded message that you can't read without going into trance again. If you accidentally shift your fingers out of position, try repositioning them one key to the right or left of the proper position and typing in the phrase you typed by accident. With a little experimentation, you can usually recapture your original meaning.

Speaking to the Dead

Most graveyards are locked up after dark, so sitting out in the cemetery is probably not an option here. It is probably not a good idea in any case, unless you are very experienced, have a very good reason for contacting a particular spirit, and have arranged for a backup in case of danger from incarnate or discarnate entities. It is much more convenient, not to mention safer, to create a connection with the dead in a warded space in your own home. I know several people who have built a small mound in the backyard to use as a focus for their ancestor work. Exercise 24 will help you build and use an ancestor altar.

Exercise 24. Setting Up an Ancestor Altar

Set up an altar with a picture of the spirit you are trying to contact. If you have access to the actual grave, gather some earth from it to help make the connection. Set out some food and drink, and light a candle. Draw a circle around yourself for protection. One African tradition instructs you to tie a piece of red yarn around your arm as a sign that you still belong to the living world.

Sit down, make yourself comfortable and prepare for trance. When you have reached the appropriate level of relaxed focus, call on your ally. In fact, I advise against journeying to contact the dead unless you already have an ally who will go with you. Visualize the place outdoors from which you usually start your journeys. When you leave it, ask your animal or spirit ally to guide you to a place where you can meet the spirit you are trying to contact. You may get good results by simply opening your awareness where you are and waiting. This is certainly the safest approach.

If you have a photo of the graveyard where the individual is buried, you can journey there. Another route is to go to the Mound of the Ancestors on the plain of Midgard and call to the spirit to come out to you. Or you can journey to the entrance of the home of the ancestors as it is envisioned in the tradition in which you are working and call for the spirit to come and meet you there.

Call for the spirit you are seeking. You may get an image or simply a sense of presence. Ask your questions, then ask the spirit if there is anything it wants you to do. If you have any sense that the spirit would like to come back with you or get too close in an inappropriate way, ask your animal ally to create a barrier between you, or draw a warding circle around yourself.

When the interview is over, thank the spirit and direct it to return to its rest. Retrace your steps and firmly close any gates you opened, until you have passed through your base camp and returned to ordinary consciousness.

Do not attempt to go through gates into Hel, Hades, or even the Elysian Fields until you have done a great deal of journeying and have completely internalized your sense of direction and controls. Even then, you should not do so without a backup, a companion who journeys with you to the gate and waits there to call you back again. Visiting the Land of the Dead is a job for an experienced spirit worker. The danger is not (in most cases) that something will try and eat you, but rather that this land, like the island of the Lotos Eaters, is a place of rest, and those who enter may lose the desire to leave again.

Practice

You can journey to the plain of Midgard, the Celtic Otherworld, or the Greek Arcadia to find an animal ally, or you can work out a journey of your own using the induction given below. Read the induction to memorize the instructions and then journey, or record it and journey as you listen. First, be sure to ward your space and assume your meditation position. Balance, ground, and center according to the process you have developed.

Sit in balance upon the earth . . .
Let each limb relax . . .
Here you are safe and secure.
If there is need, you will be able to easily awaken and return.
You hear sounds, but they mean nothing,
all that does not concern you fades away.
Anything you hear will only make it easier to look within.
Let your eyes close.
Breathe in . . . hold. . . .
and out . . . hold. . . .
Breathe in . . . hold. . . .
and out . . . hold. . . .

Allow a minute or two to pass as you count your breaths.

Now let the image of the place around you come to mind. . . .
Note the texture of the floor, then let that memory slip away. . . .
See the colors of the walls, and as you do so, watch them fade.
Remember the placement of the furniture,
then let shadow erase it all.
Feel the temperature of the air,
then withdraw awareness so that you feel nothing at all.
All images and sensations begin to ripple and flow.
All that you see, or hear, or feel dissolves and flows away,
A thought comes to you—recognize it, then let it go. . . .
Again and again, all is carried away. . . .

Now the image of your base camp forms around you. . . .
Look down, scuff your feet, feel the texture,
Look around, observe what's there—
Greet all your favorite things.

Touch them, breathe the air,
Take a few moments to enjoy being here. . . .

But now it is time to set out on your journey.
Take a moment to remember your goal–
You are looking for an ally to guide you
In the worlds within.
Take a stick or a cloak, whatever you think you will need.
Find the exit and go through.

You see a path leading away–follow it.
On either side grow shrubs that brush against our clothing.
As we move onward, they become taller.
Now they are trees, growing ever closer together and higher until they arch overhead.
Make your way downward through the tunnel of trees,
pass beneath green-scented shadow,
fallen leaves rustle softly beneath your feet.

At last you see a circle of brightness.
Drawing closer, you glimpse a broad plain.
A great tree rises in its center.
This is the World Tree, axis of all creation,
so high its branches brush the heavens,
so wide you can scarcely see around it.
From this place you can go anywhere.

Gaze around you.
In one direction you see deep forest and mountains,
In another, a grassy plain.
You can see desert. . . and then jungle. . . .
You see the ocean and marshes,
You see meadows and hills. . . .
Each direction shows you a different habitat,
But as you gaze, one of them attracts you.
Move forward, now it is all around you. . . .
Explore. . . .

Gradually, you become aware of movement.
Is it an animal? A bird? You wait, creatures appear,
Shy or curious, they come and go around you.
Soon one of them will return,
once, twice, three times you see it.
When that happens, ask if it will be your ally.
What does it want from you?
What will it do for you in exchange?
Ask its name.

Allow about five minutes for this negotiation.

It is time to return to your base camp.
Say farewell to your new friend,
Remembering that you know the way now,
And will return soon to speak again.
Ask it to set you on the path back to the World Tree.
Retrace your steps until it rises before you.
The Tree grows larger as you approach it,
From here you can see the path
that leads to the Wood Between the Worlds.
Follow that path,
let the green shadows enfold you.
Swiftly and easily, move up the trail
through the tunnel of trees.
Now the trees are farther apart,
you can see the sky above you.
Soon they dwindle to bushes that brush your garments.

If you are drumming, beat four times quickly and then very rapidly to signal return.

The entry to your base camp is before you.
Pass through and sink down upon the familiar ground.
Then that image too begins to fade. . . .

Reality is flowing around you.
You see light flickering on water,

You hear the ripple of a stream.
Gradually it gives way to an image of the room around you,
Feel your weight in the chair.
Twitch your fingers and toes.
Breathe in . . . and out . . . in . . . and out. . . .
Let the air of that place become the air of this place.
Sigh and stretch, open your eyes
And return.

If you are already working with power animals, you may want to make contact with an ancestor spirit. You can call for a specific person, or ask for an elder from a specific time or place, or simply ask for "the one who can help me."

If you are recording the journey, use the first six stanzas of the induction above to begin, then continue with the following:

Gaze around you. . . .
A plain stretches away to either side,
Long grass ripples in the wind.
But as you gaze, you notice what looks like a small hill.
You move forward, it grows larger.
Now you can see that it is a barrow,
Higher than you are tall,
Oval in shape and covered in grass.
Move around it until you see where the earth has eroded away
to reveal an opening framed by massive stones.
It is a door into darkness,
A passage to the Land of the Dead.
The air that flows from that opening is chill. . . .
But you have come here for a reason.
In your mind, renew your purpose–
You are looking for an elder,
An ancestor, one of the Mighty Dead
Who will advise and counsel you.

Center yourself and call. . . .
Ask for the wise mother or sage father,

The elder or ancestor who can teach what you need to know.
Wait, and presently they will come.
Wait until one comes and stays with you.
Ask for a name and origin, explain your need.
If the elder agrees to help, ask what he or she wishes as an offering.
Take some time to get acquainted.

Allow about five minutes to get acquainted, then conclude your journey using the last three stanzas of the induction given above.

It is time to return to your Base Camp.
Say farewell to your new friend,
Remembering that you know the way now,
And will return soon to speak again.
Ask it to set you on the path back to the World Tree.
Retrace your steps until it rises before you.

Continue the return journey as above from "The Tree grows larger as you approach it," to "Sigh and stretch and return."

Chapter Seven

Getting Along in the Culture

If you reject the food, ignore the customs, fear the religion and avoid the people, you might better stay at home.

James Michener

You have found the way to the worlds within and you have a guide. You're all set for further explorations. Or are you? Experienced travelers know that reaching your destination is only the beginning. Once you arrive in a new land, you must learn how to live there. C. S. Lewis observed: "The logic of a fairy-tale is as strict as that of a realistic novel, though different" (1966). Likewise, there are rules for getting along in the inner worlds, just as there are for travel in the world we know, but they are not the same.

The tale of "The Giant Who Had No Heart" is a classic example of beliefs about how friendships with Otherworld beings are established and maintained. In the story, the youngest son has set out to find his lost brothers. He meets a starving raven.

> "Oh dear friend, give me something to eat, and I will help you in your utmost need," said the raven.
>
> "Very little food have I," said the prince, "and you don't look as if you could help me much either, but a little I must give you, for you want it badly, I see," and then he gave the raven some of the food he had with him (Booss, 1984).

Next, the boy encounters a salmon out of water, and then a famished wolf. He puts the fish back into the stream, and lets the wolf eat his horse. The wolf then becomes his steed and his advisor. Later, the wolf carries him across the lake to the island where the giant's heart is hidden. The raven flies to the top of a church steeple to retrieve the key to the well. The salmon brings up the egg that contains the heart from the bottom of the well. Many other cultures have similar stories, all of which make enjoyable reading. They also make a point: Those you help along the way may become your friends, and those friends may one day help you.

In a chapter 5, I mentioned a similar tale—the story of the girl who went to visit the goddess Hölle. When she falls down the well, the girl finds herself in a lovely land where it is summertime. As she wanders along exploring this new environment, she comes to an apple tree loaded with ripe apples, which the tree begs her to pick and take their weight from its branches. After she picks the apples, she goes on her way and comes to an oven, which asks her to remove its baked bread. Of course, the girl obliges. Having seen that our heroine is good and helpful, it shouldn't surprise you to learn that, when she comes to a cottage in the forest, she proves to be a good servant to the old woman who lives there, sweeping under all the furniture and shaking the featherbeds vigorously, unaware that, when she does so, it snows in the world above. When the girl goes home, showers of gold fall into her apron as she passes through the door.

Myth and folklore are full of stories about animal helpers. The hapless Psyche is aided by mice to sort the grain she has been ordered to collect by Aphrodite. Puss-in-Boots smoothes the way for his young man, helping him to a high marriage and riches. The animals and birds that help the heroines in Disney's *Snow White* and *Cinderella* are archetypes that should be familiar to everyone.

The Care and Feeding of Fetches and Allies

Like any relationship, the connection with an inner guide needs to be developed and cultivated. Once you have made a good contact, repeat the journey to the place where you met your ally at regular intervals until you can see and hear it easily. To fully develop the connection, you must meet your ally on all levels and learn to relate to it in a variety of ways–by studying it, through images and actions, by developing your connection, and by taking responsibility for its welfare.

Study

Study your animal. If possible, observe living examples on film or at a zoo. A good library or the Internet will provide you with images and information. For instance, if you are working with a raven, Berndt Heinrich's *Ravens in Winter* and *The Mind of the Raven* are excellent sources. For wolves, try *The Wolf: Ecology and Behavior of an Endangered Species* by L. David Mech, *Of Wolves and Men* by Barry Lopez, and a Nature Company book entitled *Wolf: Spirit of the Wild* edited by Diana Landau–a picture book presenting cross-cultural views of wolves, along with poetry.

Did you end up with a moose? *Giants of the Northern Forest* by Bill Silliker will give you a good introduction. You can find information on almost any creature by searching the Internet or a visiting your local library, the Nature Company catalogue, or Amazon.com. For a sense of how Native American cultures look at relationships with spirit animals, see *Animals of the Soul* by Joseph Epes Brown, which discusses Lakota lore, and *Make Prayers to the Raven* by Richard Nelson, about the beliefs of the Koyukon tribe.

Bear in mind, however, that power animals and allies, no matter how helpful, are not "tame lions." Nor are their real-world analogues.

Don't assume that, just because your very own "Ricky Raccoon" has guided you all over the Otherworld, the cute raccoon climbing your garden wall is either safe or friendly. The evidence from shamanic cultures indicates that the spirit world also has its dangers. Be careful and respectful in your dealings with Otherworld powers, and don't overestimate your own abilities.

Images and Actions

Collect pictures and statuettes of your helper. Try drawing and painting it (see figure 1). In shamanic traditions, it is common to paint images of spirit helpers on magical gear or jewelry, and to collect their teeth, bones, or fur (if the species is not endangered). Set up a spirit altar with images of your ally, which you can contemplate when you begin your meditations. Experiment with a "moving meditation" in which you play recorded drumming or appropriate music and dance for your animal, imitating its movements. If the species from which

FIGURE 1. Ritual drum with a raven image, decorated and photographed by the author.

your ally comes lives in your area, find out what it would find safe and tasty, and set out an offering. Otherwise, such offerings can be put out on your altar for consumption by the spirit.

Developing the Relationship

Many people who work with spirit animals develop strong and continuing relationships with clearly defined figures. Others may find that their guide appears in different forms for different journeys, or may develop a large circle of "invisible friends" that specialize in helping with different kinds of spiritual work. Shamanic guides simplify and speed journeying, provide illuminating and useful information and advice, and can extricate you from trouble.

Do not be surprised if your ally scolds you like an old grandmother or advises you like an uncle. Allies, especially those in animal form, often seem to look upon us with a rather amused tolerance, as if we were rather stupid children with whom they must make do for lack of anything better. Generally, their teasing is gentle. Certainly, their counsel is worth heeding. Sometimes, depending on the character of the ally, there may be a sexual element to the interaction. Old Man Coyote, for instance, often tries to seduce his students. This is neither negative nor shameful. You can simply refuse–on the other hand, it could be an interesting experience.

As your connection deepens, you may find you are aware of your ally's presence even when you are not in trance. Lorrie, whose principal ally is an otter, finds herself powerfully attracted by the fish counter at the supermarket. People who work with ravens become sensitized to "shiny things" (which is at least better than dead things, which ravens also find attractive). This awareness may develop into an internal commentary. There is nothing wrong with listening to the voices in your head, as long as you do not answer out loud when other people can hear you. Remember that, in the physical world, *you* are the expert. You don't have to do something just because your invisible friends tell you to. On the other hand, their advice is often well worth considering.

Allies can lead you to desired destinations in the world within—the temple of a particular deity, one of the nine worlds, or a place where you can get the answer to a specific question. Sometimes, of course, it is best to ask your ally to lead you where you will learn "what you need to know."

One of my favorite fictional examples of interaction with a power animal is the episode of *Star Trek: The Next Generation,* in which Data tries to get in touch with his unconscious. He begins a series of paintings in which the image of a raven becomes ever more apparent. Then he induces a trance journey in which he walks through the corridors of the ship. He comes to a crossroad, where he meets a blacksmith working at a forge who hammers out a wrought-iron raven feather. This becomes a real bird that leads Data on a tour of the universe.

On spirit journeys, your ally is your best defense against danger. If you encounter anything disturbing, it can help you get away ("Chewie, get me out of here . . . "). Once, when I was guiding a friend whose ally was a horse on an interactive journey, she encountered a hostile entity. "What should I do?" she asked. I suggested she ask her horse for help. There were a few moments of silence and then, "Oh—she kicked it!" When I told this story in class, one student reported that, when she ran into trouble, her heretofore unassuming ally grew to giant size and saved her. Ember countered that, when she got into a jam, she grabbed her ally by the scruff of the neck and hauled *him* out. Well, it *was* a rabbit, and a Very Young Rabbit at that. . . .

Sometimes, as suggested earlier, the best help your friend can give you is to zap you back to ordinary reality. If this happens, remember the advice I gave you about returning from trance. If a sudden return leaves you disoriented, retrace your route back to the point where the trouble occurred and return in a more deliberate fashion.

Responsibilities

Like any other relationship, your connection with your inner ally needs to be nurtured. If you have pledged to take specific actions—journeying with your "friend" on a regular basis, or making certain offerings—you must do so or renegotiate the contract. You will also develop a special relationship with your ally's real-world analogues, and may find it helpful to contribute to wildlife funds or shelters that protect them. The more closely you identify with your ally, the more you may be affected by what happens to its species.

Treat anything that has to do with your ally very carefully. As a case in point, I offer this example. A friend whose ally is a red-tailed hawk found a dead hawk on the street, took it home, and put it in the freezer until he could decide what to do with it. Obviously, this find was a great gift, and he wanted to make the most of it. While he tried to make up his mind, he figured the bird was safe enough wrapped in plastic behind the frozen foods. This went on for about two years. From time to time, his family would wistfully wonder when he was going to free up the freezer space, and his children's friends were fascinated by tales of the hawk in the freezer.

One day, his wife, needing the space for some ice cream, decided that enough was enough and threw the bird in the trash. By the time my friend found out what had happened, the garbage had been collected. He is normally a very calm and controlled person, and the anguish he felt astonished him. It was not the fact that the bird was gone that bothered him—it had been doing him no good in the freezer, after all—but the fact that the body had been disposed of without honor. The guilt of sacrilege hit him with a gut-level intensity; his whole relationship with his ally was endangered, and, by extension, a significant part of his spiritual identity.

When he got over the first pain and rage, he calmed down enough to do a journey and ask his ally what he would accept as compensation. After some rather cutting remarks, Mr. Red-Tail directed him to make a donation to the local bird-rescue organization, which had a raptor shelter. He told my friend that, when a hawk feather came to him from an outside source, he would know that he was forgiven.

Almost a year later, he received a package in the mail from a friend in another country. It contained a perfect hawk feather and the following story. Apparently, his friend had found a sick bird on the road, which, despite her care, died. The friend (who had no knowledge of my friend's problem) took several feathers from the bird, one of which she sent him. She also sent a photo of the pyre on which she had ceremonially burned the body. This act apparently served as a vicarious funeral for the first bird as well. Sadder but wiser, my friend was able to resume his relationship with his ally.

From this experience, I derive the following advice. If you find a dead bird or animal, treat it reverently. Freezing will kill mites and other parasites that can cause disease in humans, but if you have what another friend's significant other refers to as "something pagan in the freezer," set a limit on the time you will leave it there. If you do not dispose of it in some other respectful way, give it an honorable burial. If your ally's species is endangered, do not purchase body parts, unless they are clearly very old. We do not wish to encourage the illegal trade in hides and bones. You should also be aware that, unless you are a registered member of a Native American Indian tribe, it is illegal to possess feathers from raptors or migratory birds.

Fetches and Shape Shifters

Even when humans ceased to worship animals, they continued to see them as powerful. Personal, family, and clan guardians in animal form were retained in names and symbols such as coats of arms. In many cultures, people believed that a soul part was seen in animal form. In medieval Scandinavia, there were many tales about the *fylgja*, or "follower," known in English as the "fetch." In more recent times, this came to be called the *vardøger* or *vård* (guardian). The fetch is considered a projection of the soul, and appears as a double or in animal form, the nature of the animal revealing the character of the owner. In human form, the fetch is a doppelganger, and it is bad luck for its "owner" to see it. The fetch can be seen by animals and those with second sight.

According to Scandinavian folk tradition, evil people have evil fetches. There is a story about a Norwegian farm girl who had second sight who arrived late to a dance. When she looked through the window to find out how the evening was going, she saw everyone followed by his or her fetch. The scoundrel who starved his horses was followed by a horse that was skin and bones; the glutton was followed by a fat pig; the cheater was followed by a fox (Kvideland & Sehmsdorff, 1988, #9.3). The fetch was often seen as an alter ego.

The fetch can also be an alternate shape into which one shifts for astral travel. Taking animal form for spirit journeys is one of the skills ascribed to Odin. In the saga of *Hrolf Kraki*, a warrior called Bodhvar Bjarki sends out his fetch to fight in the shape of a bear.

> Hjorvard and his men saw a great bear advancing in front of King Hrolf's troop. The bear was always beside the king, and it killed more men with its paw than any five of the king's champions did. Blows and missiles glanced off the animal, as it used its weight to crush King Hjorvard's men and their horses. Between its teeth, it tore everything within reach, causing a palpable fear to spread through the ranks of King Hjorvard's army.

When Bodhvar's friend Hjalti goes to find out why Bodhvar has not turned up for the battle, he finds Bodhvar "sitting idle," and wakes him. Bodhvar tells him, "In truth, I can tell you that in many ways I can now offer the king far less support than before you woke me." And indeed, when they return to the battlefield, they find that the bear is gone, and the battle is turning against them (Byock, 1999).

In *A History of the Norse Kings*, we are told how the Danish king Harald Gormsson sent a "troll-wise" man forth in the shape of a whale to scout around Iceland, where he was repelled by land spirits in the form of an ox, a vulture, a serpent, and a rock giant (Sturlason, 1990).

Invoking Your Ally

Perhaps the most widely used cue for invoking an ally is song. As you found in chapter 4, music can help you shift to a specific state of consciousness. In shamanic traditions, power songs are used to call the spirits who will help the shaman in his or her work. In a culture like our own, where music is often considered a mysterious and arcane skill to be practiced only by professionals, being asked to compose a song can be very threatening. In our classes, this assignment has provoked some of the greatest resistance.

I will not try to tell you that writing a song for your ally is essential. The concept of conditioning yourself to respond to a sequence of stimuli matters more than any single cue. But music is both powerful and traditional, and I strongly encourage you to give it a try. The harder you have to work to produce some kind of song, the more your ally will value it. Make it an offering.

Since your ally song will invoke a being, it should probably be somewhat more focused and explicit than your trance-inducing power song. Try a more formal tune and a more poetic form, possibly with several verses. The verbal music of rhyme and meter are especially important if you cannot carry a tune in a basket and will be intoning, rather than singing, the words.

Ally songs can be as simple as nursery rhymes. If you have no better inspiration, try a simple four-beat, four-line format with rhyming couplets:

> Raven sitting on the tree,
> do you have a word for me?
> Raven, Raven, dark and bright,
> Guide my journeying to-night.

In this example, the second two lines become a chorus that is repeated after every couplet. So the next stanzas might go like this:

> Raven, sitting on my arm
> will you keep my soul from harm?
> Raven, Raven, dark and bright,
> Guide my journeying to-night.
>
> Raven black and Raven white
> will you grant me spirit sight?
> Raven, Raven, dark and bright,
> Guide my journeying to-night.
>
> Raven flying round a-bout
> lead me in and bring me out!

Raven, Raven, dark and bright,
Guide my journeying to-night.

When calling my Raven, I always start with the same lines, but later verses can appear in any order. This meter goes well with a strong drumbeat, and I enjoy dancing about while beating the drum and singing, thus gaining the benefit of both sound and movement.

Another simple form is a ballad meter, in which four-beat lines that can end with any sound alternate with three-beat lines that rhyme. Here is one for the great moose who helps me with soul retrieval:

Through the wood you break the trail,
Striding strong and slow,
Antlers mighty to defend,
Show me where to go.

Review the earlier advice about finding a tune. If necessary, find a collection of obscure folk music and borrow a tune that you are unlikely to hear elsewhere.

Modes of Transit

You know how to get to the Otherworld, and now you have a native guide. But how will you get around once you arrive? The first, and generally safest, way to get around in the Otherworld is by walking. Those who are accustomed to teleporting may find this annoyingly slow, but it has certain advantages. When you travel slowly, you have time to observe the landmarks, which will make it easier to retrace your steps on the journey home. You are also much less likely to miss significant sights or encounters. So much of our mundane lives are spent in a preoccupied rush. We should try not to rush our spiritual lives as well. Fortunately, whatever the shape of our bodies, when we journey within, we are all limber and strong. In the Otherworld, you can walk swiftly, and distances will contract as needed. It is, therefore, generally no trouble to journey and return in the allotted time.

There are some places where walking will not serve, however. If you encounter a river, you must find a way to cross it. For some, the preferred method is to change into the shape of something that can swim easily. On the other hand, you may want to find a boat—especially if your ally can neither swim nor fly. (Of course, allies can sometimes change shape as well.) If simply looking around doesn't reveal a boat, ask your ally how to find one.

The same advice applies to flying. If, for instance, you need to go up the World Tree, you must either fly or climb. Here, shape-shifting is the obvious solution, but it is amazing what transformations can take place in the inner worlds. The raven that turned into a black 707 jet that could carry the whole group comes to mind.

Sometimes, however, the best way to get somewhere is not by making your way around or over the obstacles, but by finding a direct passageway. Remember the advice on finding passages *into* the inner worlds given in chapter 5. To further fine-tune your journeying, choose images that relate directly to the purpose at hand. If you want to contact a deity from a particular mythology, use images from that culture. For Norse deities, for instance, use the "map" of Yggdrasil and the nine worlds. If you are studying the Runes, an image of the rune itself can expand to become a doorway. A Hebrew letter can do the same. Meditating on the *tattwa* symbols of the four elements from Hindu tradition can move you into an appropriate elemental landscape. When studying Kabbalah, construct a journey with symbols appropriate to a given *sephira* to move into that sphere.

Geometric forms can be used as maps independent of cultural context. Try contemplating crosses, interlaced designs, or endless knots. With your finger, trace the pathway through a labyrinth, or lay one out and walk it (see figure 2). The passages that work best for each individual may depend on cognitive style or neural organization.

Rules of the Road

An ally, whether animal or other, can guard and guide. By the time you have read through a collection of fairy tales, however, you will realize that there are certain rules for getting along in the Otherworld. When you travel in a foreign land, you get along much better if you observe

FIGURE 2. Diagram of the Cretan labyrinth.

the mores of that culture. The same is true when you journey within. Once you have an ally, of course, you can call on him, her, or it as soon as you set forth. If you encounter someone or something strange, your ally can help you. Here are some guidelines:

1. When heading into the wilderness, mark your trail. Breadcrumbs are a poor choice, as the denizens of the woods will eat them. Try a thread, or stones.
2. Look before you leap. Don't agree to go with a strange being without knowing where you are going and why.
3. Help those who ask. If you cannot, explain why, or ask for assistance from your own helpers. Don't put conditions on your help.
4. Share what you have.
5. Be polite to everyone and everything.
6. If something wants to join you on your journey, accept its company unless your ally advises otherwise.
7. Be brave, and don't forget the rest of the Boy Scout virtues. Be clean, trustworthy, loyal . . .
8. Be honest and sincere, but don't offer more information than necessary. At times, you may have to disguise your meaning with circumlocutions or kennings.
9. Appearances can be deceiving. What looks fair may be foul, and vice versa. Judge not by looks, but by deeds.

10. Take responsibility for your actions and keep your promises, whether they relate to situations within the journey or in the waking world.
11. Before you sleep on or in something, ask. On the other hand, if you are able, offer hospitality to those in need.
12. A gift requires a gift—so be careful what you accept, as you may have to pay for it. On the other hand, it may be useful later. Be careful about making bargains. The story of the woman who promised Odin to "Give me what lies behind your girdle" without knowing she was pregnant comes to mind.

In general, you should not eat fairy food. As Ember put it in a poem:

> Sir, I would not dare insult you,
> But my mother taught me well.
> Food of Fey or foreign magic
> May be laced with Charm or Spell.

Of course, any of these rules may have exceptions, especially the last one. Lorrie reports that, on a visit to the home of the giants, Aegir and Ran tried to offer her sushi. "I refused, citing the Rules, and Ran blandly pointed out that my ally seemed to think it was all right—as Otter was cheerfully plowing through the raw fish at a rate heretofore only seen in cartoons." Another friend tells of being in the kitchen of Fensalir, home of the goddess Frigga, and refusing to eat some goulash. The goddess informed him that she had made that goulash he was refusing and respect demanded that he eat it—so he did. In the first instance, the actions of the ally and, in the second, the presence of a goddess indicated that it was all right to bend the rules. When in doubt, ask your ally. You can find a useful discussion of this topic in "Journeying and Fairy Tales" by Jenny Blain at *www.thetroth.org/Articles*.

Road Warriors

Sometimes, following the rules is not enough. What do you do if you are tripping merrily along and something scary steps out to bar the way?

If you recognize the being from mythology, there may be traditional methods for dealing with it. You can oppose Medusa, for instance, by mirroring her own horror back at her, but you must evade a troll or trick it into the sunlight. For other things, almost any kind of weapon will do. If you didn't expect opposition, however, you may have only a few moments to manifest something. Fortunately, in visions, you *can* create something out of nothing. You just have to be able to think fast and choose the right tool for the job. In traditional cultures, journeys tend to take place in familiar mythic landscapes in which both the dangers and the defenses are known. A background in folklore, fairy tales, and mythology can be very useful, as is an ability to think in metaphors.

Here are some ways to deal with "scary monsters" suggested by Lorrie Wood in the beta test of the trance class:

> **Hide**: If you are watching where you are going, you will presumably see the monster before It sees you. Look around for something to hide behind, or better still, a passage through which you can escape.
> **Trick it**: Look to Nature for ideas. If you cannot escape notice entirely, visualize yourself larger, scarier, or veiled by the appearance of something that does not look like prey. If this doesn't work, you can try President Johnson's favorite tactic: "Let us sit down and reason together."
> **Run/Fly**: Use appropriate in-trance transport. One student reported that all our insistence on walking had made it harder for her to teleport—on the other hand, she experiences states more deeply now that she's walking than she did when teleporting.
> **Use tools**: Use the Tools at Your Disposal in the Context You Understand! This is where you use those weapons with which you have been furnishing the base camp you created in chapter 5. But Lorrie points out that not everything we're going to come up with as a way of vanquishing beasties or unsnarling tangles is going to have all these nice ancient layers of mythic reality. "No, sometimes what rings true is that you turn into Sailor Moon, whip out a light saber, or call on some other image that has deep

resonance in your psyche. While this may be considered somewhat poor form and embarrassing, it's not wrong, per se, and should not be dismissed on that basis. In short, just because it's out of place doesn't mean it's wrong."

Eject!: This is the equivalent of the convulsive start with which we wake from a nightmare that is too terrible to endure. In an emergency ejection, you jerk yourself completely out of trance. This can also be done with the help of your ally. As anyone who has ever wakened from a nightmare in this way knows, it can be both disorienting and painful. For ways to deal with the effects, see "Back Again" in chapter 5.

Fight: The alternative to flight is fight. However, there are some situations in which the recommended course is to let the critter eat you, and/or to make it your helper (as was discussed in the previous chapter). The problem is how to decide whether what you have encountered is a monster or a possible ally. Frodo's comments about Aragorn [in Tolkien's *The Fellowship of the Ring*] may provide a useful guideline here. "You have frightened me several times tonight, but never in the way that servants of the Enemy would, or so I imagine. I think one of his spies would–well, seem fairer and feel fouler, it you understand." (1956) In other words, don't reject something just because it is ugly or has big teeth, or trust something because it seems beautiful. Try to sense its emotions or psychic atmosphere, and ask yourself whether it challenges you to be greater or tempts you to be less than your best.

When in doubt: "Use the Force, Luke!" Trust your instinctive responses to get you through.

True Names

Names can be very important when traveling in the Otherworld. Ask your prospective helper what it wants to be called. It may likewise ask what it should call you. This is another lesson we learn from fairy tales. Remember the story of Rumpelstiltskin. When the girl called the dwarf by his true name, his power over her was broken. In Egyptian myth, the goddess Isis gained power because she learned the secret name of Ra.

Words have power, and some of the most powerful words we will ever encounter are our names. In Ursula LeGuin's *Earthsea* books, knowing someone's true name, as opposed to his or her use-name, gives you power over that person, and even over a dragon. In "True Names and Other Dangers," Vernor Vinge explores the idea of true names in the context of the computer world. Finding out a hacker's legal name gives you ultimate power over his online persona and activities. Anything that might want to hurt you, however, usually has a far more intimate handle on you than any handful of syllables can bestow. Who you are can't be confined to anything as simple as a label.

We each have many names throughout our lives. Our surnames indicate our family's origin. At birth, our parents give us one or more names. They may be traditional in the family, or given to honor a friend. They may represent the current interests or enthusiasms of one of the parents. When my son was in preschool, the class list included children named Arwen, Darshan, Chaka, and Aragorn. Admittedly this was in Berkeley, but it was still a sign of the times. Before my birth, my mother was intrigued by the goddess Diana and sculpted a head of Diana that I still have–hence my first name. I share my middle name with her older sister and her best friend. My surname came from my father's family, which is English. Catholic tradition adds the name of a saint, usually the one on whose day the child was born, as a middle name. Traditional Chinese and Roman names reflected a person's birth position in the family–Eldest Sister or Octavius. Researching the meaning of our names helps us to understand our origins.

Many of us also acquire nicknames as we grow older. In some families, the oldest boy is known as Son. If he is named after his father, he may be known as Junior. One friend's name was mispronounced as Bagel by a younger sibling, and he was called Bagel until he was grown and had children of his own. Another acquired the nickname Froggy from the thick lenses in her glasses. Native Americans got their names from significant characteristics or events (Deed-names), and might change names several times during their lives. The Germanic peoples had a real gift for giving nicknames that described personal characteristics—Ragnar Hairy-Breeks, Ivar the Boneless, and Aud the Deep-minded.

Taking a new name may indicate a change in identity or in status, as when a woman takes her husband's name on marriage or a couple decides to jointly adopt a new surname. An English monarch may choose a new name on ascending the throne. Actors often take stage names, as when Bernie Schwartz became Tony Curtis. When someone enters a convent, the worldly name is left behind and a "name in religion" given. When people join the Society for Creative Anachronism, they choose a medieval name as part of developing a new persona who will inhabit the Current Middle Ages. Many people who engage in magical practices find it useful to have a magical name for use in meditation and ritual. In some esoteric traditions, initiates choose or are given magical names that are used only within the circle. Others may take Craft names for use in pagan activities to prevent being "outed" in a hostile community.

Your name serves as an extra level of protection between your mundane persona and your magical personality. If you live in a conservative community or have a job that requires that you hide your participation in an alternative religion, a magical name can protect your identity. People may adopt pagan "noms de plume" for writing or public appearances. If you work in a culturally based tradition, a name taken from its language can help you identify with the culture. Some choose a pagan name because it expresses who they feel they really are. This chosen name may become the one by which they are known to most of their friends.

In trance work, the choice of a magical name is important because it can serve as a powerful trance trigger. When you call yourself by your magical name, you cue your unconscious to leave the preoccupations of daily life behind and move into a magical reality. I have one friend who, in addition to his birth name, had a "witch" name that he used in the pagan community, as well as one he used only when doing trance work. To get him out of a trance state, I had to call first on his magical persona to give back the pagan persona; then ask the pagan persona to give back the everyday person. This may sound cumbersome, but it enabled him to make a smooth and gradual transition back to ordinary consciousness.

In shamanic practice, names and epithets can be used to affirm spiritual power. An affirmation in which the shaman uses epithets to boast of previous successes often comes at the beginning of a healing ritual, although the shaman may use description and kennings to convince the disease spirit of his power without giving it his true name. The conversation between Bilbo and Smaug in *The Hobbit* is a good example of a response that is at once courteous, affirmative, and protective:

> "I am the clue-finder, the web-cutter, the stinging fly. I was chosen for the lucky number . . . I am he that buries his friends alive and drowns them and draws them alive again from the water. I came from the end of a bag, but no bag went over me . . . I am the friend of bears and the guest of eagles. I am Ring-winner and Luck-wearer, and I am Barrel-rider . . . "
>
> That, of course, is the way to talk to dragons if you don't want to reveal your proper name (which is wise), and don't want to infuriate them by a flat refusal (which is also very wise) (Tolkien, 1956).

Names can also be used to indicate to others the role you are playing. Even the god Odin prefers not to give his own name when dealing with other powers. When he calls the archetypal Seeress from her deep sleep, he tells her his name is Vegtam, son of Valtam (Way-Ready, son of Battle-Ready). Apparently, the disguise is a good idea. When the Völva deduces from his questions that this is really "Odin the Old," she kicks him out and refuses to answer any more questions. He names himself Bolverk (Evil Work) to the thralls he is about to trick when he tries to gain the mead of poetry. In the hall of Vafthruthnir, he calls himself Gagnradh (Good Counsel) and boasts, "Wide have I wandered, dared many deeds, often challenged the Powers" (*Vafthruthnismál*: 3).

Practice

1. **Hanging out with your friends:**If you have recently acquired an animal helper or ally, develop the relationship by making regular journeys. Hang out together. Play. If you already have a good relationship with an invisible friend, look for another guide in human or other form, such as an ancestor. Look for an ancestor who will help you (this does not need to be an actual blood relative) by seeking the Mound of the Ancestors and calling for a helper to come forth. To look for a teaching spirit, ask your animal helper to take you to the Upper World. Whatever kind of helper you find, take some time to establish your friendship. Journey to see him/her/it at least once a week. Set up an altar with images and offerings as a focus for meditation. Ask for help with your problems.
2. **Singing:** Write a song to invoke the presence and help of your ally. The words can describe and praise the ally's characteristics and virtues or say how you hope it will help you. If you are already comfortable with music and poetry, challenge yourself to create a song in which the meter, sounds, and melody reflect the movements of the animal. Listen to "Carnival of the Animals" by Camille Saint-Saëns, "On the Trail" by Ferde Grofé, or "Peter and the Wolf" by Tchaikovsky for examples of the ways in which music can "describe" an animal. Review the discussion of "onomotopoiea" in any standard poetry text. Try singing both with and without a drumbeat. If your ally is an animal, sing and dance in imitation of its movements.
3. **Power names:** Choose or create a magical name to use in trance work and incorporate it into an affirmation of power. You can borrow a name from another language (as long as you understand its meaning), use an English composite, or make up a word. In some traditions, the magical "name" is a noun or phrase like Seeker after Truth. Or use a word that expresses one of your ideals in another language–*Shantih* ("Peace" in Sanskrit) or *Wynn* ("Joy" in Old English). Names that incorporate the name of a god or goddess, like *Thorsvin* ("friend of Thor"), work well. To call yourself by the name of a deity without qualification, however,

can be both presumptuous and possibly dangerous. You may say I am hardly the one to talk, but the name Diana was given to me by my mother, not chosen by me. While I am known by it in the pagan community, I have different names for use in magical work. I also recommend you avoid the "Lady Pixie Moondrip" school of pagan nomenclature. You can find it in a brilliantly funny article written by the late Leigh Ann Hussey at *www.widdershins.org/vol3iss4/m9710.htm* that includes the Random Craft Name Generator.

4. **Affirmation:** A magical affirmation is a way for the conscious mind that plans an operation to communicate with the unconscious and cue up the abilities needed for the work. It is usually voiced before beginning an activity like healing. A typical affirmation might begin: "I am (Magical Name), and I am a (healer, trance-worker, witch, or other title appropriate to the work at hand)." There is a certain temptation to use the formula, "(____) is my name, and (____) is my game." Whether this works or simply reduces you to hysterical laughter depends on your personality; however a rap-style format and delivery for an affirmation can, in fact, be quite effective.

   Continue your affirmation with statements that describe the skills you have (or would like to have)—World-walker, Spirit-speaker, and the like. Refer to your helpers and guardians—"Athena protects me," "Raccoon guides me." If you have done the work before, boast of your successes or affirm that you will do the job in the same way as some legendary figure—"As Odin healed Balder's lame horse, so I will heal (name)." Your Affirmation of Power will change and grow as you do.

Chapter Eight
Mapping the Inner Worlds

It is not down in any map; true places never are.

Herman Melville

From earliest times, spiritual explorers have tried to map the worlds through which they journey. Do these maps portray actual inner landscapes and, if so, are those landscapes personal or do they reflect a shared reality stored in the collective unconscious? The project to map extraordinary reality being conducted by the Foundation for Shamanic Studies may one day help to answer that question. In the meantime, I have found that many people feel working with a graphic representation of their inner journey helps them to organize their perceptions and travel more swiftly to their goal.

Real Maps and Imaginary Places

Or, do I mean "imaginary maps of real places"? When we try to map our inner processes, we question the very nature of reality. One of our most useful tools for doing this is words. As we all know, however, even words are not always consistent in their meaning. Yet they give us a chance to define the personal realities we experience in a way that others can understand. We start from a baseline experience of consensus reality–the objective world that we are given, as opposed to the world we desire or imagine. Then we use the terms and images that describe our common physical experience to develop a verbal and visual vocabulary we can use to communicate our experiences of non-ordinary reality.

Maps are particularly useful when dealing with a shared visionary state. Most mystical traditions have attempted to map their cosmologies. In shamanic cultures, the topography of the inner worlds is part of the education of apprentices. Shamans must know where they are going and what to expect when they get there.

Over the centuries, the visions of successive travelers have been combined into a consensus reality that then conditions the perceptions of subsequent journeyers. Thus, people in shamanic cultures are better able to deal with unexpected experiences in the Otherworld, because they are already familiar with the terrain.

The Magic Mountain and the World Tree

A cultural worldview can be mapped. For instance, the Saami (Lapps) of Scandinavia represent the Upper, Middle, and Lower worlds on their drums, along with the beasts and spirits found in each location (see figure 3).

> . . . the drum depicts a microcosm with its three zones–sky, earth, underworld–at the same time that it indicates the means by which the shaman accomplishes the break-through from plane to plane and establishes communication with the world above and the world below. . . . Lapp drums represent the three cosmic zones, separated by boundary lines. In the sky, the sun and moon are discernible, as are gods and goddesses (probably influenced by Scandinavian mythology), birds (swan, cuckoo, etc.), the drum, the sacrificial animals, and so forth; the Cosmic Tree, a number of mythical personages, boats, shamans, the god of the chase,

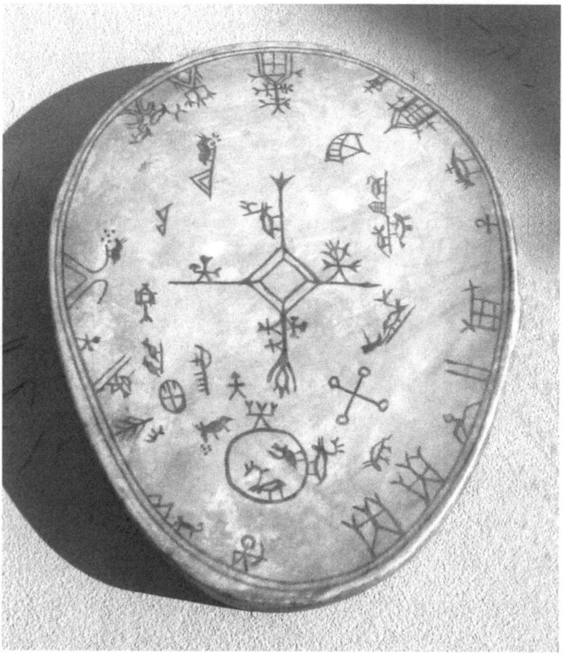

FIGURE 3. Saami drum depicting the Upper, Middle, and Lower worlds. Photo taken by the author.

> horse-men, etc., people the intermediate space (the earth); the infernal gods, shamans and the dead, snakes and birds are found, with other images, in the lower zone (Eliade, 1964).

When I first painted my own drum, I chose a concentric rather than a vertical plan, and discovered that, by changing the part of the drum I struck with the stick, I could invoke the beings and places I wanted to reach. By beating my way from one place on the drumhead to another, I drum my way through the worlds.

A vertical arrangement of worlds seems to represent a psychological reality. Three cosmic zones are common, though they may be subdivided into seven or more levels. Metaphors of "sinking," "going deeper," or "going inward" seem to be attempts to describe the journey into our own depths, the foundations of consciousness. Metaphors of ascension, from climbing a tree or a mountain or "rising on the planes," to being literally taken up, as in the wall painting I once saw in a medieval monastery that portrayed Christ's Ascension as a pair of feet sticking out of the bottom of a cloud, are more likely to represent an external or "superior" spiritual reality.

The symbolic "mountain" of the Altaic peoples of Siberia has seven or nine levels that may reflect levels of trance. Sometimes these worlds are connected by a pillar or the trunk of a cosmic tree. This idea is often related to the concept that the world has a center, or navel, that serves as a point of access to the worlds above and below. During their initiatory illness, future shamans may find themselves climbing this cosmic mountain. Once they know the way, they can return on later visits to the Otherworld. As Eliade observes:

> By a sort of symmetry, the underworld has been imagined to have the same number of levels as the sky. . . . the Altaic shaman successively passes through the seven underworld "obstacles" (pudak). Indeed it is he, and he alone, who commands experiential knowledge of the underworld, for he enters it as a living man, just as he mounts and descends through the seven or nine heavens (Eliade, 1964).

This cosmic mapping is not limited to shamanic cultures. In Dante's *Divine Comedy*, the Inferno into which Dante descends, passing from level to level into the bowels of the Earth, is balanced by the Mountain of Purgatory he must climb (see figure 4).

In Greek tradition, the *omphalos* (navel) of the world was marked by the altar at Delphi, where the upper levels of the temple were dedicated to the Olympian Apollo. The cavern beneath belonged to the chthonic Dionysos. Although by Classical times, the oracle channeled Apollo, she also descended to a subterranean chamber to prophesy. Given that the seeress continued to be known as the Pythia (python priestess), it is probable that the oracle was originally that of the Earth goddess, and sought her inspiration from the depths, not the heights.

Hindu epics state that Surya, the Sun God, circumambulates Mount Meru every day. In the late nineteenth century, when Aryans were believed to have had their original home–Urheimat–in northern Europe, Mount Meru was seen as the "center of the world." The Ira-

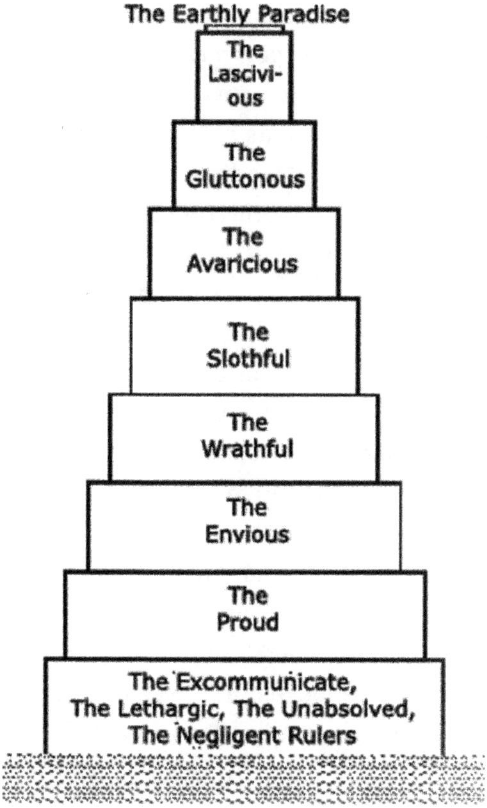

FIGURE 4. Diagram of Purgatory. Redrawn by the author from a diagram in *Purgatory*, translated by Dorothy Sayers.

nians claim that the Aryans came from Mount Hara. Har is another name of Shiva, who has his abode in this mountain. Although I do not know if there is an etymological relationship, Hár, the High One, is also a byname of the Norse god Odin, who lives in Asgard at the top of the World Tree. Some beliefs local to that area of the Himalayas associate mythical Mount Meru with a mountain called Kailasa near Lake Manasarovar in Tibet.

The Mesopotamian ziggurat was a cosmic mountain—a symbolic image given physical form in a flat landscape. Its seven levels represented the seven planetary heavens (as at Borsippa) or bore the colors of the world (as at Ur). The mountain was the navel, the world axis (although the navel may also be represented by a stone). The tree, which is also, by extension, the Tree of Life, may grow on the mountain, or become a map in itself, as in the two otherwise widely divergent traditions of Viking Age Scandinavia and medieval Kabbalism.

In Norse mythology, the World Tree is known as Yggdrasil, the "steed of Ygg (Odin)," that he "rode" when he hanged himself from its branches in the ordeal in which he acquired the runes. As described in the *Prose Edda*, "The ash is of all trees the biggest and best. Its branches spread out over all the world and extend across the sky. Three of the tree's roots support it and extend very, very far. One is among the Æsir, the second among the frost-giants. . . . The third extends over Niflheim. . . . " (*Gylfaginning* 3). References elsewhere in the lore allow us to identify the location of nine "homes" or worlds in relation to each other and the Tree. Various scholars have attempted to map the Tree based on these references. I give my own version in figure 5.

The world we live in is called Midgard, or Middle Earth. Its name suggests that it should be located in the center, midway between the top of the Tree–where we find Asgard, the home of the gods–and Hel–the home of the ancestral spirits, in the depths. The other seven worlds are arranged on the central axis or to the sides.

By contrast, in the image or glyph of *Otz 'Heim*, the Hebrew Tree of Life, our world, Malkuth, is placed at the base of the Tree. According to one tradition, it was originally located much higher, below the Supernal Triad in the empty area called Da'ath. Legend holds that it was demoted from this place on the Tree at the time of the Fall of Adam and Eve. These days, the glyph is usually represented not as a tree, but as a diagram of ten spheres connected by arrows, rather like a flow chart. The map can also be laid out upon a human figure, as in the "Adam Kadmon" or Divine Man (see figure 6).

Maps and diagrams are used in many spiritual traditions as aids to meditation. Tibetan mandalas and Navajo sand paintings teach students to invoke the powers of the Otherworld in magic and healing.

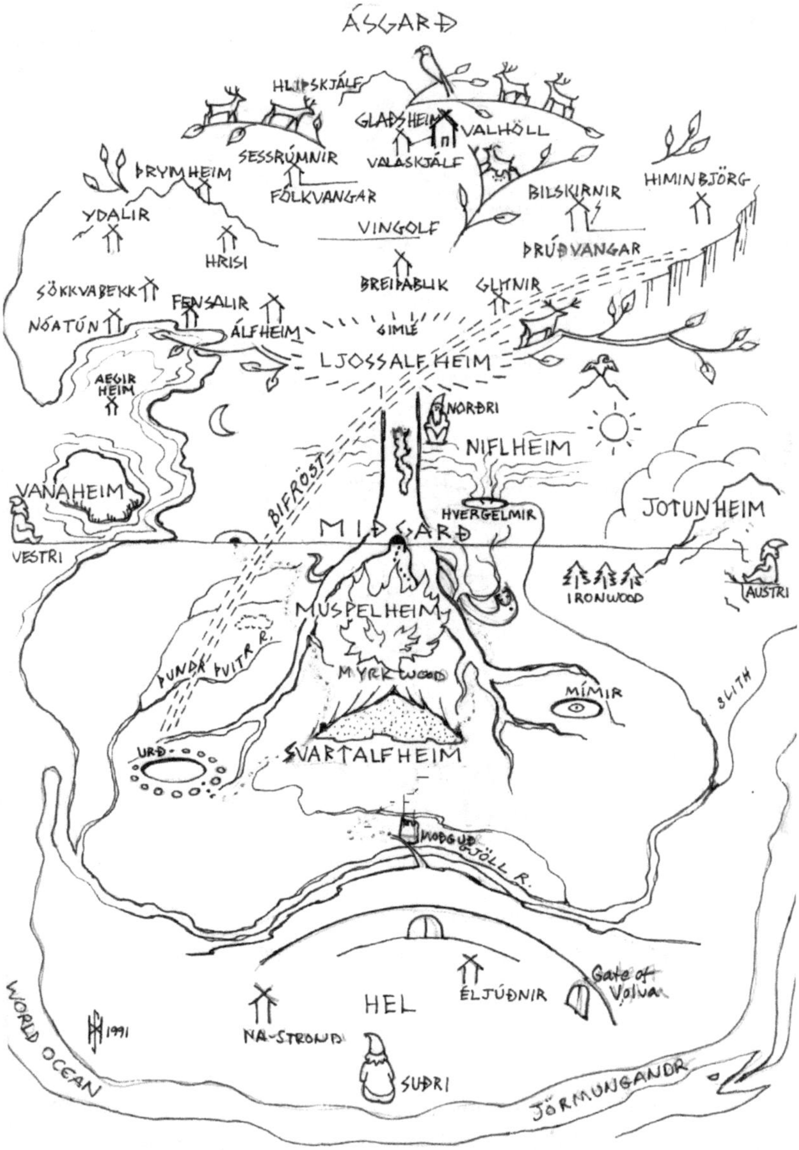

FIGURE 5. Yggdrasil, the Norse World Tree. Drawing by the author.

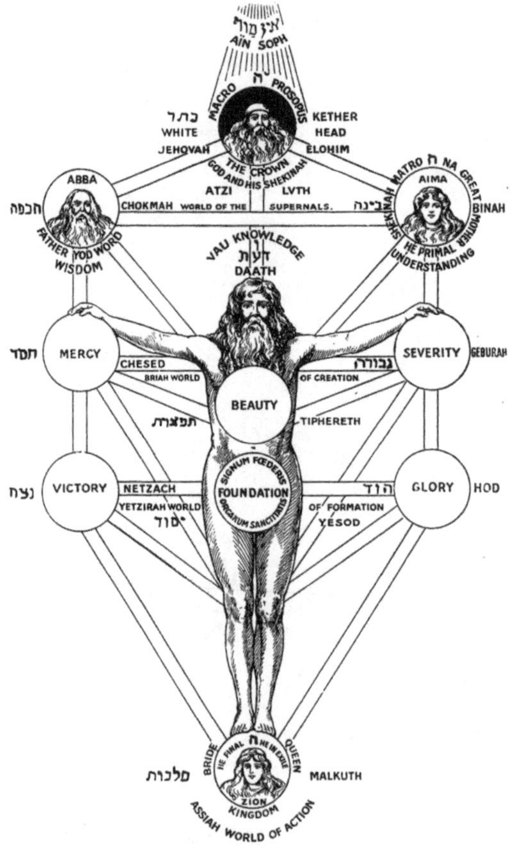

THE SACRED TREE OF THE SEPHIROTH

FIGURE 6. Adam Kadmon, nineteenth-century engraving reproduced as frontispiece to A. E. Waite's *The Holy Kabbalah*.

Mapping Inner Realities

Before we can begin creating and using maps as an aid to journeying, we must consider what a map is. The maps we use to find our way around the "real" world are abstract and symbolic representations of physical reality. We know that a freeway does not actually look like a red line, nor is a town a blue dot. We learn to interpret the symbols as representations of the relationships between physical places. They show us direction and distance, and indicate landmarks to follow. Once you understand its symbolic language, you can use a map to guide you around places you have never been. Maps indicate the sequence in which you reach points on a journey and, by their arrangement and proportions, may indicate importance as well.

Those of us who grew up looking at maps of the world produced in America may not have considered the implications of putting Europe and North America at the top, or realize how the projection exaggerates the size of the northern lands. The medieval view of the world reflected a very different set of assumptions. The ancient Greek tripartite division of the known world was the basis for the map included by St. Isidore of Seville in his seventh century *Etymologiarum sive Originum libri XX* (figure 7). Jerusalem is in the center, a traditional ecclesiastical view of the world. Although scientists as early as the Pythagoreans and Aristotle argued that the Earth is spherical, the notion of a flat Earth persisted in ancient Greece and continued to be widely believed well into the late medieval period.

The famous map of the United States as seen by a New Yorker shows New York City and the Northeast swollen in size, while most of the rest of the country dwindles, except for a few places, like Florida and Los Angeles, that have made it onto Easterners' radar. This map (see figure 8), drawn by Daniel K. Wallingford for the 1936 Times Book Fair, inspired the 1976 Saul Steinberg cartoon, "The World from Ninth

FIGURE 7. St. Isidore's map of the world.

Avenue," which appeared on the cover of *New Yorker* magazine. In a view like this, physical size represents psychological significance. The attitude at which the illustration pokes fun is quite real. When I was in school in Maine, I found it very hard to convince my roommate, who was from Vermont, that the state of California was larger than the state of New York.

Maps can be completely symbolic or partially representational (relief maps, for instance). Political maps show boundaries, or divide the country into "red" and "blue" states. A good atlas will contain maps that show elevation, geology, vegetation, weather patterns, industry, religion, language, and every other possible characteristic of an area. A flow chart is a map that can show the relationships and movement of energy within an organization. We map social, economic, and physiological systems, seeking to display graphically how things get from here to there. The moving route lines on the maps featured in old adventure movies and resurrected for the *Indiana Jones* films provide instant exposition as well as educating the viewer.

You can find a good selection of maps of imaginary worlds in J.B. Post's *An Atlas of Fantasy*. J.R.R. Tolkien's detailed and elegant map

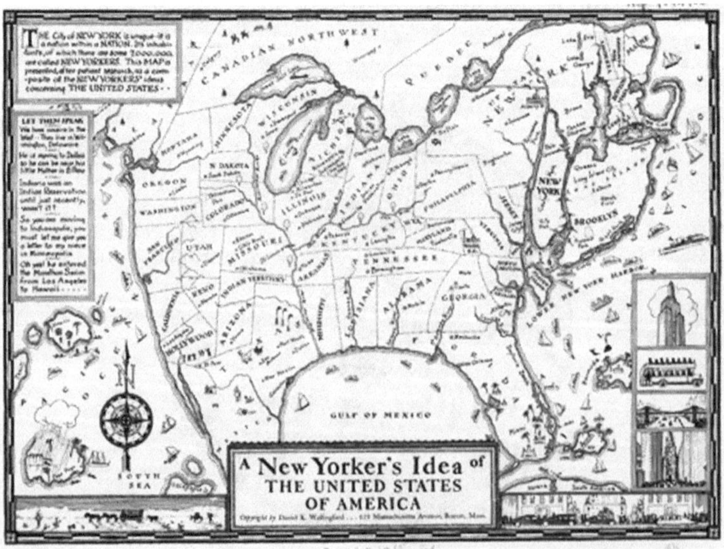

FIGURE 8. A New Yorker's view of the United States by Daniel K. Wallingford.

contributed to the verisimilitude that eventually resulted in travel posters inviting us to "Visit Middle Earth." Every fantasy series since then has featured a more or less credible map of the story's topography. Most writers, as well as many readers, find a map useful, although some feel it cramps their style. For years, Marion Zimmer Bradley resisted letting anyone make a map of Darkover because, as she told me, she "might want to put the city somewhere else next time."

Some writers go beyond two dimensions. The "Marauder's Map" used by Harry Potter and his friends in J. K. Rowling's series is interactive. In Susan Cooper's *Over Sea, Under Stone*, what appears to be a map of the Cornish coastline is, in fact, a perspective drawing. What are first taken to be blotches refer to positions of the Sun and Moon in relation to landmarks whose shadows or alignment point the way to the hiding place of the Grail.

Participating in Dungeons & Dragons and other role-playing games has introduced an entire generation to the concept of mapping imaginary worlds (as well as developing alternate personae, working with invisible friends, and improving group collaboration skills). By the time you have worked with a couple of examples provided by the game designers, you are ready to create your own, like this map of "Umbria" drawn by my son, based on the East Bay Area opposite San Francisco (see figure 9).

Exits and Entrances

Before passing on to practice, let's take a moment to consider a more abstract means for passing from one "world" to the next. Instead of the representational symbolism of a map, you can use a symbol as a mnemonic—a trigger that, upon contemplation, expands into meaning. When a symbol whose meaning has been thoroughly internalized is used as a focus, it can become a doorway through which you pass to an appropriate sector of the Otherworld.

For instance, if you are studying the Runes, an image of the rune itself can expand to become a doorway, or be fine-tuned even further by adding another rune to create a bindrune (essentially a runic

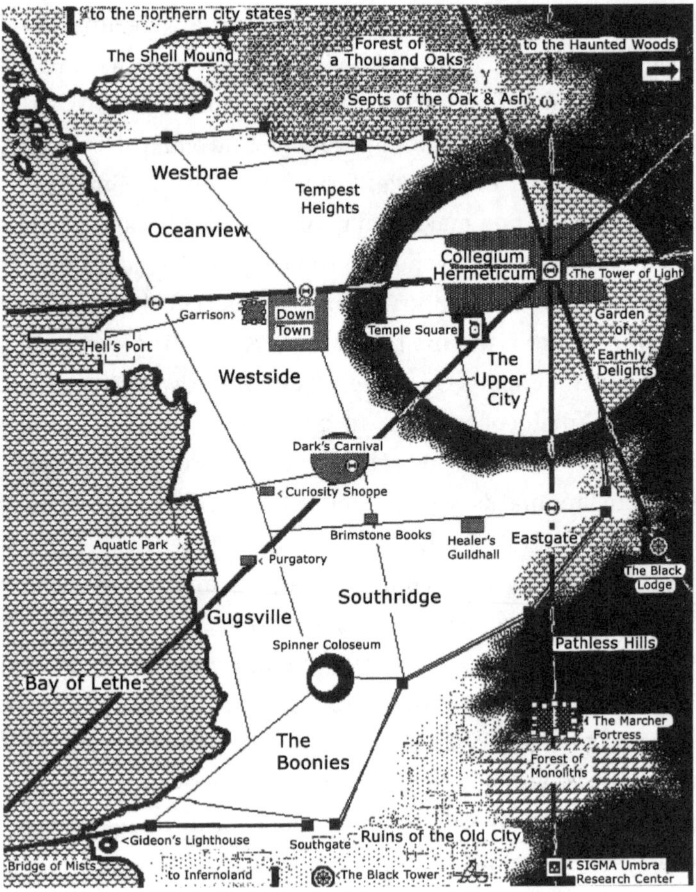

FIGURE 9. "East Bay Umbria" by Ian Grey. Used by permission of the artist.

monogram) that combines their meanings. For example, the rune *Ingwaz* ◇ bears the name of the god Ing, another name for Freyr. The rune *Gebo* X means a gift, or an exchange of energy. Contemplate Ing by drawing the rune on a piece of paper and staring at it until you see it when you close your eyes. Then allow the diamond shape to expand until it becomes an opening through which you can step. You will move into a landscape associated with the god, where you can seek him. But if what you need is Freyr's help with jobs or income, add the Gebo rune to the corners as in figure 10. Silently articulate your intention and need as you move through the doorway once more, looking for symbols or beings that can help you learn to give and receive the prosperity you need. When you have finished, look for the bindrune, and step back through it.

A Hebrew letter or an astrological symbol can be used in the same way. Meditating on the *tattwa* symbols of the four elements from Hindu tradition can move you into an appropriate elemental landscape. When studying Kabbalah, constructing a journey with symbols appropriate to a given *sephira* will move you into that sphere.

Geometric forms can be used as transfer points independent of cultural context. The question of whether these symbols are universal or

FIGURE 10. Ingwaz/Gebo bindrune, by Diana L. Paxson.

dependent on your cognitive style is still open to debate. Are there some sigils that will move you into a certain state–of place or consciousness–as automatically as taking a freeway exit? Or does the effect depend on understanding the significance of the symbol?

Road Signs

George Hersh describes the relationship between symbol and meaning like this:

> There are many classes of elements of language and one of these is the class of signs: entities that "stand for" other entities or relationships or qualities or processes. Words can be signs or they can be empty place-holders, slithy toves before Humpty Dumpty provides meaning. Signs can indicate states, Beingness can be a state, and a state can be determined or defined within a multidimensional universe of locations.
>
> Since the three most important aspects of selecting a state are location, location, and location (as in the choice between Hawaii and North Dakota), it is useful to maintain mnemonics of location associated with states that you wish either to visit or to avoid, and states to which you wish to consign inconvenient others by express parcel post. In trance, thoroughly rehearsed glyphs, signs, tokens, mnemonics are useful to evoke urgently needed entities, events, processes, or places. Remember that a GPS works because we have placed reference satellites around our world. We ground-truth our point of view by checking in with the local surveyor's monuments of recorded time. Now, as to the relative complexity or lack thereof in our magical signs, is a sign a sign post, a map, or a swift kick in the flying ointment?
>
> (I divide expert magic workers into three broad classes, the rote workers, the obsessive/compulsives, and the poets. The rote workers have obtained a large or small collection of spells and procedures which they are loath to alter at the altar from the way they are wrote or wrought. They hold fast to the idea that repeti-

tion is possible and safe. They like rubber stamp signs kept in black silk wrappings to insulate them between uses. The obsessive/compulsives elaborate procedures and elaborate the elaborations, never discarding anything and ornamenting whatever they add. Dee's tables and pentacles and Crowley's artistic variations thereon are excellent examples. I use the term "obsessive/ compulsive" because those who use the term "anal" have a nasty record of croaking "ribbit" all the way back to the pond. Bindrunes are relatively simple instruction sets for the compelling by the compulsive. The set of switchable luminous lines that allows minimal alphanumeric representation is a superb example of the bindrune in action. The poets are fond of stealing from each other and from anything that holds still enough to grasp. They build lovely nonce structures and can be your best friends in unforeseen emergencies. However, sometimes it doesn't rhyme or scan and the Blatant Beast eats you.)

Do our symbols map or direct or label or indicate or diagram the roads to our various destinations? Sure they do, but be careful not to mistake a map fold for a trade route. Are the magical elements of great power and effect by virtue of their forms? Sure, but so are the Venuses of Willendorf and Milo. Intent must be linked to form for magic to ensue.

Labyrinths

One symbol that has haunted the human imagination for centuries is the labyrinth. The sacred significance of this symbol spans the world and goes back to the dawn of time. Labyrinths appear in the art of cultures from Crete to the Pima Indians, from a medieval example in Chartres Cathedral (see figure 11) to two (indoor and outdoor) at Grace Cathedral in San Francisco. Recently, there has been a resurgence of interest in the labyrinth. You can order one online or go to the Labyrinth Society (*www.labyrinthsociety.org/*) and learn to build your own. You can create a portable labyrinth with duct tape on a plastic tarp or with paint on canvas. For an excellent discussion of labyrinths past and present, along with instructions for building one, see *www.crystalinks.com/labyrinths.html.*

The very simple stone spiral that used to lie among the redwoods at Fernwood Campground in Big Sur took only a few minutes to reach the heart of the mystery. In Oakland's Sibley Park, the original labyrinth in the bottom of a disused quarry appears to have given birth to a family, spiraling across the hillside (figure 12).

One of the oldest and most prevalent forms is the seven-fold Cretan labyrinth, an endlessly running meander based on the Greek key design (figure 2). It is said to be the design that imprisoned the Minotaur, although in the *Iliad*, it appears on Achilles' shield as the image of the dancing floor designed by Daedalos for Ariadne. In the Middle Ages, this was elaborated into an eleven-fold form, which is the one found in both the Chartres and San Francisco cathedrals.

Walking the labyrinth combines visual and kinesthetic stimuli. As you spiral in and out, hopefully approaching the center only to swing back toward the periphery and around again, it is natural to find in your action a symbol of the spiritual journey, in which you yearn

FIGURE 11. A labyrinth design from Chartres Cathedral.

FIGURE 12. The Sibley labyrinths, photo by Diana L. Paxson.

toward the peace and union of the center only to be distracted by the needs of the world. And when you at last arrive at the still point within, the demands of your body eventually and inevitably bring the experience to a close and send you back again. That point at the heart of the labyrinth has been likened to the womb of the Great Goddess from which we are reborn, or a journey to your own center. Some have used walking the labyrinth as part of a ritual, in which they journey to look into the Well of Wyrd. A Samhain ritual with a triple labyrinth placed a priestess of the Maiden, Mother, and Crone at each center, offering words of wisdom to those whose paths led them there.

When I walk the Sibley labyrinth, to sight and motion I add song, replacing "Spiral in to" with "Spiral out from" on the return–

Spiral in to the center,
spiral in to the earth,
Spiral in, all together,
to new life, to new birth.

Practice

1. **Mapping perceptions:** From memory, draw a map that shows someone how to get from your job or school to your home. Get a city map and compare the two. Go online and print a map from Google or Mapquest. In what ways are all three maps the same, and how do they differ? What elements does your own map emphasize and what does it leave out? At what points does your map change in scale?
2. **Making a mental map:** Draw a map that shows the route you take to reach your base camp or starting point, and the route from there to a point you have visited in the Otherworld. Do you find that some locations are perceived more consistently, or are harder to remember, than others?
3. **Exploring the Otherworld:** Choose a sector in the Otherworld to explore, such as Arcadia or Vanaheim, or the place where you meet with one of your allies or guides. Draw a map that shows the nature and relationship of its major landmarks. Note that the terrain of the inner worlds is mutable; from time to time, sizes and locations may change. Locate things where you usually find them.
4. **Opening symbolic doorways:** Choose a rune or sigil from one of these Web sites and use it as a doorway for a journey, or use those given as inspiration for creating your own. Write down your experiences. *(en.wikipedia.org/wiki/Sigil_(magic); www.sigilgarden.com/)*

Chapter Nine

Fellow Travelers

They therefore went up through the regions of the air, sweetly talking as they went; being comforted, because they safely got over the river, and had such glorious companions to attend them.

John Bunyan, Pilgrim's Progress

Solo travelers can choose their own routes and set their own schedules. The freedom you have when you travel alone is sometimes half the value of the experience. And yet, from the Canterbury pilgrims to the people who climb Mt. Everest, travelers have also found good reason to journey in company. If adjusting your pace to that of another is sometimes frustrating, a companion can also help you over a rough spot, and watch your back or the luggage while you go to the loo. And at the end of the day, it is good to have someone with whom to share what you have seen and done, to imprint your experience on your memory by describing it and understand it more fully by hearing another perspective.

The same thing applies when you wander the inner worlds—perhaps even more so, given the subjective nature of the experience. Although a vision shared by two may be no more than a *folie à deux*, you can avoid a great deal of self-delusion by getting a second opinion. And when your own strength or skill falters, you may be very grateful for some backup.

Most of the material in previous chapters was written from the point of view of someone studying alone. If you are working with a class, however, you have been participating in group work and may have some ideas about how it can contribute to your progress. (Even if you are in a class, however, the rate and extent of your learning will be affected by the intensity of your personal practice.) If you are working alone, you may not have an opportunity right now to do trance work with others. But if you continue working along these lines, at some point interactive energy work and trance skills will be important for you to know.

And there is another reason for exploring these skills. In the Western Tradition, the primary purpose of spiritual development is not to escape the world, but to serve it—the perfection of your soul or the attainment of magical power is desirable, but incidental to the main task. As Evelyn Underhill observes, "In the mystics of the West, the highest forms of Divine Union impel the self to some sort of active, rather than of passive life . . . not spiritual marriage, but divine fecundity is to be their final state" (1961).

Perfect Trust

Although perfect love may not be required for trance work with others, the second half of the traditional Wiccan watchword of "perfect love and perfect trust" certainly applies. When we talk about trance, we use phrases like "opening up." Much of the work in the first two chapters was devoted to warding and shielding a safe space in which to do so. We create these outer barriers to replace the inner ones that prevent us from perceiving the world of the spirit. Our souls may be naked, but we are still in a well-insulated room. But when we work with others, we have to take down some of those barriers and let others come in. Some things can only be done when we are open to each other, but being open also means being vulnerable.

We all have our own energy signatures, which may sometimes be distracting or incompatible in a group or class setting. In addition, if someone is in physical or emotional pain, its resonance can upset any unshielded person nearby. When the purpose of the session is to do your own work, you are quite justified in protecting yourself by moving away from the individual causing a problem. An alternative is to put up a light personal shield.

But what if your goal is to establish rapport with the other person? As you will see in the next chapter, many of the purposes for which we use trance skills, such as healing, involve working with other people. You must be able to take down enough of your own shielding to establish rapport and make a connection without abandoning all your protections.

When one person gives blood directly to another—an action that requires a great deal of trust—medical personnel watch carefully to make sure the donor retains enough blood to survive. When doing psychic work, you can be tempted to give all, as the Ranger Marcus does in order to heal Ivanova in *Babylon 5*. I can recall an instance when a person warding and supporting a seer in an oracular ritual sent so much energy that, when we were finished, everyone had to spend another half hour re-energizing *her.*

Even when you work with others, you must retain your own focus and identity. Bear this in mind as you work through the exercises at the end of this chapter. As you address each one, experiment with thickening and thinning your defensive shields until you work out how to maintain the minimum necessary level of protection.

Since, in this chapter, we will talk a great deal about the exchange and sharing of energy, it may help you to review the discussion of Sensing Energy in chapter 4. There, the focus was on learning how to sense the flow of energy in your own body. Here, you will build on that awareness until your inner senses can tell you what others are doing spiritually, just as easily as your outer senses tell you what they are doing in the physical world.

Evaluating Flight Status

Of course, you are also responsible for the ways in which you affect others. One factor to consider, therefore, is your own physical and emotional condition, especially if you are the one piloting the plane. This is where the concept of checksums introduced in chapter 4, becomes really useful. By now, you should be pretty familiar with the ways different factors affect your ability to do trance work. As part of your preparation, ask yourself the following questions:

> **Did I get enough sleep last night?** If you fall asleep when someone else is leading a guided meditation, the loss (or, if you snore, the embarrassment) is yours. If you do so in an interactive meditation, you also diminish the experience for your partner. Depending on how you respond to stimulants, try drinking a cup of coffee before beginning work. If your problem is fatigue in general, you may be able to work with a strong partner who can carry part of your load as well as his or her own.
>
> **How long has it been since I ate?** Food levels can have a dramatic impact on both energy levels and perceptions. A growling stomach can be a major distraction when you are trying to journey. When I am doing oracular work and notice that empty feeling in my middle, I know that my fuel guage is approaching empty and it's time to head for home. More insidious are variations in blood-sugar levels. If you eat a candy bar just before beginning work, you may be raring to go, but if the session is intense or lengthy, this quick high may be followed by an equally quick crash. It is better by far to substitute, or at least accompany, the sugar with some protein that will burn more slowly and more steadily. Check your hydration levels as well, especially in hot weather.

Are my hormones or biochemistry doing anything I need to watch out for? As with blood sugar, hormonal variations can have a major impact on temper and perspective. Become familiar enough with your own biorhythms (and, if you are a woman, with the effects of your Moon cycle) to anticipate problems. If you know that your physical state is likely to make you weepy or short-tempered, try to compensate, or at least warn your companions.

Are my emotions stable? This area can be the hardest one to evaluate, and the most important, especially when you will be in rapport with someone else. You may have tamped down your resentment at your boss or your anxiety about your mate so thoroughly that it is no longer present to your conscious mind. But, when you open the door to trance, you open the door to your unconscious. Everything you experience will be colored by those feelings, and anyone connected to you will feel them as well. Of course, nobody's life is perfect and, if we all waited until we had no worries, we would never get any spiritual work done at all. What you *can* do is to try to know yourself, to recognize and "own" your feelings and manage, rather than repress, them. Before beginning group work, spend a few minutes reviewing your day. Bring to consciousness any difficulties. Accept them, and then release them to be dealt with later. If necessary, warn your partner that the feelings are yours and not his or hers.

I remember an instance when one of our seers had a fight with her boyfriend a half hour before we were supposed to begin an oracular ritual. When she told me that she was still too upset to work, I was both disappointed and grateful. Losing her from the lineup meant the rest of us had to work harder, but, fortunately, we had other people who could take up the slack. I congratulated her on making the correct and responsible decision. The moral here is: If your own emotional turmoil is dominating your awareness to the exclusion of all else, it is not a good time to be around, much less linked to, other people who are taking down their shields.

Establishing Rapport

In order for people to do trance work together, they must be in rapport—a term that comes from the French *rapporter*, "to bring back." According to neuro-linguistic programming pioneer Robert Dilts:

> Creating rapport is generally defined as the establishment of trust, harmony and cooperation in a relationship. "Harmonious mutual understanding," "agreement," being "in tune" and "in accord," are some of the words used to describe the process or state of being in rapport with another. The process of body mirroring to create rapport is one of the earliest and most well known NLP techniques (although mirroring is not a guarantee of the creation of the state of rapport because a person can still easily stay in his or her own "first position" and not necessarily enter the "we" experience).
>
> The NLP notion of rapport was derived from the work of Milton Erickson. As a hypnotherapist, Erickson created and entered into a special state of rapport called the "therapeutic trance." In 1978, a student noticed that, as Erickson was in the process of leading a client into a trance state, Erickson himself exhibited the characteristics of trance, including pupil dilation, change of muscle tonus and breathing. When asked if he was entering trance when he hypnotized his clients, Erickson's response was "invariably." To this reply the student asked, "Who is hypnotizing who in that case?" Again Erickson replied "invariably," suggesting that the state of rapport is a loop of mutual influence and interaction in which each element is influencing, and influenced by, the other elements (1998).

Most of the time, rapport is unconscious, a shared perspective and harmony that are felt without having to be defined. In Ken Kesey's novel *Sometimes A Great Notion*, there is a passage that demonstrates perfect rapport in action.

> As the trees fell and the hours passed, the three men grew accustomed to one another's abilities and drawbacks. Few words actu-

> ally passed between them; they communicated with the unspoken language of labor toward a shared goal, becoming more and more an efficient, skilled team as they worked their way across the steep slopes; becoming almost one man, one worker who knew his body and his skill and knew how to use them without waste or overlap. . . . Until the three of them meshed, dovetailed . . . into one of the rare and beautiful units of effort sometimes seen when a jazz group is making it completely, swinging together completely, or when a home-town basketball squad, already playing over its head, begins to rally to overtake a superior opponent in a game's last minute . . . and the home boys can't miss; because everything–the passing, the dribbling, the plays–every tiny *piece* is clicking perfectly. When this happens everyone watching *knows* . . . that, be it five guys playing basketball, or four blowing jazz, or three cutting timber, that *this bunch–right* now, right *this moment*–is the best of its kind in the world! But to become this kind of perfect group a team must use *all* of its components, and use them in the slots best suited, and use them all with the pitiless dedication to victory that drives them up to their absolute peak, and past it (1965).

When people work together in this way, they achieve a psychic connection, a concept that puts them very close to the definition of religion itself. Religion is a term that comes, according to St. Augustine of Hippo, from the Latin words *ligare*, "To bind or connect," and *re-*, "again," an interpretation which is accepted by most modern scholars. According to Sarah Hoyt,

> This interpretation, given by the Roman grammarian (end of 4th cen. A.D.) Servius (*Religio, id est metus ab eo quot mentem religet, dicta religio*) was supported by the Christian philosopher Lactantius (about 313 A.D.) who quotes the expression of the celebrated Roman philosophical poet Lucretius (c. 96 to 55 B.C.) r*eligionum animum nodis exsolvere*, in proof that he considered ligare, to bind, to be the root of *religio* (1912).

Thus, its etymology implies obligation as well as reconnection. Religion can therefore be seen as a means to recreate and support a network of mutual obligations between humans and between humans and the gods.

In shared trance work, we use the techniques we learned on our own in a group setting–chanting together, breathing together, and using imagery to create an experience that is greater than anything we could achieve alone. When group meditation is consistently practiced in a spiritual tradition, this shared experience can transcend the experience of any single event or individual. As Dion Fortune observes, the more energy put into an image and the more people use it, the stronger its resonance in the world of the spirit will be.

> When a number of devout worshippers are gathered together, their emotions concentrated and exalted by ritual, and all holding the same image in imagination, the outpoured force of all present is formed into an astral simulacrum of the being thus intensely pictured. . . . When this process has been repeated regularly over considerable periods, the images that have been built up remain on the astral. . . . Consequently subsequent worshippers need be at no great pains to formulate the simulacrum; they have only to think of the god and they feel his power (1962).

Practice

1. **Circling energy**: With a group of people, form a circle and clasp hands. Following a leader's direction, ground and center. Breathe slowly in and out in unison. As you breathe in, focus your energy in your solar plexus. As you breathe out, direct it to flow down your left arm and through your hand to the person on your left side, while you draw in energy from the person on your right. Continue to breathe rhythmically in and out until you can feel the energy rise and fall and flow. At this point, you may begin to intone "AUM." As the energy intensifies, let the chanting grow louder, and let the tone move upward as you allow your linked

hands to rise. When it peaks, let go of each other's hands with a shout.

2. **Playing ball:** Sit facing a partner. Rub your palms together until they tingle, then hold them a few inches apart, adjusting the distance until you can feel the pressure on your skin. Move your hands back and forth, shaping the energy until you feel it strongly, then "toss" it to your partner. If you are the partner, try to sense where the ball of energy is and catch it. Add your own energy, reshape the ball, and cast it back to your partner. Play with the energy, moving it back and forth until both of you feel it come and go. Now try it with your eyes shut.
3. **Circle dancing:** This exercise is based on a form of Native American group dancing popular at powwows. Unlike most European circle dances, it is usually done without holding hands. Form an evenly spaced circle and put on a CD or ask your drummer to give you a slow, regular 4/4 beat. With your arms hanging at your sides, move to the left in unison, step-together-step, step-together-step. Try to maintain the same distance between yourself and the people on your right and left. Extend your awareness until you can sense where they are without having to look. Continue until you no longer have to check on your position, and you feel yourself and the others moving as a single organism.
4. **Blind dancing:** Assemble a group in a large, open space with a nice smooth floor. Have everyone put on a blindfold, as the leader starts a CD of soothing instrumental music with a slow to moderate pace and a defined beat. Move with the music, extending your awareness to sense the positions of the other dancers. It is advisable to have one or two warders who keep their eyes open and can reorient people who are in danger of running into the walls.
5. **Interactive journeying:** Sit or lie down next to a partner. Agree on a place to which you will journey. This can be the base camp for one of you, or a location in the Otherworld from a tradition with which you are both familiar. Or you may decide to look for a place where you can find the answer to a question. Talk about the kinds

of perception that work best for each of you—aural, visual, tactile, kinesthetic. Direct your partner to ground, center, and breathe. Focus on your shields and intentionally lower and extend them to include each other. When you are breathing in unison, start narrating a journey to an entrance to the Otherworld, taking care to include sensory imagery that works for you both. When the journey is well established, turn it over to your companion with words like: "We're going down a path. There are a lot of grey rocks; I can hear them crunch beneath my feet. Can you see or hear the rocks? Tell me, what do you see?" Continue passing the narration back and forth until you perceive each part of the scene as soon as, or even before, your partner begins to describe it. When you reach your goal, retrace your steps, noting the landmarks that will show you the way. When you return, write down your experiences and then compare notes.

6. **Shadowing:** Sit or lie down next to a partner. Breathe together until you are breathing in unison. Extend your awareness and your energy field to include that of your partner. Without speaking, visualize a journey or a scene. Make it as vivid and powerful as you can. Then increase the rate of your breathing and return. Have your partner write down what he or she experienced or saw and compare notes. Repeat the exercise with the roles reversed.
7. **Scoring spiritual energy:** To improve your ability to identify and evaluate other people's energies, not to mention broaden your spiritual experience, visit a number of religious services of different denominations and "score" participants on type and level of energy. High Church or festival services that feature multiple clergy offer a good opportunity to compare people from the same tradition. Check for kinds of energy as well as levels—some traditions or congregations may raise a very cool, but very focused, energy; others may be "hot" and expansive. Attend a sports event and evaluate the energy of the crowd. If there are cheerleaders, note how they raise and focus the energy. How do the levels for those supporting the two teams vary and change as the score

changes? How does each side feel when the game is over? Attend a live entertainment event and try to get a seat close to the performer. Great artists are "turned on" by the response of the audience. Their energy flows out, is amplified, and returns in an ecstatic circuit. When they achieve rapport, artist and audience journey together to other realms.

Chapter Ten
Destinations

Certainly, travel is more than the seeing of sights; it is a change that goes on, deep and permanent, in the ideas of living.

Miriam Beard

Trance work can take you to many destinations. Once you have created a base camp, it becomes your jumping-off point for exploring your inner universe. You can journey to destinations known and unknown, seeking aid and answers. Your ability to journey can help you endure physical discomfort. Focusing energy and establishing rapport with another person is also useful in counseling or healing. When you open up to messages from your unconscious, inspiration flows more smoothly into any creative activity you may try (like writing a book like this one).

Healing

Your work so far has shown you something about the relationship between mind and body. When your attention moves inward, the sensations of your physical body become distant and unimportant, or may even seem to disappear. Time passes differently—fifteen minutes may feel like five, or five minutes may contain a novel's worth of experience. Clearly, altering your consciousness can help you deal with your own pain.

You can direct the trance skills you have learned in many ways to help yourself or others. The art of healing the body with the help of the mind is both ancient and new. Be aware, however, that, in most cases, spiritual healing should assist and support rather than replace physical healing—at least until the doctors have done all they can. Eat all the healthy food you can digest, and take all the exercise your body will allow. Work with your doctors, and insist on learning as much about your illness as you possibly can. You cannot effectively apply your mind to healing unless you give it good information.

Problems and Soul Parts

As you have already discovered, journeying can be an excellent way to seek illumination and help with personal problems. If you do not know what you are looking for, ask your ally to show you. Or identify your goal as "a place where I can find help with X," or search for a talisman. You can also journey interactively to support someone else who is less experienced in traveling the inner worlds.

Soul Retrieval is a special kind of journeying to help another. In this practice, a shaman searches the Otherworld for soul parts that someone else has lost and brings them back to the client. In the procedure as developed by Sandra Ingerman of the Foundation for Shamanic Studies, shamans use their judgment regarding how much to tell their clients about what they have found. This is a task for an experienced trance worker. To learn more, see Ingerman's book (1991) or contact the Foundation for Shamanic Studies for information on workshops.

Experienced trancers can engage in a similar process by working together and narrating what they see and hear, preferably with the support of a third person who is not in trance.

Pain Management

One of the most immediately useful applications for trance skills is managing pain. Women who have taken classes in natural childbirth have learned how to breathe to avoid the pain caused when tense muscles conflict with uterine contractions. Deep breathing and relaxation can ease many kinds of hurting, especially when combined with something like soothing music or a visualization of flowing water that carries each pulse of pain away. If that is not sufficient try to journey Elsewhere.

One student reports that a series of dental procedures recently gave her the opportunity to refine this skill. She used controlled breathing to get deeply relaxed, then "breathed into" the pain, and finally breathed it out. "For quite a while now, I have tried 'breathing into' pain, then breathing it out. A series of dental procedures has recently presented me with a chance to sharpen (ouch) this skill. The breathing we have been practicing is really useful; I use that to get deeply relaxed, then I can access the other technique. The effect seems to be rather to stop pain feedback and help one get through the episode. Then the next episode is less and it gets longer in between. Not an instant cure, but a palliative."

The discomfort of procedures like medical tests and dental work can also be muted by journeying. A friend of mine impressed her dentist so much by her ability to trance when he was treating her that he offered to trade dental work for trance lessons. You should, however, explain what you are doing, so your doctor does not become alarmed when you fail to respond to questions.

Many of the same techniques you work with alone can also be useful when you work with others, if you can articulate the things you know how to do and create your own trance inductions. For a discussion of how to deliver shared inductions, see Appendix II. You can, for instance, direct someone else through the process of grounding, centering, relaxing, and breathing, or lead them on a journey to find a place of peace and healing.

Visualization Therapy

The use of mental/spiritual techniques in healing has a venerable history. You can find a good summary of it by Patricia Norris online at *www.healthy.net/scr/Article.asp?Id=392&xcntr.* In recent years, the medical profession has begun to explore the uses of biofeedback and visual imagery in treating conditions like high blood pressure. Researchers Carl and Stephanie Simonton built on this work in their experiments using visualization and affirmation to fight cancer. Norris summarizes their work:

> The Simontons taught patients to visualize their cancer cells or tumors as accurately as possible. They taught them that cancer cells are weak and mixed up, disorganized, and instilled confidence that bodies could naturally and normally defend against cancer. They also explained the treatment and its desired outcome, and they taught patients to visualize it as powerful and effective, capable of producing a positive outcome. Most importantly, they encouraged patients to develop visualizations of their white blood cells as being numerous and powerful, attacking and destroying the cancer. . . .
>
> They were able to isolate fourteen factors which seem to have high prognostic value, involving vividness, activity, and strength of the cancer cells; vividness, activity, and strength of the white blood cells; and the relative size and numbers of white cells as compared to cancer cells. Other important factors were vividness and strength of the medical treatment being received, the overall strength of the imagery, and the emotional investment of the patient (1985).

They also found that the most effective images were those that were organized and contextually related, carried a strong emotional connection, and were perceived as a source of continuous comfort and support. This suggests that, when you work with imagery to fight illness, you should fine-tune the content to your own preferences or those of the person with whom you are working. A child may see his protector as the Incredible Hulk or Superman. A pagan may visualize Thor striking cancer cells with his hammer or Oya incinerating them with bolts of lightning. A Christian may call on the archangel Mikael to slay them with his fiery sword. The internal struggle can be visualized, perhaps, as a battle between spacecraft inspired by *Star Wars*. When slow, gentle healing is needed, on the other hand, you may call on Gabriel or Brigid or Eir. Some have found their power animals helpful in healing themselves or others. Raven may peck out a bad spot and fly off with it. Coyote might simply gobble it down (coyotes and ravens can digest *anything*).

In order for all this to work, you must understand what you are dealing with. Today, our knowledge of the structure of the human body and its interlocking systems is extensive. As we explore ways of recruiting the mind to help heal the body, we should make use of every advantage we have. If you are engaged in healing, there is no excuse for not knowing exactly what it is you are trying to treat. Dig out your college physiology textbook, or look for a copy of the *Atlas of Human Anatomy* by Frank Netter (pricey, but available, and with lots of pictures). If you know the name of a condition, look it up online. Identify the organ or organs affected and learn how they are supposed to function. Contemplate the pictures until you can see them with your eyes closed. If a group of people are working together, you should all contemplate the image and agree on exactly what changes need to take place. Should something be subtracted, such as shrinking a tumor? Or is the need to build up layers of healthy bone? Are you trying to increase strength or calm a fever? In each case, figure out what the healing should look like. But be careful. If you have any question at all about what needs to happen, simply visualize the patient as strong and healthy, surrounded by a golden or rosy glow. Exercise 25 gives you a technique a healing circle can use at a distance.

Exercise 25. Healing at a Distance

Sit in a circle, holding hands. Perform these steps together as a group. Choose one person as your focus, usually someone related to or close to the patient. Have that person clearly describe the problem, state the location of the patient, and affirm what you want the energy to do.

Close your eyes, ground and center, and establish rapport. Begin to move the energy in a circle in tune with your breathing, drawing it in through your right hand and out through your left, so that it circles clockwise. At the same time, start intoning "AUM," staggering your breathing around the circle so that the tone is constant.

As you feel the energy grow, increase the volume and intensity of the toning. As it begins to peak, let the chanting rise up the scale, at the same time visualizing the energy you are raising as a clockwise-whirling vortex of light. Let your linked hands rise, simultaneously sensing the moment to push the energy toward the person who is acting as focus.

Let go of each others' hands, and release the energy with a shout. The focus person then visualizes the patient, receives the released energy, and passes it on, like a deep receiver who catches a pass, lets its kinetic energy whirl him around, and then propels the ball toward the goal.

Trance work can also help patients diagnose themselves, literally "journeying within" to explore their own bodies. Norris describes one patient who got a clear mental picture of which disk was out of place as he "took a trip" down his spine. Another "saw" a problem with her pancreatic duct that explained a condition that had gone undiagnosed for years. Norris defines visualization as "consciously chosen, intentional instruction to the body. Imagery is the spontaneously occurring 'answer,' qualifier and modifier from the unconscious" (1985).

When you work with others, you may choose to narrate a trance induction and lead them to a place in the Otherworld where they can meet with a guardian or healer—either someone whom you have agreed to seek before beginning, or a figure that appears spontaneously during the silent space at the center of the journey. Or you may choose to journey with them in an interactive trance in which you lead the way into the Otherworld and gradually turn over control until they are leading and you are only supporting, nudging, and encouraging. The techniques for mapping the inner worlds given in chapter 8 can also help you portray the inner landscape in which the battle between disease and healing is fought.

Working with Energy

When doing healing work, you will also make use of other trance skills. To help someone visualize, you must establish rapport and utilize what you have learned about sensing energy. If you let down your shields and help others to do the same thing, you may be able to sense energy fluctuations in their bodies, either through the palms of your hands using an aid like a pendulum, or, if you have that talent, by observing changes in their auras.

If the energy in a certain area seems angry–if you perceive it as "hot," either psychically or physically–cool your own energy and project calm. If, on the other hand, the person is weak, raise your own energy levels and project golden energy into his or her solar plexus. Just as in working with visualization, however, you must be careful. Too much energy can overburden a weak system, and too much in the wrong place can unbalance it. When in doubt, send the energy to the patient's higher self to be used as needed.

Singing for Healing

Sound vibration is another useful tool. A part of the body can be energized by bending close and intoning a note, projecting the sound waves into the organ that needs work. Open your awareness to sense the spot and experiment with volume, tone, and pitch until you sense a resonance. Raise the intensity until it peaks, then diminish the volume and pull away. You can do this for others fairly easily and, with practice, you may also be able to cause the sound to vibrate in any part of the body you choose.

Singing, especially songs that have meaning for the patient, can also provide both healing and comfort. Even an unresponsive person in a coma may be able to hear. Chants may be even more useful, as they can be repeated to put both you and your patient into a healing trance. Chant an affirmation of the healing you desire: Something as simple as "Water flowing, fever slowing/cool you keep, calm you sleep" can be chanted over and over again. Change the "you" to "I" and it becomes an affirmation that you can sing to yourself.

Healing Ethics

When you hear that someone is sick, you are often tempted to pull out all the stops and zap the problem into the middle of next week, especially when you are just discovering your ability to work with spirit. Although you are unlikely to be hit with a malpractice suit for working without authorization, ethical and practical guidelines are very important. When you consider using your skills for healing, first ask yourself these questions:

1. **Has the patient or next of kin asked for help or given permission for the work?** As a pagan, I place a very high value on free will. The ability to choose what shall be done to or for me is a basic right, and one I cannot deny to others, even when I think I know what is good for them better than they do. In my opinion, the Golden Rule should read: "Do unto others as they would be done by," rather than "Do unto others as you would have them do unto you." Thus, if Great-Aunt-Hattie-the-Baptist, who thinks anything magical is the work of Satan, is in the hospital, I will not do specific healing work on her behalf. What I *will* do is pray to *her* god and guardian angel to watch over her and help her in whatever way is right.
2. **What kind of help is wanted?** This is, more or less, a corollary to the first question. Very often, people in the community will simply ask that "positive energy" be sent. Unless the problem has been described very specifically, or you yourself have been asked to do a particular kind of work, the best response is to offer what has been requested and no more. By "positive energy," most people understand anything from a general warm fuzzy feeling

focused in the right direction to a visualization of a sphere of healing energy surrounding the person in need.

3. **How much do you know about the nature of the problem?** If all you know is that the patient has "some kind of back problem," or you've been told that someone has a herniated first lumbar vertebral disc, but wouldn't know the first lumbar vertebra if it bit you, you had better limit yourself to working on things like relaxation and pain management and not try to heal the actual problem. This is not as restrictive as it may seem. Our bodies know how they ought to function and, if we help them with support and energy, they can go about the work of healing on their own. Unless you have expert knowledge of the problem, put your energy into visualizing the desired result–your friend standing straight and moving freely and without pain.
4. **Does the problem involve possible permanent or debilitating damage, especially to the brain?** When an illness or accident may have caused permanent damage, we are faced by a very difficult situation. The brain is still a somewhat mysterious organ, and even doctors are not always certain of a prognosis. In that case, ask whether life without full mental function is what the patient would wish. A number of years ago, a brilliant and charming friend of mine contracted meningitis. For several days, his life hung in the balance and the entire community concentrated its energy on saving him. He made a full recovery–physically. But he lost his long-term memory and his short-term memory was minimal. He looked the same, and oddly enough, his personality was unchanged. But his wife had to remind him every five minutes who everyone was. It was heartrending to watch. When, after a dozen years in the VA hospital, he finally died, everyone celebrated his release. When the situation is ambiguous, my decision has always been to direct the energy to the patient's higher self to be used for the best possible outcome.
5. **Is physical survival what you should be working for?** You face a similar decision when someone is nearing the end of a terminal illness. Fortunately, today's medical profession recognizes a

> patient's right to refuse "extraordinary measures" and die with dignity. For those whose illness may be terminal, gently encourage them to fill out a Durable Power of Attorney for Health Care with a friend or a Living Will and whatever other paperwork the hospital recommends, in which they can spell out their wishes in detail. When the time does come, pray for a peaceful and painless transition. Most faiths believe in some kind of afterlife, and, whether the patient is hoping for heaven, the Summerlands, Valhalla, or another incarnation, moving on to the next step is surely preferable to hanging on to a life supported by tubes and a consciousness deadened by drugs.

If you find yourself doing a lot of spiritual healing, study the oath attributed to the fourth-century B.C.E. Greek physician Hippocrates and adapt it to your own needs. The oath as translated on the PBS show *NOVA* goes as follows. The comments are my own:

> I swear by Apollo Physician and Asclepius and Hygieia and Panaceia and all the gods and goddesses, making them my witnesses, that I will fulfill according to my ability and judgment this oath and this covenant:
>
> (When you take this oath, call on whatever deity or deities you follow.)
>
> To hold him who has taught me this art as equal to my parents and to live my life in partnership with him, and if he is in need of money to give him a share of mine, and to regard his offspring as equal to my brothers in male lineage and to teach them this art–if they desire to learn it–without fee and covenant; to give a share of precepts and oral instruction and all the other learning to my sons and to the sons of him who has instructed me and to pupils who have signed the covenant and have taken an oath according to the medical law, but no one else.
>
> (This relates to the way in which medicine was taught in the Classical period. However, the idea that you should show gratitude and recognition to those from whom you have learned and pass on your knowledge to those who will follow you still applies today.)

I will apply dietetic measures for the benefit of the sick according to my ability and judgment; I will keep them from harm and injustice.

(This is the source of the common misquote: First, do no harm. Its implications are extremely important. You should always work from the best information available to you, and you should strive not only to keep your patients safe, but to protect their rights.)

I will neither give a deadly drug to anybody who asked for it, nor will I make a suggestion to this effect. Similarly I will not give to a woman an abortive remedy. In purity and holiness I will guard my life and my art.

(This is perhaps the part of the oath that is most open to dispute today. Abortion, for instance, is more or less accepted by the medical profession, and the right to assisted suicide is being debated. Neither practice is usually addressed by purely spiritual means, but those who also work with herbs, for instance, may eventually have to make some hard choices. The decision has to be made based on your understanding of life and death as taught by your religion, and the law of the land.)

I will not use the knife, not even on sufferers from stone, but will withdraw in favor of such men as are engaged in this work.

(As I stated earlier, we should work with the doctors whenever possible. This statement tells us to use the skills we understand, and leave surgery, prescriptions, and other kinds of help to the specialists.)

Whatever houses I may visit, I will come for the benefit of the sick, remaining free of all intentional injustice, of all mischief and in particular of sexual relations with both female and male persons, be they free or slaves.

(This passage addresses the ethics of working with both a patient and the family and community. Working with a patient mind-to-mind creates an intimacy that may lead to dependence or attraction. To take advantage of such a situation is unethical.)

> What I may see or hear in the course of the treatment or even outside of the treatment in regard to the life of men, which on no account one must spread abroad, I will keep to myself, holding such things shameful to be spoken about.
>
> (Trance work especially can put us in a position where we have access to information on personal and family problems that would ordinarily be none of our business. It is essential to keep all private matters absolutely confidential.)
>
> If I fulfill this oath and do not violate it, may it be granted to me to enjoy life and art, being honored with fame among all men for all time to come; if I transgress it and swear falsely, may the opposite of all this be my lot.
>
> If I keep this oath faithfully, may I enjoy my life and practice my art, respected by all men and in all times; but if I swerve from it or violate it, may the reverse be my lot.
>
> (What goes around, comes around. You don't have to believe in the Wiccan Law of Threefold Return to know that, if you are sloppy or venal or dishonest, you will not prosper for long. This is crucial if you are doing mind work, because, although you may be able to wash dirt off your hands, it is much harder to clean your soul.)

Journeying to the Land of Sleep

At some point, most people experience difficulty falling or staying asleep. These problems may be caused by something as simple as traveling to another time zone; they may result from stress or worry; or they may be the inadvertent result of bad sleep habits. If insomnia becomes chronic, consider using trance techniques to deal with it. Knowing how to do trance work can both help and hinder you in changing your sleep habits. On the one hand, you are already expert at relaxation and deep breathing; on the other hand, you have conditioned yourself to use these cues to move into altered states *without* falling asleep.

First, let's address the physical side of the problem. Obviously, you should avoid stimulants like caffeine in the evening, or even during the second half of the day. However tempting, an alcoholic nightcap is counterproductive. It may put you to sleep, but, when the alcohol wears off, you will find yourself awake once more. A drink of warm milk or an herbal tea like chamomile can be useful. Some gentle exercise or stretching exercises about a half hour before bedtime can reduce tension, and fatigue can become a cue to rest your mind as well as your body. So can a warm bath.

Getting into bed can also become a cue. It is best to use your bed only for sex and sleeping–no reading in bed or watching TV. If you want to read before going to sleep, do it in a chair, and avoid exciting fiction. If you watch late-night TV, avoid shows that increase your anxiety.

You already know how to change your brain waves from beta to alpha, the state in which we do most of our trance work. In order to cue sleep, continue from the alpha state to delta and theta, and then to a state of sleep. Sound is a good cue for this. Choose a CD or make an iPOD playlist of music that you only use to help you sleep–something slow, dreamy, without a definite rhythm. New Age music, temple bells, or recordings of waves or rain can all provide enough interest to occupy the surface of your mind, without providing stimulation that will keep you awake. There are also many sleep-induction CDs on the market that you might try.

I recommend establishing a bedtime routine–warm milk, brushing your teeth, a warm bath, nightclothes, and music can all be a part of this routine. Write out an affirmation of intent and, as you get into bed, say it aloud. Try something like:

> I will fall asleep easily.
> I will have all the rest I need.
> I will have all the sleep I need.
> I will have the dreams I need, and remember what I need to know.
> I will wake in the morning (or, "at 7 A.M." etc.), refreshed and ready to go.

If you are using a tape or CD, turn it on and the lights off. As you relax your muscles, let your mind relax as well. Allow the images and thoughts that come into your mind to float to the surface; then let them float away. If your mind persists in throwing up reminders of things to be done, keep a notebook beside your bed and write them down so that you can stop worrying. Free-associate without trying to focus on any one thing. Moving into a sleep state is different in this regard than passing into the altered states of consciousness in which you try to discipline and focus your awareness. Here, the purpose is to let your mind drift, to become a not-very-interested observer of the passing scene. If your mind persists in being busy, try a journey to the Land of Sleep, in which you seek out all the most soporific images you can imagine—the buzz of cicadas on a warm summer evening, the flicker of a fading fire, sleeping cats. . . .

If you find that time has passed and you are still awake, *do not worry about it!* If your clock has an illuminated dial, throw a towel over it. Remind yourself that you are still getting rest, even if you are not exactly asleep. The relaxation of your body will restore you, and the hypnagogic state is close enough to REM sleep that you will get most of the benefits of sleep, even if you do not achieve unconsciousness. If you absolutely cannot relax, get up, read something boring for a while, repeat your bedtime sequence, and try again.

Internal Exercise

We have all experienced how low blood sugar, fatigue, and illness can affect our mental state, but can your state of mind affect your body as well? You do not need to deny the existence or value of the flesh to explore ways you can use trance work to heal it. In fact, to do so honors the value of your physical body. Mind and body should be partners, working together for health and happiness. Both are important, and you must give them equal attention if they are to function well. However, in cases where one partner is in difficulty, the other can sometimes be of help.

We talked earlier about the need to evaluate "flight status" before beginning spiritual work. You know that your physical state can affect how you do spiritual work. But spiritual exercises can have an effect on your physical state as well. Traditionally, this has been best understood in disciplines like the martial arts, where mental exercises that calm and center the spirit are a necessary prelude to competition.

In the past few years, visualization has been used as a tool in everything from fighting cancer to sports training. Many studies have demonstrated that psychological skill training and visual-motor behavior rehearsal (VMBR) that includes relaxation, visualization or mental imagery, and performance of the skill in a simulated stressful environment can significantly improve performance in everything from basketball to karate (Lohr & Scoggin, 1998). The essence of the practice is to see yourself perfectly performing the skill you want to improve. The term "kinesthetize" may be more accurate in this context than "visualize," since it is not enough to visualize what should be happening. You have to recreate the physical sensations involved.

In one study, athletes were divided into three groups. The first practiced physically, the second practiced mentally, and the third engaged in both physical practice and mental imagery. The third group showed the most improvement; however the group that only used mental imagery did better than the athletes who only practiced on the court. Obviously, an inner understanding of how to make a basket must be supported by physical strength to be truly effective. It is also clear, however, that mental work can improve physical coordination and focus.

What else can it do? At a football game, the players are not the only ones who work up a sweat. While they do their work on the field, spectators sway and twitch, hearts racing as they sympathetically mirror every play. We experience the same effect as we watch a chase scene in a movie, or even as we read an exciting scene in a novel. Many of us have experienced dreams with marked physical sensations–falling, running, or flying. All of these involve passive participation. If we take an active role in these mental simulations, what more might we achieve?

Obviously, one use for "kinesthetization" is to improve your golf game. But it may have a use in controlling the effects of debilitating illness as well. A few months ago, a woman I shall call Elaine contacted me for help dealing with chronic and debilitating pain from several problems with her spine. She had been very athletic in college, but inactivity had lowered her metabolism, causing weight gain that increased the back pain. She tried isometric exercises she could do lying down; although they helped maintain some muscle tone, her metabolism still seemed to think she had gone into hibernation and continued to hoard every calorie. She had some experience in journey work, but she hadn't thought to apply this skill to inner exercise.

I suggested she try exercise 26. (One word of warning: If this works as intended, it will place some stress on your system and raise your heartbeat, so check with a doctor if this is likely to be a problem.)

Exercise 26. Journeying as Exercise

Begin by refreshing your memory regarding the kinesthetic aspects of your chosen activity–review the moves, remember the texture and weight of equipment such as balls or bats. Prepare yourself for journeying in your usual fashion–ground and center, relax and focus. Build up an image of the place from which you begin your journeys, paying special attention to the sensory details. When you have done so, move into the world within.

Ask your ally to lead you to a place where you can play your favorite sport, or build up an image of the field in your mind. Take the time to put on appropriate gear. See and feel yourself playing the game. Focus particularly on the sense of movement. An added bonus is the fact that you can make a perfect score when playing your inner game! Play until the game is complete (or you feel tired), and then take off the gear or change clothes as appropriate for the journey home.

Exercise 27 gives another, somewhat easier, alternative.

Exercise 27. Dancing Away Your Troubles

Put on your favorite dance music and party. Build up an image of a disco bar, or a Viennese ballroom, or any appropriate setting. Dress yourself appropriately (you can also design yourself a body to fit the occasion). If needed, find a partner and step out onto the floor. Let the music direct you and involve your senses. When one piece of music ends, wait for another to start, or leave the floor and go home.

Obviously, both these exercises will be easiest for people who have actually played sports or danced, and have the kinesthetic memories available for recall (although I have always wondered where the extraordinarily vivid physical sensations of flying I've experienced in dreams come from). If the prospect of football makes you blink and the thought of dancing makes you blush, put on a CD of nature sounds and try kinesthetizing a brisk walk along a beach or a run through the woods.

Who Were You When?

One interesting use of journeying skills is to explore other lifetimes. This does not actually require that you believe in reincarnation, by the way. I have never been sure whether my own experiences in this area are a glimpse into actual past lives of my own, the lives of other people whose experiences were relevant to me, or a message from my own unconscious. I just know I have found them both interesting and useful.

You can do this in a number of ways, all of which involve a set of images that cue you to move backward. Try the technique in exercise 28 to move backward through time.

Exercise 28. Journeying to Explore Other Lifetimes

Begin by settling yourself as you usually do for journeying; ground and center, relax and breathe. Articulate your intention, seeking information on a life that will help you understand a particular problem, or simply show you something you need to know.

Move from your base camp to a transitional device that will take you back in time. This can be an elevator in which the buttons indicate centuries, or a ladder, or a time machine with a dial. Ask the machine to take you where you need to be and watch the numbers change. When you come to a halt, let the door open and step out into the scene on the other side.

Orient yourself by looking down at the ground, and from there build up awareness of your surroundings. To learn more about yourself, look down at your feet, examine your hands, then your clothing, then your other physical characteristics. This may be enough to tell you who you are and what your life is like. Explore and experience, and then find your way back to the elevator or other device, press the "up" button, and return to the present.

When you do this exercise, be prepared to take your revelations as you find them. You were probably not a priestess in Atlantis in a past life; the memories you bring back may not be very exciting, or even very significant. One (female) friend's most vivid memory was of being a mercenary soldier in someone's army, and pissing against a tree. Another remembered being a bus driver. One of my journeys brought me images of cooking over an open fire sometime in the Paleolithic Age–interesting, but not life-changing. On the other hand, if you want to know why you are so attracted to Egyptian art, memories of serving in the Temple of Isis may provide an explanation. You can also journey with a friend in search of a lifetime you shared.

You can learn even more by asking how you died, but it is probably wisest to do this in a group or with a partner, as the experience can be traumatic. This kind of exploration can work well for a group as a guided meditation narrated by a leader who can bring back anyone who appears to be in distress and help people deal with the emotional impact of what they learn.

Reliving a death is not always as harrowing as you may expect, however. I experienced one lifetime in which my point of view was that of a scholar at Oxford during the Reformation. This particular scholar was unpopular because he focused on his studies and ignored other people's feelings. He was eventually burned for refusing to put the authority of the Church above the truth as he saw it. Fortunately, the experiential part of my experience ended before this gruesome scene played out. I still do not know if this was one of my own past lives, but it did help me recognize certain potential problems in my relationships in this life and motivated me to try to correct them.

Practice

Pain Management: Here are some simple techniques for managing pain.

1. Practice detaching your awareness from your body's sensations using a stimulus that is annoying rather than painful or destructive, such as holding an ice cube or something prickly in your hand.
2. Ground and center, and relax each limb. Relaxation is extremely important, since tense muscles will increase pain. Begin your rhythmic breathing, counting each breath, focusing all your attention on the numbers. Count 1-2-3-4, 2-2-3-4, etc. See how high you can count.
3. Let all physical sensations slide in and out of awareness and disappear.
4. Put on a CD or tape of drumming. Lie on a comfortable surface, ground, center, and relax, keeping your attention on the sound. "Ride" the beat.
5. Ground, center, relax, and start the breathing pattern you use to journey. Go to your base camp, call your ally, and ask him/her/it to take you to a place of healing. Explore it, memorize it, then return and write a description.

Trance dancing: Trance dancing has been around since the first hominid beat out a rhythm on a hollow tree. Most cultures have some form of dance in which the body becomes one with the rhythm and the mind wings free. You can do this alone at home by clearing some space and putting on the music you like best. In fact, if you are insecure about dancing, it is probably best to start alone. The music can be anything from tribal drumming, to sixties acid rock, to the latest technopop, as long as it has a good line and a perceptible beat.

> Do a few stretches to loosen up and then stand, close your eyes, ground, and center. When you feel balanced and relaxed, focus on the music. Identify the beat and begin to sway. The first time, that may be all you want to do. When you are ready to explore further, let the music suggest movement. Try steps, arm movements, loosen your spine and sway. Relax into the music and let it carry you away.

Once you are comfortable dancing on your own, see if any of your friends want to go with you to a rave. There is a whole scene out there with clubs that specialize in "trance" music, which incorporates elements of electronic New Wave/industrial music, electronic techno-disco, and music from the psychedelic age. Dance styles emphasize fluidity and keeping the beat. Beyond that, although there are some popular moves, there don't seem to be any rules. Raves may also feature performers with glow-sticks and some pretty spectacular dancing, but the scene is generally very accepting of newcomers. Most people are too wrapped up in their own experience to care what you are doing, and the energy raised by a whole roomful of people trancing can produce a powerful contact high.

Past-life problem solving: Identify a personality problem that does not seem to have its origin in this life, and journey to seek another lifetime whose events can throw light on the problem. You can do this alone or with a friend in interactive trance. When you reach your goal, focus on as much sensory detail as you can. When you feel you have learned something, return and write down as much as you can remember.

Chapter Eleven

Your Place or Mine? Getting Closer to the Gods

Thanne longen folk to goon on pilgrimages
And palmeres for to seken straunge strondes
To ferne halwes, kowthe in sondry londes . . .

Geoffrey Chaucer, Prologue, *Canterbury Tales*

Trance work can take you to a lot of different places, some of them very strange indeed. Ever since humans discovered that their spirits could travel while their bodies remained stationary, one of the most common reasons for journeying has been to get in touch with the divine. Another approach to contacting the divine is to bring Spirit, or a spirit, into your world by channeling or possession. Both ways can enrich your life, but, on the whole, seeking out the gods in their own realm is a little easier to control.

When a spirit uses the human "software" to communicate through a medium, the words can be understood by anyone, but the message may be limited or even distorted by the concepts and vocabulary of the person transmitting it. Dion Fortune once observed that

> . . . the communication brought through a medium depends to a large extent upon the capacity of the medium to act as a suitable channel. There are two aspects to this: one is the grade of the medium, which reflects the medium's own evolutionary development; and the other is the degree of education and general culture of a medium. If a medium is ill-educated and has few symbols available for the mind, then the inner-plane communicator can only work with what he has. . . . Someone has described the process of an inner-plane communicator trying to work through a poor medium as being analogous to Michelangelo trying to build his famous statue, David, out of tins of soup (1985).

When you journey to the Otherworld for information, on the other hand, the message comes through more clearly. The downside is the difficulty of bringing it back to ordinary consciousness. Articulating what you learn is what the exercises in this book have been teaching you to do. You can use the same journeying skills you used to find a power animal or spirit guide to make contact with an entity such as a goddess or a god. But what do you do when you find one? You may enter a state of consciousness in which you lose your human identity in contemplation of the divine. This is a transcendent and transformative experience, the goal of mysticism. For most people, however, spiritual contact is translated into images the human mind can understand.

A Question of Gods

Before we discuss how to contact the gods, let me explain what I mean by "gods." In contemporary usage, the term "God," complete with capitalized pronouns, refers to "the" Supreme Being—a non-corporeal, perfect, and omni-everything Entity Who is the Source of All. In practice, we assume this definition describes a deity worshipped by a monotheistic religion. In Western European cultures, "gods" without capital letters are usually defined as personified supernatural beings that may be associated with a natural force or area of life, or the images that represent them.

Of course, people can view the nature of Spirit and our relationship to it in many ways. Panentheism is a belief that deity is both immanent in Creation and transcendent. Pantheism identifies Creator with Creation, and holds that the universe is itself divine. Dualism divides Spirit into two, often opposing or polarized forces–Good and Evil, or Male and Female (also called *ditheism*). This belief begins to move us toward polytheism, the belief in multiple deities. Henotheism holds that all of these beings are aspects of the ultimate Divine Being, or that many gods exist, but an individual should worship only one. Monolatrists believe that gods have power only over those who believe in them. Kanentheism is a term coined by the philologist Max Müller to mean the worship of one god at a time. Finally, in suitheism we have the belief that not only do gods exist, but that we are divine as well. The ethical question is whether one says "I am God," or "I am god but so are you," which is implicit in the statement "Thou art God; Thou art Goddess," as a corollary of the immanence/transcendence paradox.

However, despite the efforts of monotheistic religions to define God as a being beyond human understanding, the human mind is programmed to interpret mental input in terms of its own experiences. In a language in which sentient beings are assumed to have gender, the use of a masculine or feminine pronoun ("Him" or "Her") inevitably personifies the divine. Thus, in medieval Christianity, the supernal God became an old man with a white beard, and his son, who really did start out with a human form, is portrayed as the Good Shepherd or presiding over the Last Judgment. For most people, the Holy Spirit, represented more abstractly by a dove or a flame, remains a relatively theoretical part of the Trinity.

In many religions, a multitude of saints (many of whom took on the attributes of the local gods they replaced) are called up to express other aspects of the divine. Islam has one god, but honors saints and prophets. Buddhism, which prefers to focus on the search for enlightenment rather than "silly speculations" regarding the existence and nature of its Source, nonetheless includes myriad divine beings—among them, in Tibet, the "converted" native gods.

I believe the existence of this ultimate source is a fact, but, like the sea, it is too vast for human comprehension. In *A Wizard of Earthsea*, Ursula LeGuin's mages learn that each part of the ocean has its own name, which they must know in order to work magic. This idea may be the theological equivalent of "Think globally, act locally."

If your primary spiritual focus (whatever your religion) is a singular supernal deity, you may want to move directly to chapter 12. On the other hand, if you are willing to accept that what you perceive is only a part of a totality, you can use the practices in this chapter to establish contact with Jesus as easily as with Apollo, or the Virgin Mary as well as Athena. For that matter, the descriptive terms used to honor the God of the Abrahamic religions, such as "Father" or "Lord of Hosts" can serve as by-names through which to establish a connection.

But what if the deity you would like to contact is in fact Apollo? What are the "lower-case" gods? In current usage, "theology" means the study of religion, with the assumption that the focus of faith is the monotheist's personified God. As the restored pagan traditions mature, however, works of (poly)theology are beginning to appear—most notably, John Michael Greer's groundbreaking (and extremely readable) book, *A World Full of Gods*. This new polytheology is not prescriptive, however. Paganism, unlike the "religions of the Book," assumes that, " . . . propositions about the existence of gods may best be assessed through experience and inference, in much the same way that thoughtful people assess any other proposition" (2005). In this chapter, we will use experience and inference to explore ways to get in touch with the gods and goddesses.

Do the Gods Create Us or Do We Create Them?

In the old days, it would never have occurred to anyone to ask this question. The gods simply *were*—as much a fact as earth or sky. Modern pagans, on the other hand, have to test and question. As with so many other things, in a religion that is generally tolerant of ambiguity, the answer is probably "yes." The question has no universally accepted, much less "orthodox," answer. My own feeling is that, while the shapes that the gods wear come originally from human minds, the power that fills them comes from beyond.

Sometimes those shapes were once worn by living women or men—heroes can become demigods; loa evolve from ancestors. But that is not the whole story. When people hold an image in their minds, they empower it, and it leaves an imprint on what occultists of an older generation called the "astral plane." In *Applied Magic*, Dion Fortune states that

> In religions where the gods or the saints are freely represented in pictorial form, the imaginations of the worshippers are accustomed to picturing them as they have seen them represented.... When a number of devout worshippers are gathered together, their emotions concentrated and exalted by ritual, and all holding the same image in imagination, the outpoured force of all present is formed into an astral simulacrum of the being thus intensely pictured.... When this process has been repeated regularly over considerable periods, the images that have been built up remain on the astral.... Consequently subsequent worshippers need be at no great pains to formulate the simulacrum; they have only to think of the god and they feel his power (1962).

This is the process that has transformed the Statue of Liberty from the personification of a virtue to a focus of enlightening energy. Whether we call it the collective unconscious, the psychic equivalent of a morphogenetic field, or the astral plane, there does seem to be some connection between human minds, some critical mass in consciousness that explains how fads and crazes sweep through a culture. The research behind the "Hundredth Monkey Effect," the idea that when a sufficient number of beings have learned something, the knowledge will expand to the entire community, has been questioned. Given the current ease of human communication, it is difficult to be certain that no contact has occurred between people who come up with the same idea in different places. Nonetheless, I do have anecdotal evidence for the appearance of certain parallel details—like the belief that the goddess Frigga's favorite colors are white and pale blue—in the meditations of individuals with no previous contact with the heathen community.

Whether beliefs are acquired through physical or psychic means, and whether they exist solely in the human mind or in a "place" that transcends it, there does seem to be a point at which the appearance, personality, and powers of gods acquire an existence independent of the person or people who first imagined them.

A survey of traditional polytheist cultures reveals a world that is indeed "full of gods"—emerging, evolving, or fading away. This also seems to be the experience of pagans today. Gods can begin as concepts—like the Roman Concordia—or as human beings—like the old Danish kings eventually subsumed into the figure of Freyr. In traditional African religion, the ultimate deity has no contact with humankind, and the affairs of the world are managed by the *orishas*, believed to have once been women and men. The voodoo ceremony of *Retirer d'en bas de l'Eau* (bringing a soul back from beneath the waters of Guinée) starts a soul on the path to becoming a *loa*. Those who give good value in return for offerings continue to receive them and ultimately join the pantheon.

In theory, there is nothing to prevent you from setting up an altar to Superman, or creating a god-figure of your own. In practice, however, the most productive relationships are those that draw upon the traditions of a religion. A "god" is therefore a persona, whatever its origin, to whom we may relate in order to connect with the world of the spirit. And the longer and more widely a deity is worshipped, the easier it is to make contact.

Divine Relationships

In practice, of course, none of these definitions really matter. Polytheism is experiential, not theoretical—based on encounters that we perceive as transcending our usual experience of the world. For these contacts to have meaning, however, they must be incorporated into our lives. They must become relationships modeled on the relationships we already understand.

Someone who grew up with affectionate parents may see a deity as a father or mother. Yet even those with dysfunctional families understand the concept of ideal parents, and may be even more likely to seek in a god or goddess the wise and loving father or mother they never had. In some traditions, this relationship is formalized, as when an adherent of Santeria is initiated as a "child" of one of the orishas. Relationships with the patron or matron deity sometimes found in Wicca may be of this type, or may be closer to that of the Roman patron and client.

The teacher/student relationship is a variation on this that can occur with other figures such as ancestors or animal allies. A god who needs a job done may recruit a student, or students who need information or skills for which they can find no human source may seek out a relevant deity. This kind of connection is less likely to be exclusive, and you may have several different teachers over time. Or it may eventually evolve into a different and closer kind of connection.

Another common relationship is that of a spouse or lover. The nun who becomes a Bride of Christ or the Voodooist who marries Erzulie are likewise formalizing the kind of relationship implied by the passionate, sometimes erotic, imagery through which mystics have tried to express their experience of the Divine. This, however, brings up another question. Most "theisms" contain some doctrine that describes the "spiritual marriage" as a form of spiritual obligation. Monogamy (perpetual or serial), polygamy, and polyamory all have their spiritual equivalents. Some people may develop close relationships with several deities; others, while honoring all, may pledge themselves to only one.

A common model in the heathen tradition is friendship. Much of the *Eyrbyggja Saga* follows the career of a Norwegian called Thorolf Mostur-Beard, who " . . . was a close friend of Thor, and had charge of Thor's temple there on the island" (Palsson and Edwards, 1989). When he runs afoul of the king, he holds a great feast and asks the advice of "his friend Thor" regarding whether to stay and fight or try his luck elsewhere. Thor tells him to go to Iceland. When he makes landfall, Thorolf casts overboard the pillars of the high seat from his old temple on which the figure of Thor is carved and settles where Thor sends the pillars to shore. In many of the other sagas, we find similar relationships. The deity with whom you have this kind of connection is called your *fulltrúi* in Norse tradition—your "fully-trusted one," not a bad definition for a best friend.

In the Middle Ages, Christian saints were known as the "friends of God." The Carmelite nun St. Theresa of Avila was a mystic whose deepest desire was to live a life focused on deep interior prayer. However, her devotion to her deity led to a long and vigorous career in which she wrote voluminously on mysticism, and reformed, founded, and governed a number of convents. Her approach to mysticism is noted for its practicality and emphasis on personal friendship with Christ. However, she is said to have observed that, if God treated all his friends the way he treated her, it was no wonder he had so few of them!

St. Theresa's comment notwithstanding, most Christian devotional practice encourages a relationship in which God, whether seen as an all-powerful Father or a Divine Lover, is immeasurably superior—the One, as C. S. Lewis points out in the introduction to *The Four Loves*, whose love is a gift and for whom our love must necessarily be based on need. Friendship between beings so different in power and nature is a logical impossibility.

In other traditions, too, the relationships may be more one-sided. In some Kemetic (Egyptian) traditions, you are not allowed to argue with your patron god. In Voodoo, devotees are known as *serviteurs*, because so much of their worship involves literally serving food or in other ways assisting loas who have possessed mediums. This enforces the sense that the role of humans is to serve the deities, to meet their needs and fulfill their desires so they will, in turn, grant their blessings.

The other important point about divine relationships, however, is that with the exception of monogamous marriage, we are generally not limited to just one. A parent, for instance, can love many children. Given the way modern families split and recombine, it is quite possible to have multiple parents and many siblings. If you are fortunate, you also have a multitude of friends, to whom you relate in different contexts and different ways. As with your relationships with other humans, however, not all of your relationships with deities will be the same. The number of deities you can effectively serve, work with, or worship (however the relationship is defined) will depend on your personality and your needs, and the resources available to you, including time, energy, and altar space.

Friendship and Devotion

Your animal ally is your helper and guide in Otherworld traveling, a companion to assist you on your way. You usually call or encounter it fairly early in a journey, and together negotiate where to go and how to get there. The goal of your journey, however, may be a meeting with a spirit or teacher in human form, or a goddess or god. Once this happens, a relationship can develop that may be similar to the one you have with your animal ally, but with the potential for a much deeper involvement. Let us consider, therefore, how to meet divine beings and how to build a friendship once you have met them.

Note that I say "friendship" rather than "devotion." Certainly there will be moments in which your awareness of the deity becomes an overwhelming sense of presence in which consciousness of your self and all other concerns are swept away. This is the divine union reported by mystics all over the world (see chapter 12). These experiences are memorable. They confirm your faith and nourish your soul. But they are not necessarily *useful.*

The discussion of divine relationships will sometimes use metaphors based on sex. Images of rapture and arousal are common in the poetry of the great mystics, and a mystical ecstasy may in fact produce a response that is physically, as well as metaphorically, erotic. For the same reason, the Tantric tradition and others use sexual arousal as means to attain mystical union.

In Hinduism, the ecstatic, romantic relationship that leads to the gods is called *bhakti*, the path of devotion. It is characterized by the same kind of emotional intensity we experience in the first stages of falling in love. Some people, in marriage and in religion, have the ability to sustain this intensity for extended periods of time, though they may suffer correspondingly if, for a time, the sense of connection disappears.

Nonetheless, although a transcendent sexual experience can illuminate your life, it is not necessarily the best basis for marriage. In your relationships with the gods, moments of rapture may come. As in married sex, they remind you why you fell in love with your partner and nourish your relationship, but your day-to-day productive living depends on developing communication and ways of working together for the good of the world and your own. Beyond the ecstasy of adoration, there is a great deal to be said for simply relating to your god or goddess as a partner or a friend.

This is, at least, a good place to begin. Indeed, if your relationship progresses from acquaintanceship to that of a *fulltrúi*, or an exclusive and passionate devotion to a single deity, it will certainly become something different. Although the claims of the gods may not be as all-encompassing as those ascribed to God, the Greek tragedies, among other pagan sources, state quite clearly that no man can fight them.

I believe that our perception of the Divine is like light seen through a stained-glass window. The specific wavelengths that pass through the pieces of colored glass enable us to comprehend something of the deity's nature. It is an interface that allows us to endure a contact that, in its pure form, would blind us. We work with deities as distinct and individual personalities, because that is the level at which it is easiest to communicate and get things done. There will be times, however, when the barrier thins and we may glimpse the glory of the light on the other side.

Recognize that not all gods are a good match for all people. If your attempts to connect consistently result in bad luck or miscommunication, don't pursue the relationship. The advantage of polytheism, of course, is that there is always another road to the Divine. And the same spiritual practices may not be appropriate for everyone. Just as some of the trance exercises in this book will work better for some than for others, we all need to find our own way to the gods. Some may find great satisfaction in building elaborate altars or creating images or regalia. Some may write songs and prayers; others may find fulfillment in doing the god's work in the world.

Indeed, working together, progressing side-by-side toward a shared goal, is the essence of friendship. Of course, craftwork and writing are also forms of labor that I have spent many happy hours pursuing. It may be, however, that the reason I am focusing on friendship in this chapter is that the deities with whom I connect seem to be very goal-oriented, and want my help to get their work done in the world.

Communication

Once you have established a good connection with a deity by journeying, you begin to bring back information and instructions. As the relationship develops, you may see the deity in your dreams, or receive intuitions or messages while awake. Hearing voices in your head is not necessarily a problem. What matters is what you do with the information you receive.

It is natural and healthy to ask where the information comes from. It may be from the deity, or it may be from your own unconscious—especially if you are being told to do something you really *want* to do. Or, depending on your relationship with your unconscious, you may be receiving suggestions that sap your self-confidence and leave you worse off than before.

Faith is not the same thing as credulity. When you enter the Temple of the Mysteries, you are not required to leave your brain at the door. Apply the same standards you would use for communications coming from outside to judge internally derived information. When a psychic communication is ambiguous or questionable, there are several possibilities to consider:

1. A spiritual being is sending a message and it is coming through clearly.

2. A spiritual being is sending a message, but the "signal" is being distorted by its passage through the mind of the person channeling it and/or the person hearing it.
3. Some part of the medium's psyche that resonates to a divine archetype is giving a message that is coming through clearly or distorted (see above).
4. A suppressed part of the medium's psyche is giving the message (see above).

In general, you cannot know for certain which of these is true—although, when people in different places come up with the same information independently, it does tend to suggest that you are either dealing with a real third-party source or the collective unconscious.

Does it really matter? You must apply the same standards to information coming from people in trance as you do to any other communication. The responsibility for deciding what to do with the information remains your own. Just because you think a deity wants you to do something does not mean you are required to cooperate, although, if the source is one whose advice is usually helpful, you should at least consider it. "Coyote made me do it—" is not an excuse.

Sometimes, the difficulty seems to result from a divergence of perspective. Deities have their own priorities, and do not always seem to understand the restrictions of modern life. Thus, you may have to explain to Oshun that, if she wants a solid-gold dresser set for her altar, she is going to have to come up with the gold. This is not as frivolous as it probably sounds. For a spirit to speak clearly to a human often seems to require a limitation of its powers. Deities that have not been honored since ancient times may need to be updated on the resources and constraints of the modern world. However, the more you work together, the more of your knowledge the deity will acquire—or perhaps it is the interface between you that expands. The real question is not where the advice or information comes from, but whether it is good, and likely to help you live a more productive life.

One student who has worked both as an oracle and with gods describes her experience thus:

> When I take the high seat (to serve as an oracle), the unexpected and often confusing nature of what I see and hear helps to confirm that it is a "real" experience and also when people afterwards explain what the messages meant to them–though of course I have no way of knowing if this is wishful thinking on either of our behalfs. However, when I have been in direct contact with a god/dess if the matter has been important, I have been left in no doubt of the validity of the context–somewhat akin to having a mountain screaming in your head! The above are rare moments and always important ones–I also have weaker more frequent contact, but again it is usually the unexpected nature of it that makes it real, whereas when I see things it's only later that I realize they weren't actually there. (Oh dear, that sounds bad. :) For example seeing my grandfather after he had died or the third cat that lives in my house without a corporeal body.)
>
> Essentially, I am saying there is an otherness in general about my experience with contact with the gods, which I recognize. However, as a psychotherapist I also am prepared to accept the concept of the Jungian overview–and as I also use hypnosis a fair amount, I know the depth and creativity of the subconscious mind. Which is what? I think it is about belief–as long as we don't succumb to the desires of wishful thinking.

I would certainly agree.

Israel Regardie recommended that anyone intending to do serious occult work go through a course of therapy first. When you do trance work, you stir up your unconscious mind, and problems you may have repressed can wake up and bite you. Be aware of the possibility and be prepared to consider, understand, and reintegrate (or in some cases heal) anything disturbing that surfaces. Some of the difficulties that are most likely to surface in a relationship with a god are control issues, fears, and problems relating to authority. Contact with deities may also activate dysfunctional patterns of relationship with parents or lovers.

This is one reason why keeping a journal and recording your dreams is useful. Psychic discomfort can be disturbing, but it is also an opportunity to grow and heal. Take this opportunity to do some thinking about any problems you have had in your life and look for patterns of response. Ask why you have chosen (or been chosen by) the deity with whom you are working. Are you seeking to recreate a good relationship, or looking for an alternative to a bad one?

Developing the Connection

When communication is well established, the deity may move closer, so that you have an ongoing sense of inner companionship. At times, this can become an inner dialogue (especially when you are shopping for altar decorations). Contemplation using an image or altar as a focus brings deities into a middle dimension between your world and theirs. Be aware that, as the connection deepens, it may come to dominate your life in the same way an intense human friendship or love can. The term "chronically god-bothered" comes to mind.

Relationships with gods and spirits, like relationships with other humans, vary. Sometimes, they become long-term commitments, as close and rewarding as a good marriage. You may eventually recognize this kind of relationship with a formal ceremony of dedication. Or you may work with a god or goddess for a limited period to address a particular problem or achieve a certain goal. Some relationships are intense for a time and then slowly fade. Others develop into the kind of friendship that can survive long periods without communication, then spring to life immediately when there is need. Take it slowly and let the connection develop naturally. A formal dedication, especially, should be approached with the same care and caution you would bring to marriage or adoption.

Some people dedicate themselves to deities with the same spontaneous abandon as a couple eloping to Las Vegas. If the relationship doesn't work out, they are later stuck with the messy process of getting a spiritual divorce. Some deities may release you cheerfully, but others are possessive and will not want to let you go. On the other hand, some people have had the disconcerting experience of being passed from one god to another. Be careful, therefore, about the oaths you take. Choose your gods carefully and negotiate the terms of your relationship. And if you make a promise to a deity, be sure to *keep your word!*

You must also consider how this connection will fit into your other relationships. Some people are naturally monogamous–just as they only have one human lover, they will only be able to work closely with one god. But if the relationship with the deity becomes overwhelming and ecstatic, the human spouse may become jealous, and with some reason. If you have both a spouse and a primary deity, consider carefully how to balance what you owe to each, and be sure to meet both sets of needs.

Some people are polyamorous–either in their human or divine relationships, or in both. They may work with several gods in sequence, or with different deities in different traditions or for different purposes. Needs must also be balanced here. Some gods are delighted to encounter deities from other traditions through the medium of a human mind; others are possessive and must be kept strictly separate.

As a relationship develops, your awareness of a deity may become intrusive. The gods seem to enjoy interacting with us; when the door is open, they will try to come through. Once you have turned on your spiritual cell phone, you'll never know when you are going to get a call. You may simply have a sense of companionship, or a deity may "speak" in your head, sometimes to a degree that is distracting. This can be exciting. It can also be exasperating, especially if the deity does not seem to recognize your other responsibilities and commitments. You may need to work on articulating your needs and capabilities, both to yourself and to your god.

As in any other relationship, you must set boundaries. Some deities are polite and gentle, but others may become very pushy indeed. "Not now, darling, people are watching–" is a reasonable response. Make clear to your inner companion that while you are at work, driving, operating heavy machinery, or talking to another human, is not an appropriate time for communication. Observe the same rules you would for talking on a cell phone and, if necessary, develop inner cues that will let you "hang up."

This does imply, however, that you are willing to receive calls at a more appropriate time. Trance work in general, and divine companionship in particular, are addictive. Once you become accustomed to spiritual contact, you may feel a build-up of pressure and an increasing need if you go without it for a time. If you want your deity to leave you alone while you are at work, be sure to make time for communication when you are at home. If a deity has trouble following these rules, you can threaten to close your head to him or her entirely. The more accustomed you become to using cues–like images or a song–to invoke the presence of a deity or spirit, the easier it will become to make contact at will, and the less likely it will be that these contacts will occur at inconvenient times.

Much of the advice on the care and feeding of allies goes for divine friendships as well. Create an altar to serve as a focus for contemplation. This can bring deities into a middle dimension between our world and theirs. Set aside certain times for work and worship. Fulfill any pledges you have made regarding obligations and offerings. And make the time to journey within to meet the gods on their own ground.

Practice

Establishing communication: Use the practice in exercise 29 to establish communication with a deity or spirit.

Exercise 29. Journeying to Meet a God

Relax, breathe, and prepare to journey in your usual manner. Make your way to your base camp and call on your ally. Explain that you want to meet a god or goddess who may become a temporary or long-term patron (this can be a deity to whom you already have an attraction), and ask it to lead you to a place where this deity may be found. If you already know with whom you want to work, ask for the deity by name. If you are, in addition, familiar with that deity's cultural context, ask your ally to take you to, for instance, the Celtic Otherworld.

From your knowledge of this culture, build up in your mind's eye a terrain through which to pass. Remember to look for or build in passage images to take you deeper within. If you are not familiar with the culture, go where your ally leads you. You may find that the images you encounter will seem appropriate only when you have done the follow-up research.

Presently, your ally will stop, or you will feel that you have reached a place of power. This may be a temple of some kind, or you may find it useful to build up in your mind the image of a temple (think of an astral "Sims" program). If a deity has not already appeared, look for or imagine a source of light—a shaft of sunlight or an altar flame. Imagine this brightness expanding to human height, and then acquiring human form. Gradually the brightness fades and you see the figure of the deity standing before you.

When the figure becomes solid, offer it a respectful greeting. Ask any questions you have. If you are working on a problem, ask for help and counsel dealing with it. When you have "spoken," open your awareness to receive an answer. It may come as words, as images, or as straight information—a certainty about what you are to do. You will have a sense when the communication is complete. Say thank you and visualize the deity becoming radiant light once more and then disappearing. Leave the temple and retrace your steps back to your base camp, and so back to mundane reality.

Honoring the God: To honor your god or goddess, create a prayer, chant, or song. A prayer can list by-names or epithets of the deity, or catalogue its deeds. It can employ a refrain that consists of simple repetition of the name. It can summon the deity, or simply praise it. For example, Thor can be invoked as follows:

Redbeard, firebeard, bringer of lightning,
Life-giving stormlord, lover of feasting,
Father of freedom, fighter most doughty,
Donor, defender, dearly we need thee,
Hear us, hero, hasten to help us,
Gifts thy great goats gallop to bring.

Use this formula to create your own prayer or chant:

Hail (best-known name), (descriptive epithet),
Child of (parent), lover of (spouse)
You who dwell in (name of hall),
You who (summarize several relevant deeds)
With your (characteristic tool or weapon)
Come swiftly to aid me
As I (summarize problem being addressed)

Rather than asking for help, you can simply end with praise:

Don ar, defender, hear how I praise thee
For the gifts that thy great goats have galloped to bring.

Songs can be simpler–a few descriptive or affirmative lines in free verse or simple poetry:

Brigid, bright one, beauty upwelling,
Bless me, embrace me, blaze now in my heart.

If you are not musically inclined, your song can be as simple as a one-note line that dips and rises at the end, like plainsong. You can also adapt tunes from traditional music of the culture to which the deity belongs. In fact, simply sitting and listening to this music is a good way to move into a mental space in which your deity will draw near.

Contemplation: One way to develop contact with your deity is through the contemplation of images. Find a safe space in your house and create an altar. Read everything you can find about the deity and his or her culture. Journey to meet with your deity as many times as necessary to find out how the altar should be made and decorated. What color does the deity like? What are his or her favorite plants or animals, food and drink? What tools and weapons should be there? What kind of incense and candles? You can find a lot of this information in the literature on the relevant tradition, but sometimes the deities have other ideas.

Start with an altar cloth in the appropriate color and go on from there, adding miniatures of appropriate items, a vessel for offerings, etc. Combine the results of your research and your journeying. Find a picture or statuette of the deity, or draw one yourself in the guise in which it has appeared to you. Set it in the place of honor and keep it covered with a cloth when not in use.

As your altar evolves (for it will never be completely finished, and its contents will change as you and your relationship with the deity change), make time simply to sit and gaze at it. If ideas for improvement come to you, note them down, then return to your contemplation. Look at each item and meditate on its meaning. Gaze at the image until your vision blurs and you see it grow and take on the radiance of life before you. Murmur your praise chant until awareness of the deity is all you know. Some deities, of course, are much more at home in wild places than in a house, no matter how lovely the altar may be. If possible and appropriate, spend some time meditating on your deity in a natural setting like the woods or seashore.

Chapter Twelve

Going Nowhere, Being Everywhere

> Their one passion appears to be the prosecution of a certain spiritual and intangible quest: the finding of a "way out" or a "way back" to some desirable state in which alone they can satisfy their craving for absolute truth. . . . Hence, they should claim from us the same attention we give to explorers of other countries in which we are not competent to adventure ourselves, for the mystics are the pioneers of the spiritual world. . . .
>
> Evelyn Underhill

We have spent a great deal of time considering how to go "somewhere"—journeying, traveling, trance-porting ourselves from ordinary reality into the Otherworld. There is another type of trance work, however, whose goal is to go nowhere and become nothing. As a spiritual practice, this type of meditation builds on the grounding, centering, and focusing you learned earlier to bring renewal and peace. If practiced faithfully, it can also lead to a state of consciousness called the "core," "zero," or "unitary" experience. In this state, you are unaware of anything, and yet are everywhere and everything. This is the state of ecstatic mystical union with the Absolute that some say is the goal of all the practices we have explored so far.

Those who have had this experience and who seek to replicate it are called mystics. Mysticism is found in all religions, whether as a primary goal or a nervously tolerated occasional phenomenon. It is not, however, limited to or dependent on religious practice. Those who have taken drugs, especially in a sacred setting, may also find them a doorway to these experiences.

Why should we seek these experiences? According to a recent article in *Scientific American Mind*, there is evidence that meditation can improve your ability to focus on tasks, stimulate your brain to offset the effects of aging, improve your immune system, counter depression, and promote a positive outlook on life (Biello, 2007). A study conducted by McCready and Greeley in the 1970s found that as much as 10 percent of the population has been touched by the Divine–usually forceful and active people who become even more effective as a result (Greeley, 1987). Living with someone whose life has been so transformed, however, can be hard. Not every husband or wife is willing to share a spouse with (a) God. For many, divine union is a spontaneous occurrence, remembered for a lifetime. It transcends all differences of faith or creed. For those who have encountered the intangible and unprovable Uncreated Light, the experience becomes a yardstick against which all other perceptions of reality must be measured.

How can the techniques for entering and managing the altered states of consciousness we've discussed here help you achieve a state that is, by definition, so totally open and vulnerable that, in it, even awareness of your self may be lost? The contradictions seem impossible to reconcile, and yet teachers from Buddha to Ignatius Loyola have taught disciplines intended to help people attain that goal. Indeed, there has been far more written about the search for union with the Divine than about the less overwhelming (but sometimes more useful) methods used to journey. It would be presumptuous to promise that in one chapter I can do more than point to the beginning of the mystic quest, but we can look at some useful practices, and I will refer to some of the more helpful texts for those who want to continue this study on their own.

The Mystic Way

The road the mystic follows is perhaps the most difficult spiritual quest, and it offers, perhaps, the greatest rewards. The mystic soul surrenders all in order to gain all. But that surrender can require a heroic level of discipline. Some achieve *Samadhi* only after many years of austerity. Others encounter the Absolute quite unexpectedly, and begin spiritual practices to find their way back again.

William James noted four identifying characteristics of a mystical experience: ineffability, noetic quality, transience, and passivity.

Ineffability: What happens while you are in this state is so far beyond ordinary experience that it cannot be communicated in words. This does not stop the mystics from trying to convey what it was like through metaphor and image, but they are always frustrated by the inadequacies of human language.

Noetic quality: "Noetic" refers to *gnosis*, or knowledge, especially that derived from inner sources. The consciousness of the mystic is illuminated. Mystics perceive the truth that underlies all appearances, a revelation of ultimate meaning, and remember having had these insights after returning to ordinary reality. They may not, however, recall exactly what they were.

Transience: This is, of course, the problem. These sublime states rarely last more than a half hour. For some, the experience may come only once, and yet be sufficient to inspire an entire lifetime. Others experience it at unexpected intervals. Some of the great Christian saints and Hindu mystics have apparently existed entirely in this state, except when they were required to "come down" to attend to worldly affairs.

Passivity: Although austerities, contemplation, chanting, and other practices can help us to get our egos out of the way and

> encourage ecstatic experiences, when they happen, we have no control over them. Imagery of fire and flood, sexual union, or any other metaphor of being overwhelmed and carried away, is common in the literature of mystical experience. In this sense, these states are the opposite of the tightly controlled states achieved through ceremonial magic. Although magical practices may bring us to the edge of mystical revelation, they cannot help us once we jump in.

To the list given by James, I would add ecstasy or euphoria. Ecstasy often, although not always, accompanies the experience of union as reported in the literature. For many mystics, the only appropriate metaphors are those drawn from sexual love. It is clear that, although these experiences are of transcendence, they can activate the brain's pleasure receptors to produce the ultimate high. Just as the pleasure of sexual orgasm may be an evolutionary device to encourage people to procreate, the "rush" produced by a Close Encounter with the Divine and other, less overwhelming, spiritual experiences argues for the existence of something beyond ourselves with which we are programmed biologically to seek connection.

The road to regular enjoyment of these rewards is neither straight nor easy. Evelyn Underhill describes the stages of the journey in the Christian tradition:

> First comes the *awakening*, the first ecstatic experience of the Divine. Seen by this illumination, all the imperfections of the Soul and the vanities of her previous life become apparent, and the budding mystic turns to the second stage of *purgation*, in which she strives through discipline and if necessary self-mortification to get rid of whatever elements in her life stand between her and the Divine Perfection. If she is successful, she achieves a state of *illumination*, in which she is often aware of the Divine Presence and lives in its Light. This is a state in which many of the great mystical writings are produced. However this happiness may be interrupted or followed by the *Dark Night of the Soul*, times in which the apparent absence of Deity leaves the

> Soul all the more desolate by comparison with what went before. If the Soul can work through this to a point at which ego is conquered and it neither asks nor desires anything at all, it may be followed by *union*, a state of identity with the Ultimate in which the connection and perspective are felt most of the time (1961).

The Eastern mystical tradition describes an additional state in which the individuality and self-awareness of the soul is annihilated and absorbed into the All. Western mystics tend more toward seeking the perfecting of the soul within the Divine. Rather than retiring from the world, they are more likely to engage with it in an even more effective way because they are aware of how unimportant most of the things that get in the way of true fulfillment really are.

The Gods and God

In the literature of mysticism, the object of adoration is defined as the Supreme Being of the tradition to which the mystic belongs. The Hindu seeks union with Brahma, the Sufi with Allah, Christians with Christ. However, the more personified your deity, the harder it may be to go beyond personality. As Agehananda Bharati puts it, " . . . so long as the gods and goddesses of your cherished pantheon face you, meet you, make love to you, talk to you, give you advice, you have consummated your mythology, but you have not become a mystic unless you become these gods" (Bharati, 1982).

Here, Bharati does not refer to the state of god-possession in which the personality of a deity overshadows or replaces that of the medium in order to act in the physical world. Such a sharing of consciousness can be ecstatic and illuminating for both the medium and the others taking part in the ceremony, but only a small portion of the deity's essence can be poured into a human vessel at one time. It is, by definition, a limitation of the deity's power. In the union with a divinity sought by mystics, on the other hand, the human partner becomes part of the expanded consciousness of the deity. And even then, that consciousness is limited by the deity's perspective until there comes a time when the god stands aside, pointing toward the Greater Light of which he, too, is only one vibration.

So what is this "Divine" that we are talking about when we try to discuss mysticism? Lorrie Wood has made a good attempt at conveying the distinction between gods and God in comprehensible terms:

> A polytheist god is *roughly* the same weight class as an orixa—with a lot of leeway for, say, a smallish orixa compared to largish alf and so on.
>
> Putting things in neat boxes is more Roman than heathen. This really annoys me, because frankly, I wish more things came in pigeonholes.
>
> But where was I? Ah.
>
> Contrariwise, the God that is referred to as *Olodumare* (et al) is closer to how a pantheist may talk about God: the Universe, sentient, incarnate. In Kabbalah they talk about Ain Sof, and me, I talk about the Force, but as soon as you name it, you've lost it. The Big All-That is only perceivable in the most abstruse of glimpses, in states so far removed from consensual reality and consciousness that the best you can do is wave at it and say words that only make sense to someone else who has *also* seen the elephant, the Grail, Nirvana, what-have-you.
>
> This can be extremely disheartening.

Terms like "Ground of Being" and "Ultimate Source" attempt to convey the scale of the contact experienced, but cannot account for the emotion that comes with it. When you are dealing with something that transcends the comprehension of your human senses, you may do best to resort to paradox—a realization that the Supernal Light is also the Divine Darkness, everything you have ever imagined and nothing you can comprehend. Or perhaps you should begin with pronouns, since, for all their transcendence, these experiences are intensely personal, and say, "This also is Thou, neither is this, Thou. . . ."[4]

---

4. Charles Williams, possibly derived from a line in the Upanishads. Note 9 in *Outlines of Romantic Theology* (Berkeley, CA: Apocrophile Press, 2005), p. 53.

You can get some idea of the depth of the experience by reading the accounts of those who have had it, just as reading the journal of a traveler in an exotic land can almost make you feel you have been there. In the same way, the writings of mystics like Rúmi or Richard Rolle can stimulate some of the feelings they experienced in their raptures. In fact, such an experience may literally be "stimulated" by these readings. Neurological research into mysticism indicates that *remembering* an ecstatic spiritual experience can stimulate the same areas of the brain (although to a lesser degree) as repeating it (Kornfield, 2000). You will find quotes from many of these writers in Evelyn Underhill's book on mysticism. Use her book as a guide to explore them in more detail. Just as a travelogue can fill you with longing to return to a place where you have never been (at least in this life), these reports by travelers in the inner worlds can activate a longing for a spiritual homeland that lies beyond the circles of the world.

After the Ecstasy, What?

Now let us look at the downside of enlightenment. For, despite the hype, the life of a mystic is not necessarily all hearts and flowers. In his excellent book, *After the Ecstasy, the Laundry*, Buddhist teacher Jack Kornfield focuses on the difficulties of maintaining an intense spiritual practice while living in the world. It is not by chance that most of the great mystical literature has been produced by people living within a monastic support system that takes care of things like cooking dinner and paying bills.

Nor does enlightenment itself result in holiness. Kornfield quotes Suzuki Roshi as saying, " . . . there are no enlightened people, there is only enlightened activity" (Kornfield, 2007). Depending on your beliefs and opportunities, the personal and permanent conviction of the reality of the divine that comes from a mystical experience can impel you to sell all you have and devote yourself to serving the poor, or to join a convent, or to go singing and dancing through the world, or to continue to carry wood and draw water. The moment of ecstasy fuels the engine, but you are still the driver. It is up to you to choose where that energy will take you.

Mystical experiences may make it very difficult for you to live in the world, especially if you are unfamiliar with them. Like the lover obsessed with the beloved, the soul struck with love for the divine may become very frustrated by anyone or anything that distracts it from the quest for union. Family and friends who are accustomed to dealing with your flaws may be upset or even resistant if you suddenly take the path of virtue. In his novel *Patience of a Saint*, Andrew Greeley portrays the trials of a hard-drinking Chicago newspaperman who suddenly is hit by the Divine Clue-by-Four. As his life becomes more complicated and his immediate friends and family have difficulty dealing with his conversion, he complains: "Now I have nothing–no job, no wife, no mistress, no family, no friends, my parish priest sends me to a psychiatrist who wants to lock me up. . . . And it's all the Lord God's fault" (1987). This is being god-bothered with a vengeance. When your perspective has been so overwhelmingly altered, you have to find a new way to live in the world.

Doing and Being

There are two ways to seek the divine. One, of course, is to do nothing and simply hope that God, or Brahma, or the Great Pumpkin, or whatever, will one day decide to give you a call. It could happen. On the other hand, there are millions of people for whom it does not. The other is to practice the kind of meditation that makes it a bit more likely.

Being, myself, of an active temperament where spirituality is concerned, I advise you to try the exercises given below. They may not turn you into a mystic, but they will almost certainly alter your consciousness. You have already taken the first steps on this path, but the purpose of earlier chapters was to prepare you for other kinds of journeying. Now, as you revisit skills like contemplation, you will address them as ends in themselves.

The path may be a long one, and you may find yourself wondering whether it leads anywhere. Are the self-proclaimed mystics deluding themselves and the rest of us? When you engage in meditation without apparent result, are you wasting your time? There is, of course, no way to prove what causes the mystic's raptures, but neuroscience can now demonstrate that, when people engage in meditation, *something* is going on in the brain. In recent years, a number of scientists have tried to identify a "God spot"—a location in the brain that is activated during religious experiences. Various studies have targeted the temporal lobe and the limbic system. Meditation by both Buddhist monks and Catholic nuns slows down activity in the parietal lobe and increases it in the prefrontal cortex, reflecting a transfer of focus from the outside world to inner experience. Other areas stimulated by mystical experience include the caudate nucleus (associated with feelings of love) and the insula (involved with body sensations and social emotions, which may explain the ecstatic sensations). Speaking in tongues, on the other hand, seems to decrease activity in the frontal lobes. So far, it appears that, rather than being localized in one area of the brain, spiritual states involve an extensive neural network (Biello, 2007).

It is important to remember that having an experience of the holy does not make you holy yourself. These encounters may motivate you to act in ways that your religion teaches are likely to encourage a repetition, but, as the Buddhist saying makes clear, after Enlightenment, you still have to carry wood and draw water. Spiritual gifts can even be a distraction. The evidence for holiness is found in the way you act on the world, not the way in which the Divine acts upon you. The fact that, for many years, Mother Teresa labored to express God's love to the sick and dying of Calcutta while remaining unable to feel that love herself is, to my mind, further evidence of her sanctity.

Opening Your Head

William James describes deep meditation as a practice in which "We pass into mystical states from out of ordinary consciousness as from a less into a more, as from a smallness into a vastness, and at the same time as from an unrest to a rest" (James, 1958). To do this, you must get your ego and all the stress and clutter that occupy your waking mind out of the way. You now know that grounding, centering, relaxing, and releasing can free your mind to focus elsewhere. Before you begin to address the exercises in this chapter, review those skills. Whether you are driving across country or only to the corner grocery store, you start the car in the same way. When you turn the corner, however, you may be moving in a direction you have not gone before.

When you meditate to open your mind to a completely passive trance, the objects on which you focus are there only to distract your surface mind until it too can let go. The two most common methods are contemplation and chanting. Statues, religious art, mandalas, yantras, or abstract designs are traditional objects of contemplation. They have the advantage of being transportable and silent. A natural object like an interesting rock or a shell can also serve as a focus through which, like William Blake, we can

> . . . see a World in a Grain of Sand
> And a Heaven in a Wild Flower,
> Hold Infinity in the palm of your hand
> And Eternity in an hour. ("Auguries of Innocence," ll. 1-4).

A more diffuse awareness comes when you seek a natural setting like a garden, or a forest, or the banyan tree under which Buddha sat until he achieved Enlightenment. Many mystics report that their doorway to the core experience was contemplation of the beauty of the natural world. Scenes and symbols can both stimulate associations and carry meaning, however, contemplation of which can keep you connected to the outer world.

A practice common in Eastern traditions is the chanting of mantras. Mantras have meanings that can be contemplated, but, as you repeat them, your focus shifts to the articulation of the syllables themselves, resulting in self-hypnosis. *Tat svam asi!*, "Thou art That," is a mantram of the elephant-headed Hindu deity Ganapati (Ganesha) that expresses the fundamental identity of micro- and macrocosm. Daniélou gives its meaning as:

> Thou [the living being] art the visible form of That [the supreme essence]" (*Ganapati Upanisad 2*). Human existence is the coor-

> dination of the absolute and the relative, of That and Thou. True knowledge is the realization of this unity. The image of Ganapati constantly reminds us of the reality of this apparently impossible identity. Man is truly the image of the cosmos. All realization lies within himself. Through the study of our inner impulses and of our inner stucture we can understand the nature of the universe (Daniélou, 1985).

The paradox of this identity makes it particularly useful as a focus, and the phrase flows more smoothly when repeated than the related phrase, "This is also Thou, neither is this Thou." Daniélou's *Gods of India* includes a selection of mantras for various concepts and deities that you can try. Many traditions employ a rosary to help stay focused on the task. The act of moving a bead with each repetition keeps you from losing track.

You can also use the simple chanting of a name as a mantram. Even your own name will do, because the repetition strips the syllables of meaning and, therefore, of identity. Chanting a god-name can take you *to* the god, and then *through* the god to the reality behind all images.

Wordless sound can provide an even more abstract focus. Appropriate pieces ranging from recordings of Tibetan temple bells to New Age compositions are widely available. Set your CD player or iPod on repeat and let the vibrations pulse through you.

Choose one of the practices given below that attracts you, or try them all in turn, working for at least a week on each one. You will get better results if you view them as ends in themselves, rather than as means to an end. In fact, that is what they should be. This kind of meditation has been demonstrated to produce a number of useful effects, from lowering stress to improving focus. Meditating only to hit the jackpot of a "peak" experience will lead to frustration and make it almost impossible to reach your goal. When you seek the Holy Grail, to journey is as important as to arrive.

Practice

1. **Preparation**: Review the methods for grounding, centering, relaxing, and focusing that you learned in chapters 2 and 3. If you have gotten careless, practice until you can move into a state of readiness swiftly and dependably before beginning the other exercises.
2. **Contemplation of images**: Copy or draw a simple design—a spiral, a maze, an infinity sign, a Celtic knot, or a symbol of your choice. Make sure the lines are distinct and dark. Place it against a wall where you can see it while sitting in your favorite position for trance work. Set a lit tea-light below it and turn out the lights in the room. Make sure you will not be disturbed and ward the room. Then sit down and ground, center, and relax. Articulate your intention—something like opening your awareness to Divine Wisdom—and the amount of time you want to spend in meditation. Then release all sense of purpose and simply gaze at the image, following its lines in and out and around, recalling your awareness when it wanders, until you and the image are one.
3. **Chanting**: Choose a name, mantra, or phrase to chant. If you find it helpful, create a longer prayer as a lead-in to your chosen phrase. For example, in Kabbalah, the god-name associated with Kether, the highest of the *sephiroth* on the Tree, is E-HE-IEH, "I am that I am." A prayer for that god-name might be:

   Holy, holy, holy, Maker of All
   Heaven and Earth are full of Thy Glory,
   Glory be to Thee
   Oh Thou who Art . . .

   Sing or chant this for a while, then shift to the god-name itself.
4. **Intoning**: You can do something similar by *galdoring* (intoning) a bindrune. Try linking the runes ᚹ *Wunjo*, (Joy) and ᛃ *Jera* (harvest, and therefore fulfillment) to ᛁ *Isa* (Ice, stasis) for a serene state, or to ᛊ *Sowilo* (sun, victory) to achieve a spiritual breakthrough. Begin by chanting the runes one after another—

"Wun-Yo-Yare-Ah-Ee-Sah"—while visualizing them. Gradually run the syllables together until you have something like "Wun-Yare—Ee—Sah . . . " Chant this while visualizing white peace. Or chant "Wun-Yo-Yare-Ah-So-Wee-Low" until you get "Wun-Yare—Ah-Sol. . . ." Intone these syllables while imagining a sudden blaze of radiance.

Chapter Thirteen
Road Hazards

Only he that has traveled the road knows where the holes are deep.

Chinese Proverb

Not all journeys, including those we make in trance, go smoothly. Bilbo's advice applies to the world of the psyche as well as to the world of the imagination: When you leave the Shire, the road may take you to Rivendell, but it also can lead to Mordor. Stanislav and Christina Grof have observed that, although a psycho-spiritual crisis can be triggered by a variety of physical, social, and psychological events:

> ... one of the most important catalysts of spiritual emergency seems to be deep involvement in various forms of meditation and spiritual practice. These methods have been specifically designed to activate spiritual experiences. We have been repeatedly contacted by persons whose unusual experiences occurred during the pursuit of Zen, Vipassana Buddhist meditation, Kundalini yoga, Sufi exercises, or Christian prayer and monastic

> contemplation. As various Oriental and Western spiritual disciplines are rapidly gaining in popularity, more and more people seem to be having transpersonal crises–yet another reason that the correct understanding and treatment of spiritual emergencies is an issue of ever-increasing importance (1989).

To mix journeying metaphors, sometimes the trouble is no more than a frustrating squeak somewhere in the chassis of your car and you can proceed with caution. But sometimes the car breaks down and you need road service to get home again.

Although I hope the disciplined approach presented here will help you to avoid these problems, know that they can occur. Be aware of the kinds of psycho-spiritual problems that sometimes arise, as well as the kinds of help it is reasonable to expect from friends, spiritual teachers, and professional therapists. Whether you are on a physical or a spiritual journey, my basic advice is the same:

If you sense a problem, slow down: If necessary, pull over, stop, and try to figure out what's wrong. If an exercise or practice is upsetting, do it less often or stop until you understand where the problem lies. One of the most common ways to aggravate a problem is to allow the urgency of your quest to push you away from supportive help into solitary misery.

If you lose your way, retrace your steps: Find out where you went wrong. Don't be ashamed to ask for directions. If more advanced exercises don't seem to work for you, go back to the beginning and start again, more slowly. Compare notes and find out if others have had the same problem or can advise you from their own experience.

If you break down, call for help: Or at least call a friend. It is very hard to gain perspective on a situation when you are struggling to survive it. First, you must admit that there is a problem, and that you have to take the first step toward dealing with it. Even experienced spirit workers sometimes have to turn to each other for the same help any one of them would give someone they themselves were working with. When the problem is severe, to seek a trained professional is sense, not surrender.

The Issue Tour

For most people, most of the time, consciousness is a surface affair. We float on top of a lake, or live on the first floor of a house, without ever worrying about what may be in the depths below. Dreams may reveal some of it, but, unless they keep you from sleep, they are easy to forget once you get involved in the business of the day. When you open the door to your unconscious, however, and release feelings or memories you have suppressed, your spiritual journey can turn into a "first-class tour of your issues." To return to our metaphor, you may find that your car has no brakes, or that your last turn landed you in a very strange part of town and the street signs have all disappeared.

I have a friend whose mother died when she was sixteen, forcing her to become an instant adult. She coped by suppressing her own personality and replacing it with a persona she eventually identified with the goddess Frigga. When she began to practice in the Norse tradition, she was happy at first to define herself as Frigga's priestess. As she did more trance work, however, other elements began to emerge. She realized she did not know herself at all. Once having come to that knowledge, she could no longer stay safely behind the mask. So she began an intensive program of meditation with several different goddess figures, accompanied by work with a therapist.

Once you experience this kind of breakthrough, it is almost impossible to go back again. To try is likely to leave you in an uncomfortable state halfway between where you started and where you need to go. The only way out is through. When you reach the end of the journey, you will be a different person. This can be hard on your relationships.

As of this writing, my friend's work continues. On some days, she struggles at the edge of despair; on others, her meditations with the goddesses produce insights of stunning clarity. She takes two steps forward, one step back—or sometimes even two steps forward, three steps back. But little by little, she is beginning to understand. Sharing her experiences with others in her spiritual community via an online journal has been a valuable outlet for her; their support is helping her to keep on.

Spiritual Emergence or Spiritual Emergency?

Many of the best-known problems of spiritual practice are classified under the heading of "spiritual emergencies." These can occur as part of a process of spiritual emergence, or develop spontaneously–in which case, magical or spiritual practices may be adopted as a way of integrating and controlling them. When this transformation goes well, it results in an expansion of awareness that brings improved emotional and physical health, a greater freedom in making choices, and a deeper connection with the human and natural world. This awareness is usually identified as spiritual.

But the road to that desirable state can be a rocky one indeed.

Sometimes an emergency can come up suddenly, especially at festivals or conferences where people are spending several days in a very intense, unfamiliar environment, often without sufficient food or sleep. I was once on the assistance team for a young man who when he was not opening his heart to one of our clergy had been singing a song he was composing in honor of a deity, over and over again. At the end of the festival he suddenly erupted into a state of intense dissociation during which he had to be physically restrained while a group of us worked through most of the methods of psychic first-aid listed in this chapter. Fortunately, we were able to restore him to a state in which he could safely drive home, and recommended for him to work with local clergy thereafter.

The process of emergence is often gradual. In the beginning of *Ifa Quest*, Awo Fá'lokun Fatunmbi tells the story of his own spiritual awakening. He started his quest for transformation while in college. Repeated meditation walks on the beach led to a moment of intense awareness of connection with the world around him. Later, an encounter with a palm-reader opened him up to an out-of-body experience and a number of paranormal manifestations. Still seeking understanding, he eventually participated in a Native American ceremony that resulted in a series of visions, a release of Kundalini energy, and a period of successive possessions by other personalities that lasted for twelve hours. He appeared to sleep this off, but the next day was possessed once more by the African *orishas* Shango and Ogun, who would not let him go until they had a chance to talk to the Lucumi elder who was brought in to help. Because the possession occurred outside of a traditional ceremony, the Lucumi priest was unable to do any follow-up work. It took Fatunmbi several more years before he was able to make contact with an African tradition in which he could integrate all his experiences and learn to use the abilities they brought with them.

Most people do not end up initiates of Ifá, but this kind of episode can lead to a new and spiritually productive way of life. First, however, you have to survive the emergency.

An emergency can be a crisis point within the transformative continuum. Symptoms like involuntary trance, intense emotional response, visions, and other sensory experiences can become emergencies when the transformation is so sudden and traumatic that it overwhelms you and interferes with your ability to function. Are you opening up, or are you going crazy?

When spiritual experiences start destroying your life instead of enabling you to live it more fully, you may need help from a sympathetic professional. Choose carefully. Look for someone who has experience in this area, who will not automatically assume that you are delusional just because you hear voices or see visions.

Musicophilia, by Oliver Sacks, gives a good description of the difference between schizophrenic "voices" and musical auditory hallucinations. His other work is also valuable for understanding organic disturbances of perception and function. Another useful work for understanding how a psychotic break can turn into a blessing is Laing's *The Politics of Experience and the Bird of Paradise*, which describes the trauma induced by the deliberate stresses of conventional medical education. You can find other portrayals in Lessing's *Briefing for a Descent into Hell* and Charles Williams's *Descent into Hell.* However, these works may be more useful if you are trying to help someone in the throes of spiritual emergency than if you are going through one yourself. Be sure to resist the temptation to grasp onto anything that feels similar to what you are going through and convert it into an absolute answer.

The classic work on this subject is *Spiritual Emergency*, by Stanislav and Christina Grof. The *Spiritual Emergence Network* (SEN) at *www.spiritualemergence.info* exists to help people who are experiencing difficulties with psycho-spiritual growth. There you will find a database of trained therapists and graduate students who can help. (They can also be reached at 415-453-1106.) The Association for Transpersonal Psychology is sympathetic and supportive, and its members are prepared to view these experiences as opportunities for growth. You can also find help at the *Shared Transformation* Web site (*users.aol.com/ckress/st.html*).

The list of experiences that may result in a spiritual emergency include:

Dark Night of the Soul: An intense depression that may focus on a feeling that the self is dissolving, or that you are being suffocated, or are dying. The classic experience is an intense feeling of loss, abandonment, and despair that comes when someone who has previously had a conviction of direct contact and support from the Divine loses the connection. George MacDonald's metaphor for this devastating experience is that of the moment when a mother, teaching her child to walk, withdraws her supporting hand. Many mystics eventually move through this stage to a new awareness of the Divine.

Kundalini awakening: Vibrations roll up your spine releasing a surge of energy. This may be accompanied by temperature changes, flashing lights, or powerful emotions. This phenomenon may be activated by yoga and other practices from the Eastern traditions, and those traditions are the best source of information on how to deal with it.

Shamanic crisis: Visions characteristic of shamanic mythology, such as a journey to the underworld, death, dismemberment, or annihilation. Mircea Eliade's *Shamanism* includes many accounts of these experiences, which are less devastating when they occur within a culture that can provide a context for the imagery involved.

Unitive consciousness: This is an experience in which you become united with nature, the cosmos, or the Divine (see chapter 12). This is the goal of mysticism.

Psychic opening: Personal boundaries dissolve and you become open to telepathy, clairvoyance, out-of-body experiences, or channeling. This can be extremely disorienting, especially if the possibility of these phenomena was not previously part of your worldview.

Past-life memory: Episodes from your earlier or previous lives activate emotions and feelings unconnected to present experience. Hypnotherapy and past-life regression can provide access to the history, but the process should be careful and gradual.

Near-death experience: An illness or accident causes an out-of-body experience and your consciousness shifts perspective.

Close encounters: Apparent contact with spirit beings or aliens.

Possession: Involuntary hosting of an alternate, alien, or divine persona that takes over.

Any one of these experiences can be viewed as psychotic, and may in fact be so. That does not prevent them from also being potentially transformative. The difference is not so much in the experience, as in whether you find your way out the other side. Therapists or teachers who know the territory can be of great help here, as can support groups of people who have had the same experiences. Family and friends should be brought into the picture so they understand what is going on, and can judge whether or not the condition needs more dramatic measures.

Get a medical examination along with your psychological treatment to make sure your symptoms do not have a physical cause. Unfortunately, experiences induced by brain tumors, emotional meltdown, and all the combinations in between can be perceived as being caused by something outside yourself.

It is also essential that

> . . . the person in crisis is open to the idea that the problem resides in his or her own psyche and that this person does not "project" and blame everybody and everything else in the world for his or her own difficulties. And, naturally, he or she has to be willing to confront powerful experiences (Grof and Grof, 1989).

The lightbulb has to *want* to be changed.

Roadside Assistance

Some problems require professional assistance and possibly an extended course of therapy. But what do you do if it's midnight on a lonely road, and you're the only one available to help a stranded traveler?

First, make sure individuals at risk do not present a danger to themselves or others. This may require removing them from a situation, or possibly restraining them for a time. Note that even a professional cannot legally restrain or force treatment on anyone, except under a clearly defined set of circumstances. And you may be legally required to notify authorities whether the afflicted individual wants this or not.

Identify the symptoms, and decide whether you need to call 911 or get to an emergency room. Attempt to figure out the cause and the context of the episode. Question friends about the person's background and history, religious background and tradition. Have these symptoms ever appeared before? This information may help you figure out how to communicate and how to proceed.

Bringing Someone out of Trance

When someone is stuck in an altered state, and you have eliminated drugs, alcohol, or allergic reactions as the cause, try stimulating the physical senses to bring the person back to ordinary reality. Some traditions employ strong scents—Vicks Vapo-rub, smelling salts, or burning yak hair. A strong taste can help. A crystal of rock salt on the tongue stimulates both taste and texture. Sour salt also works well. Eating and drinking can help, especially if the food has a strong or familiar taste or is high in sugar (although before giving anything sweet you should make sure the person is not diabetic).

Temperature is another stimulus. Pour warm or cold water over the wrists, or apply a washcloth to the back of the neck. Sensations like running the teeth of a comb over the palm of the hand can help. For those who can walk, the motion will help reconnect them to the body. If you can get them to talk, ask them to describe physical sensations like the softness of the couch or the cool touch of the air. Have them name things in the room. Once conversation is established, focus on mundane things. Talking about financial matters like rent or income tax is often an effective way to bring someone down.

Follow-up

Once your subject is stabilized, recommend whatever additional help may be needed. For experiences with a cultural component, as when Fatunmbi was possessed by an *orisha*, recommend contact with experts in the appropriate tradition. If the first one encountered denies the validity of the experience because it did not follow the rules, keep looking. Encourage a review of the literature on similar experiences, and recommend communication and connection with others who have undergone the same thing.

In the Catholic Church, people who have mystical experiences are supposed to find a priest who can act as their spiritual director. *Spiritual Mentoring*, by Judy Harrow, offers guidance for pagans with similar experiences. If all you can do is to connect those in need with someone to whom they can debrief periodically and who can provide a reality check, that's better than leaving them to flounder alone. Better still is to establish a network of family and friends that will support them through the crisis, and treat it as an opportunity for growth and healing.

R. D. Laing's approach to treating schizophrenia has been successful in some cases, although not all types of this illness are appropriate. Stanislav and Christina Grof recommend creating safe situations in which powerful experiences can be welcomed and explored. The more room there is to do this, the more quickly you will be able to work through to equilibrium. Of course, this is not always possible. Try muting and slowing down the process by suspending meditation and spiritual practices and avoiding exposure to stimuli that activate the process.

Shifting to a diet heavy in protein can reduce sensitivity. Dion Fortune observes that, in Eastern monastic traditions, a vegetarian diet and fasting are intentionally used to help students open up to spiritual contact. However, a state that is manageable in the supportive environment of an ashram may make you dangerously vulnerable when you are living "in the world." Focus on housework or other simple tasks to root yourself back in ordinary reality.

Alcohol and sedatives are sometimes helpful as well, but can become addictive. In extreme cases, prescription drugs may suppress the symptoms without solving the problem. In Asia and medieval Europe, people undergoing spiritual crises were sheltered in monasteries. Contemporary Western European culture has no culturally supported institutions for this kind of care. As more people explore changing consciousness, however, this may change.

Therapists and Therapy

While it is true that therapy for a severe problem requires a professional, not all therapists are equally effective. Patients and their families have both the right and the responsibility to evaluate their treatment. When a therapist and a client are well matched and work together for as long as necessary, long-term improvement is likely. If you are in therapy, consider carefully before stopping or changing treatment. And be sure to check your therapist's degrees, training, qualifications, license, and beliefs. No reputable professional will object if you ask questions.

When in doubt, before or after starting treatment, don't hesitate to ask for a second opinion—preferably from a competent professional who is not a personal friend of your therapist.

Degrees and licenses themselves do not guarantee competence, but a lack of them is a warning sign. Since therapy is confidential, a therapist, unlike someone who installs windows, cannot give you a list of references. However, if a therapist works with several people in your community and you know who they are, you can at least see if they seem to be making progress.

Your best efforts may not guarantee a good match, so continue to evaluate the relationship as you work together, bearing in mind that just because you are still hurting doesn't always mean there's something wrong with the treatment. If the therapist doesn't challenge you to take responsibility for your life and redirect you from endless blame of others—if you can't stop rehashing of old problems long enough to work on your own issues—how are you going to grow?

A useful resource for evaluating therapy is *Beware the Talking Cure*, by Dr. Terence Campbell. His book provides a list of questions that can help you decide whether it's time to start, stop, or change your therapy. A Web site called StopBadTherapy (*www.stopbadtherapy.com/test/therapy.shtml*) provides a checklist for evaluating your therapy experience.

Clearly the most important requirement is that therapists not immediately assume that any visionary or paranormal experience is evidence of insanity. *The Diagnostic and Statistical Manual of Mental Disorders (IV)*, known widely as DSM IV, specifically exempts from its list of pathologies those that occur in the context of culturally supported experience. Unfortunately, not many therapists appreciate the implications of that exemption.

The Institute for the Study of Peak States in Canada suggests you use therapists trained in the specialties of basic wholehearted healing, addiction, and schizophrenia. Specialists in transpersonal psychology are also likely to be sympathetic.

Practice

If you are experiencing psychic trauma associated with trance work, you have two choices, each with its own drawbacks. You can attempt to shut the process down, living a simple life and avoiding spiritual work entirely. Or you can find or develop a support network with whose help you can work your way through. This network may include psychologists, body-workers, hypnotherapists, and others. You may also have to be willing to endure things getting worse before they get better.

A major problem associated with trying to shut down spiritual awareness is the temptation to surrender to obsessive/compulsive avoidance behavior. If you live in fear of an unwanted experience, your existence can become an endless succession of defensive rituals that leave no room to enjoy life. A corresponding danger is that those trying to help you may adopt a single explanatory structure and become equally dependent on it.

Appendix I

Notes for the Tour Guide

These notes are for group leaders who are using this book as a text for a class. In many cases, guides will be no more than half a step ahead of the other travelers. Do not let this worry you overmuch, as long as you do not feel compelled to pretend to know more than you do. In these situations, you may prefer to call yourself a coordinator rather than a teacher. Your job is to organize and focus the process. The learning itself will be cooperative and consensual. However, you may find it useful, and it will certainly bolster your confidence, if you have a trustworthy senior priest or priestess, or a sympathetic therapist, to whom you can go for advice and moral support when needed.

Organizing the Tour

To form a group, you need participants, and a time and place in which to meet. If you are already in a coven or other group, you may all decide to work through the materials together. If you do not have such a group already, you may find like-minded people on one or more community e-lists. These are a good place to publicize your class.

You can also post fliers at your local occult shop or metaphysical bookstore, or hand them out at rituals and festivals. There are, of course, certain hazards in opening up this kind of work to people you do not know. You can find out some things about people using the self-evaluation questionnaire in chapter 1, but it is probably a good idea to hold an organizational meeting at which you can get a sense of who your participants are and whether you want to work with them. To trance successfully, you must be willing to lower the barriers that ordinarily shield your soul. A working trance group necessarily develops considerable intimacy, and interacting with personalities that are incompatible (even if they are not actually unbalanced) can upset the group dynamics and even cause psychological harm.

State these guidelines clearly at the beginning of your session, making it clear that who participates depends entirely on group dynamics, not intrinsic worth. By the end of the organizational meeting, it will be clear if some people are not going to fit in. Tell them that group membership will be finalized after the second or third lesson. In fact, it is quite likely your group will self-select, with those who are not compatible quietly dropping out. By that time, you should be able to tell who has problems you can deal with, and who is too crazy, too self-absorbed, or too prone to drama to be a productive member of the group.

Copy the questionnaire and make it available online or as a hard copy for participants to fill out. Add name, address, phone, e-mail address, date of birth. Make sure everyone knows that you will keep the information confidential. From the questionnaires and the organizational meeting, you should be able to tell who is already experienced and who is an eager newbie. This may have implications for how you organize the work. If the group is large, divide members into subgroups according to need. Or assign people with complementary abilities as buddies.

Create an e-list for the group. This can be extremely useful. Encourage participants to introduce themselves online, and post any information from their questionnaires that they are willing to share. Ask people to report on their experiences with the exercises—both positive and negative. If someone has a problem, another student can often offer suggestions that may not have occurred to you.

Decide when and where you will meet. Most class groups are small enough to meet in someone's living room, as long as there are comfortable chairs and enough room for people to lie down or form pairs with some distance between them if the exercises require it. Try to make the meeting space relatively soundproof, and close enough doors to give a sense of privacy.

I recommend meeting once a month. Feel free to spread the work of some of the chapters over more than one meeting. If most members are within a reasonable commute, hold the meetings on a weeknight. Otherwise, plan on meeting on the weekend in the afternoon or early evening.

Chapter 1: Travel Planning

The first meeting of a trance class is like the point at which a group arrives to get on a tour bus. From the questionnaires, you already know a great deal about each participant. But when you meet in person, appearance, manner, and body language tell you things that people might not think to put into their answers, or that they don't really know. This is also when participants meet each other. If you had an organizational meeting, some may already know (or think they know) each other well. Others will be strangers. In either case, those who go through this class together will develop a unique relationship, just as travelers on a tour develop a special bond.

This work requires that people open up in a new way, which in turn requires a higher level of consideration and courtesy than is common in ordinary social interactions. They must be aware from the very beginning that working together requires trust. When we bare our souls, we need to be assured that our companions will not take advantage of our vulnerability. The group must be both respectful and supportive, and above all, willing and able to keep any confidences revealed. What happens in the group stays there, whether it is shared in class or on the e-list.

At the first meeting, spend some time on logistics. The questionnaires will tell you where people live. If your meetings occur on a weeknight, find out where they work. Get cell phone numbers as well as home numbers so you can check up on late-comers. Encourage participants to carpool.

In addition to this book, have everyone bring a notebook and/or a recording device (if the group agrees) to each meeting. Encourage people to eat lightly before the meeting. Develop a potluck strategy or a rotating cooking roster so that some food with carbohydrates and protein is available at the end of each meeting. Trance work can use up a surprising number of calories and solid food will help everyone to ground. Participants may also want to bring blankets or meditation pillows, eye-masks or veils.

Begin by asking everyone to give his or her name, address, relevant background, and reason for taking the class. After the introductions, explain the nature and organization of the class, highlighting the following points.

Purpose: The purpose of the class is to develop skills and conditioned responses to cues, in order to give participants the ability to move back and forth between different states of consciousness at will. This is a class for serious students, and requires considerable commitment. Many of them may already have experienced some of these states. Working through the exercises in order will help them integrate and control their experiences in a disciplined sequence.

Structure: Each meeting will include a lecture/discussion covering the importance of a given set of skills and the principles behind them. Those with experience are invited to share their insights. Each class will demonstrate appropriate exercises and discuss ways to practice them during the following month. There may be additional group exercises as well.

Method: This approach to trance work depends on mastering and internalizing a sequence of skills. Students should make a commitment to attend all classes or convince the instructor that they have already mastered the skills, or can do so from independent work with the book. Sharing of experience in class and online contributes materially to the success of the work, as people encourage each other and offer additional insights and approaches to the skills. The basic skills will be useful to everyone, but not everyone will be interested and/or ready for the later practices at the same time. Allow participants to stop at any time. Decide whether you want to offer makeup sessions—but don't guarantee them.

Assignment: The first assignment is to read chapter 1. Anyone who has not yet filled out the questionnaire should do so now. Encourage everyone to think carefully about the final question.

Chapter 2: Crossing the Threshold

With this meeting, the work actually begins. Start by introducing anyone who was not present at the first meeting. Encourage people to share their answers to the final question. Why do they want to do this work? In what ways do they think it will help them, or others? Do not, however, spend too much time schmoozing. You have work to do.

This chapter covers a number of skills. Depending on the previous experience of your group, you can extend the work over more than one meeting. You may, in fact, need three meetings: one for warding, one for grounding and centering, one for relaxation and breathing. Lead students through the exercises and discuss results and problems.

Warding: Discuss the concept of warding. Those with Wiccan training will be familiar with the concept of casting a circle. Ask how they can tell if a circle is cast effectively. Do they notice changes in air pressure? Atmosphere? Other sensory clues? Do some people cast a stronger circle than others? Have experienced group members draw the boundaries of your working space, or have several people do so and then compare the effects. Practice the Journey charm in exercise 1 (the Sith Galdor) by reading the verses and have students go through the motions, visualizing the barrier forming around them. When you do exercises in a group, aim for a consensus level of speed and intensity. Be sure students understand that, when they work alone, they can and should adjust the pace as necessary. If you will be reading the exercise directions aloud, skip ahead to Appendix II and study the instructions for reading and leading pathworkings.

Grounding and centering: Lead the group through a quick warding, then try several approaches to grounding and centering, starting with the directions in exercise 4. Develop a sequence that is acceptable to the class members and use it at the beginning of each group exercise. Try using the image of resting enclosed in an egg. If you have access to a yard, take participants outside and let them practice grounding through a tree. Ask students to share their own favorite methods with the group.

Relaxation: Discuss methods of relaxation. Ask people to describe situations in which they have felt totally relaxed and at peace with the world. Lead the group through the tense-and-release and stretching techniques in exercises 6 and 7. After each, encourage them to compare reactions. If someone has an alternative to share and time allows, try that as well.

Chapter 3: Getting Started

Students who have been doing their homework and practicing the exercises may begin to notice effects like changes in their dream patterns. Remind them to keep up with their journals, and encourage them to share their experiences with others in class or online. As before, you may want to extend the work over more than one meeting.

Toning: This is a particularly effective exercise for energizing and building group cohesion. Some participants may protest that they have terrible voices or can't carry a tune. The breathing exercises can help with voice production. The advantage of group toning is that members can simply continue to sing the same note as a drone, or sit near others with a good sense of harmony and sing whatever they are singing. The tones are supposed to shift and mutate as the group energy changes, so there is no right or wrong way to do it. Creating sound together produces a group rapport in which even those who believed themselves musical morons will find they can contribute to the tapestry of sound.

Mantras: The impact of group chanting is different from the impact of chanting alone. Lead the group in chanting AUM for ten minutes. Afterward, discuss the experience, and how it compared to solo chanting.

Clearing the mind: Encourage students to discuss their experiences with the mind-clearing technique in exercise 9, compare notes on any problems, and suggest solutions. Remember that there is no single correct way to do this work. Students who are new to the practice can often suggest excellent ideas that more experienced practitioners may not have considered. Try playing a DVD or CD of images and sounds to the class, with or without a narrated mind-clearing induction. If you want to read the induction, review the material on delivering a guided meditation in Appendix II for guidelines on how to do so effectively.

Chapter 4: Trance-Perceptions

The work in this chapter will help students develop their powers of observation and memory. The exercises can be a lot of fun, especially when done in a group. Here, however, differences in learning styles will become very apparent. Encourage everyone to take the online test at *www.www.bgfl.org/bgfl/custom/resources_ftp/client_ftp/ks3/ict/multiple_int/index.htm*, or use a similar test. Emphasize that no one type of intelligence is better than the others, although our educational system tends to focus on verbal and mathematical skills. People with other abilities often turn out to be very good at magical practices simply because they experience the world in a different way.

Vision: Practice contemplation by asking students to contemplate their shoes. Everyone in the class will have them, and they are comparable in size and complexity. Give everyone a few minutes to study their shoes, then ask them to put the shoes out of sight and write down or draw everything they can remember about them. Then have them take another look and note what they missed. On the second pass, remind students to note weight and texture, and any other details that involve senses other than vision, like smell. The Jewel Game is a similar exercise that also works well with a class. Prepare a tray full of objects ahead of time and carry it through the room, giving each student an equal amount of time to study it. Then have them write down what they observed. Try using items that appeal to senses other than vision, like packets of spices or tea.

Sound: Asking students to compose a simple chant can cause great anxiety. It helps if students can share their expertise. Those with musical skills may be able to help others with their songs. Ask students to bring drums to a meeting, and experiment with different rhythms.

Body language: Practice sensing energy with the group. Divide the students into pairs and lead them through exercise 13 in which they feel each others' energy through their palms. If particular students have physical problems in certain parts of their bodies, see if they will volunteer to lie down so other students can try to identify the part that is hurting. Have them test the energy above different parts of the body and write down their observations. When everyone has done so, compare results with the test subjects and with each other.

Checksums: By this time, you will begin to see differences in the way students are responding. Some will have dropped the class because their other commitments are too demanding. Some will have found your approach is not working for them. Some will have other reasons. You will find wide variations in how much time students spend in practice and how often they respond to online and in-class discussions. And some will have found that the first-class tour of their issues has already begun.

Make clear to everyone that psychic and spiritual development is very personal and sometimes tricky (see chapter 13). Your students' first responsibility is to monitor their flight status and, if necessary, stop or slow down. Let them know there is no shame in recognizing that the pace at which the class is moving is not appropriate or healthy for them, and there is no penalty for dropping out. They can always resume the work when they feel ready. Encourage them to use the same judgment they would in physical training. If you strain a muscle, you have to wait until it heals. If one way of doing an exercise overstresses your mind or body, find another. Encourage students to talk to you privately if they have difficulties. If necessary, help them to find a sympathetic elder in the community or a therapist to whom they can go for counseling.

Chapter 5: There and Back Again

In this chapter, class members hone their ability to navigate in the Otherworld and remember their journeys. By this time, their skill levels have increased. They can move into a state of readiness more quickly and more easily than before. The car is packed and the motor is running. It's time to make sure everyone has a camera and notebook so they can record what they see.

Fairy tales: Class members who were brought up on fairy tales will remember many examples of passages and dangers. People who read a lot of fantasy literature will also have some good examples of what to do and what not to do when wandering around in Faerie. *The Lord of the Rings* is a good place to start the discussion, as nearly everyone will have seen and/or read it. For the hobbits, the Otherworld is everything beyond the borders of the Shire.

Reverse memory: At the end of *The Lord of the Rings*, the hobbits return to the Shire—not quite by the same path they started out on, but with a definite sense of reintegrating themselves into ordinary reality. We have to do the same thing when we return from trance. The Reverse Memory practice in exercise 21 accustoms students to thinking backward. Ask class members to write down a reversed description of how they got from home or work to the meeting place, and then how they will get back again.

Building a base camp: This exercise is best done at home, as it may take several visits to create a useful "place" in the Otherworld. You can, however, have some productive discussion on the subject of what makes people feel safe, and what kinds of places they may choose. Of course, if students seek their base camp in trance, they may be in for a surprise, as the unconscious often has needs of which the conscious mind is ignorant. Encourage everyone to share their descriptions between meetings on the online list.

Snapshots: I have a collection of postcards I pass out to the class for this exercise. A pile of magazines that include pictures of places works as well. Give each student a picture, and ask everyone to write a few lines of poetry or poetic prose capturing the essence of the scene. If there is time, collect the pictures and display them. Have students read their descriptions, and see if other class members can identify the picture to which they belongs.

Sound bytes: Explain that you are going to read a passage that describes a place. As you do so, have class members recreate that scene in their minds as vividly as possible. Instruct everyone to ground, center, relax, and clear their minds. Then read the passage or poem aloud. When you are done, wait a few moments, then tell the group to breathe more quickly, open their eyes, and return. When they have all recovered, ask what they remember most vividly. Note the sensory details each person lists. See if anyone comes up with details that were not, in fact, mentioned in the passage. Possible selections are:

- Writings by naturalists and travelers like John Muir, Henry David Thoreau, Annie Dillard, or William Least Heat Moon
- Shakespeare's description of Ophelia's death in *Hamlet* (IV:vii) or the prologue to Act III of *Henry V*
- Poems from the Romantic period like Wordsworth's "Upon Westminster Bridge," the first section of "Kubla Khan" by Coleridge, any of the stanzas of "To Autumn" by Keats, "Meeting at Night" by Browning, the first stanza of Arnold's "Dover Beach," and, for something a little different, "Pied Beauty" by Gerard Manley Hopkins

You can find these all in *The Oxford Book of English Verse*, or you can try looking them up on the Web. Whatever you choose, practice reading before the class. Take your time, pay attention to the rhythms, and give full weight to the words.

Random recitals: Divide the class into groups of four or five. Ask each person to come up with a noun (at least one of which denotes a living being) or an adjective. Have everyone write down their words, then ask the group to write a description of the being.

Travelers' tale: Still in the groups, let everyone tell the story of an actual trip they have taken, being as circumstantial as possible and including the mode of transport, route, most notable experiences, and how they felt about them.

Chapter 6: Native Guides

Now students begin to put the skills they have learned together and do some purposeful journeying. Start the class with a review of previously learned skills, including relaxation by stretching, grounding and centering, and breathing. Ask them how their image of the base camp has changed. Is anyone having problems with journeying? Have they had any interesting dreams? When everyone is up-to-date, introduce the topic of animal allies. How many already have strong relationships with animal allies or other kinds of spirits? How many had these connections when they were children? How many feel they have a totem animal? Is this animal associated with their family line?

Finding your ally or spirit guide: Lead the class through a journey to the Underworld or Lower World to find an ally in animal form. If everyone already has an animal friend, lead them on a journey to find spirit guides instead. Remind them they can substitute details as needed. For instance, someone working in the Celtic tradition can look for a spiral-carved *menhir* to serve as an entrance to the Otherworld. Narrate the first directions to relax and breathe and seek their base camp (see exercise 22), then switch to drumming alone while they journey. Allow ten to fifteen minutes for the journey, then do a swift rat-a-tat-tat on the drum to alert everyone that it's time to return. Summon them back to base camp and, from there, to consensus reality. Debrief and, if time permits, encourage everyone to move to a slow drumbeat, imitating the motions of their new animal ally.

Seeing totems: Ask students to try to "see" totem animals for each other. Sit class members in a circle in low light. Tell them to unfocus their eyes and gaze through or past the figure of each person in turn. Encourage them to see an aura, pick up an impression, or wait until the person's features blur and an animal mask "slides" down over the face. Ask them to look for an animal shape superimposed or shadowing the human shape. When an impression becomes clear, tell them to write it down. Students may see more than one animal per person. When everyone has had a chance to "see" everyone else, turn up the lights and ask them to share their conclusions. If time and space allow, have everyone dance the movements of the animals people saw for them, swaying to the beat and seeing which ones feel most comfortable.

Chapter 7: Getting Along in the Culture

By this time, those who have been doing their homework may well have some interesting experiences to report. Once someone makes a connection, animal allies can turn up in some pretty strange places and ways. Share resources for finding out more about the animals. Emphasize the importance of cultivating the connection.

Lead the group on a journey in which they ask permission to wear their ally's shape as they journey to its favorite landscape or home. Compare notes when they return. Encourage them to write songs to invoke their allies. As with the trance song, this may prompt some resistance. Pair the more musically adept with those who are less so.

This meeting is also a good opportunity for class members to share memories of fairy tales. Encourage them to read and share more online. What "rules" have they observed for getting along in the Otherworld? What can they add to the list given in chapter 7? If anyone has had a scary experience in a dream-vision or journey, discuss means of protection, like a magical name. Some class members may already have magical names that they are willing to share. Discuss whether students want to create magical names for use in trance work.

Chapter 8: Mapping the Inner Worlds

Before class, e-mail students and suggest that they bring in examples of fantasy maps. Look on the Web for maps new and old to add to the examples in the book. Bring in your favorite fantasy novels and discuss the maps they contain. In what ways are the maps realistic and in what ways are they not? Which elements are emphasized, which ignored? What do the proportions and landmarks tell you about the perspective of the mapmaker?

Class work is a good way to get people to do things they might have been too busy or too hesitant to try at home. Try giving students paper and colored pencils and asking them to draw maps of how to get to their base camps. Have them map the route and then draw a diagram of the place itself. Then ask them to map the route they took to the place where they found their allies. These visual representations will be easier for some than others. Explore ways to make a "map" that does not depend on vision, perhaps by recording the sounds made at various landmarks.

Chapter 9: Fellow Travelers

This chapter is *all* about working with others. Those who have stuck with the group this far already know a great deal about each other. Members will have paired off and formed subgroups based on interests and compatibility. These subgroups are probably now accustomed to working together. For them to get the most benefit from the material in this chapter, I recommend breaking these groups up and reassigning them for the exercises.

For the group exercises, you need a tape recorder or CD player, one recording of moderately paced, rhythmic music, and one of a regular drumbeat, or your own drum. For the exercises that involve dancing, you need enough open space for everyone to move.

Begin by taking everyone through grounding, centering, and relaxation, followed by breathing together and stretching. Put people in pairs and have them perform the practice at the end of chapter 9 for playing ball. When they have gotten the idea, bring the whole group together for circling energy. Then try combining the two–ask one person to "create" an energy ball and then pass it around the circle.

The dancing practices at the end of this chapter both require a reasonable amount of open space–especially blind dancing, for which you must remove any obstacles. Some people may feel self-conscious about dancing in front of others. Dimming the lights may help them relax. If you want to explore this area further, workshops developed for business team-building include a number of exercises intended to develop trust and cohesion. A quick tour of the Internet will give you a multitude of resources.

It is probably best to address the practices for interactive journeying and shadowing in a separate meeting, since they are both intense paired activities that require comfortable places for the partners to sit or lie down. Ask class members to "score the energy" of religious services or entertainment events between meetings, and report on their findings. For best results, have everyone do each practice with more than one partner, including people they know well and people with whom they have not worked closely before.

Chapter 10: Destinations

Thus far, we have focused on developing disciplined trance skills, but those skills are not an end in themselves. Exploring the inside of your head can be entertaining, but eventually, you and your students are going to want to *do* something with those skills. From my Western perspective, I find that personal growth is most meaningful when it leads to achievement, especially the kind of work that helps others. Basic skills in trance work are thus only the preliminary to various kinds of advanced practice, from oracular or possessory work to healing. These practices all deserve volumes of their own, but, in this chapter, we can at least survey some of the possibilities.

Healing: This is an area with many variations and specialties, but you can address the simpler techniques in your class. Healing also has the advantage (or disadvantage, depending on your point of view) of being in constant demand. In any community, there will always be *someone* in need of help. If you start a discussion on the subject, group members should have no trouble coming up with situations in which spiritual healing work either succeeded or failed. Encourage everyone to speculate on how the skills they have developed might be useful in healing. Discuss the ethical problems involved and work out a version of the Hippocratic Oath to use. As a class activity, conduct a healing circle for someone who needs help—someone who has given permission. If someone in the class has a problem, do some energy or sound work then and there. If class members are interested in trance dancing, set up a session in an appropriate setting, or get a group together to attend a rave. There's safety in numbers.

Past-life regression: This exercise can be done very efficiently in a class setting with one person leading the pathworking for the rest. If the group is large, have someone act as warder. Ask everyone to think of a situation or problem for which knowledge of past-life experiences may be helpful.

Exercise 30. Past-life Regression

Direct the group to ground, center, and relax as usual, and synchronize breathing. Direct them to go to their base camps and, from there, to an elevator whose buttons are marked in centuries. It will stop at the century to which they need to go. When they leave the elevator, spend some time guiding them to notice sensory details that will provide information. Clothing, hands, and surroundings tell their own stories. Ask for smells, textures, and sounds, as well as the things they can see.

When the setting is established, give them a little space to investigate and experience it. Suggest they focus on a moment that was very important in that life. Then move on to the moment of death, specifying that they will withdraw from awareness before they feel pain. Allow a shorter amount of time to assimilate this experience, then direct them back to the elevator, telling them to call on their allies to lead them if they have any problems. Direct them to return.

People will have various reactions to this activity, especially if you include a death scene. Encourage members to comfort each other if it seems needed. Bring the group back to the present by getting them to focus on sensory stimuli–the temperature of the room, the texture of the rug–and encourage those who want to share their experiences to talk about what they learned. Provide glasses of water, or prepare a pot of nourishing soup ahead of time–the warmth will be as restorative as the calories. Get the group as a whole talking about current events, and take anyone whose experience was particularly emotional aside for debriefing. In some cases, you may need to do some individual follow-up sessions in which you take the person back to that lifetime and explore it further.

Chapter 11: Your Place or Mine? Getting Closer to the Gods

If many of your group members have previous experience with a spiritual tradition that encourages personal relationships with deity, the first part of the meeting for this chapter will probably result in a lot of "war stories." For many, it may be the first opportunity to compare notes on these experiences. For the purpose of learning, however, suggest that participants commit to working for the next month with a deity with whom they do not already have a relationship. Then go through the steps required to make contact.

Start the group on a pathworking in which you direct them to seek the temple of the god or goddess as soon as they leave their base camps, and then continue to drum without speaking. Allow ten or fifteen minutes, depending on your sense of the energy flow, and bring them back.

Discuss ways of honoring the deities, like creating altars and writing chants or songs. Not all styles of worship are appropriate for all powers. Encourage them to do some research into the cultural context of their deities. Other members of the group who already work in those cultures can serve as resources.

Chapter 12: Going Nowhere, Being Everywhere

Your work so far falls under the heading of what Charles Williams called the Way of the Affirmation of Images. This chapter, on the other hand, belongs to the Way of the Denial of Images. It is neither higher nor better than other forms of trance work, but it is different and offers an additional and potentially valuable skill.

After a general discussion, lead the group through an "open" meditation or passive trance, explaining that it is very unlikely that this will result in a mystical experience. It will, however, start them on a path that may lead there, if they persevere. The goal for this class is a state of inner quiet in which group members are no longer aware of time.

First, take everyone through a series of stretches to avoid muscle cramps, then get everyone settled in a comfortable position and lead them through grounding, centering, and breathing in unison. When the pattern is established, start intoning AUM. Try to keep it going for fifteen minutes–remember that, in Buddhist monasteries, they can do this for hours. If this exercise goes well, try working with recordings of temple bells, contemplation of an image, or some of the other suggested exercises.

Chapter 13: Road Hazards

This chapter is not the topic for a meeting, but you, as leader, should read it with special care. Anyone who has been working in a spiritual community for any length of time knows that accidents can happen. For most of the students in your group, the training will be both interesting and useful. Depending on how hard they work during the course and how many of the practices they continue thereafter, results may vary from a slight widening of horizons to a major improvement in spiritual practice.

You did what you could to weed out the fragile souls at the beginning, but the self-evaluation form cannot catch every potential problem Most of those who are not ready for this kind of work will realize it quickly and drop out. But there may be some for whom the effects are less positive–people who were already primed for trouble. This is not your fault, but it is your responsibility as a teacher to help people deal with the fallout as best you can.

If there are problems, you will likely be the one called to administer spiritual first-aid. Find out what resources are available in your community so that, if necessary, you can help your students find professional counseling. Organize a support system while they are going through whatever therapy they need.

Appendix II
Guidance Systems

Some years ago, I got a call from my friend Jennifer. British Airways had sponsored a science-fiction costume contest, and she had won two tickets to London. Would I like to come with her? I reminded her that I had been to England several times. Surely, I said nobly, she should take someone who had never been there before. "But *I've* never been there before," she replied. "Oh," I said. "You want a *guide!*"

Most of the material in this book is written from the point of view of the solitary traveler. Those who explore distant realms often return to find that their friends, like Jennifer, want to go there too, with them as guide. To do this effectively requires skills different from those you need for working alone, especially in the areas of guiding and warding.

Guiding a Meditation

One of the basic tools for journeying is the pathworking or guided meditation. Whether you are leading a group or recording a narration you have written for your own use, the following exercises may help you deliver the pathworking in a more effective way.

Words behave differently when they are spoken than they do when read silently. When you read to yourself, you can ignore awkward phrasing or weak word choice; as long as you get the meaning, you don't really care about style. When you read something aloud, however, it reveals every bump in the road. If you want to share your journey with others, *how* you present it is as important as what you say. Unfortunately the art of oratory has been well-nigh forgotten. Martin Luther King Jr., trained in the tradition of southern preaching, was one of the last public figures to demonstrate real mastery. These exercises may help you polish your own delivery style.

Exercise 31. Writing

Once you have drafted your meditation using the techniques in chapter 5, go back and polish it. Review the poetry writing exercises in chapter 5, read Shakespeare aloud, listen to recordings of effective public speakers. Now read aloud what you have written.

Note where you need to draw breath. You may need to move clauses or break up a sentence. For instance: "You are going down a pathway and you come to some rocks which are gray and rough and so you need to go around them . . ." reads much more smoothly like this: "You are walking down a path. Before you are some rough gray rocks that block the path. Find a way around them . . . "

Watch out for inadvertent tongue-twisters or words that will be hard to say, especially when you yourself are in a slightly altered state. If the word is not in English, make sure you know how to pronounce it correctly and, if necessary, write it out phonetically. In a journey to the Norse underworld, one passes the well Hvergelmir. Try to say that one smoothly while in trance! Avoid pronunciation problems by using circumlocutions: "the well from which all the world's rivers run . . ." Or try breaking up the syllables or writing them phonetically in your script—"Hver-gel-mir," or "H'vair-gell-meer." Practice enunciating anything likely to trip your tongue.

Use poetic techniques like alliteration—"the waters of the Well of Wyrd . . . "—and rhythm, assonance, and repetition—"Down and around, down and around we fare . . . "—to create powerful incantatory effects. But keep it subtle; don't distract people by the beauty of your writing to the point where they can't pay attention to what you say.

Exercise 32. Delivery

Unfortunately, when the vehicle is too uncomfortable, the traveler won't appreciate even the most beautiful scenery. Likewise, the best-written meditation can be destroyed by poor delivery. Even those skilled at meditation on their own find that leading meditations for others requires a lot of practice. The elements you must control include projection, expression, and pacing.

Think "loud and clear." Test your voice projection by reading a passage to a friend sitting on the other side of the room. Are you speaking loudly enough, and enunciating clearly enough so that your friend can understand every word? Are you keeping the energy level consistent so that the end of each sentence is as clear as its beginning? Pay attention to the quality of your voice. Read smoothly. Find the pitch that is most comfortable for you, and at which your voice can be heard most clearly.

Record your reading. Do you enjoy listening to this voice? If not, what can you improve? One element that often needs work is breath control. If you find yourself running out of breath before the next pause in a sentence, either change the way you use your breath or rewrite the sentences. You've already worked on your breathing. Now you must learn to release your breath evenly. Next, consider your expression and your use of dramatic techniques. When you are leading a ritual, is your reading so monotonous that it puts your audience to sleep? Or do you excite and move them? And do you excite them so much that they are unable to relax and move into trance?

Pick one of the exercises in Appendix III or one that you have written and read it aloud. Practice this with a group to help you understand what happens when you read in different ways (a ghost story, phone-sex call, or soap opera). You may have everyone rolling in the aisles with laughter! Once you have explored as many ways as possible *not* to read a meditation, work on finding a happy medium—a way to read that keeps people focused while easing them in the direction you want them to go. Choose a moderate pace and tone, soothing and smooth without being soporific. Be expressive, but not dramatic. Keep the rhythms and sounds clear, but don't overemphasize. Let the Greek maxim, "Nothing to excess" be your guide.

Pacing is important too. You don't want to read too quickly or too slowly. Analyze the text and note where people will need time to build up the image you are describing. Understand not only when you should speak, but when you should be silent. If your text says, "Before you is a large gray stone carved with spirals. Move forward, touch your finger to the groove, and trace the spiral . . . ," pause for the time it takes you to see the stone clearly, feel the gritty texture, and experience the sensation of moving your hand.

Spend some time thinking about presentation. Some find it easier to relax and trance if the lights are low. But it is much better to leave the lights on than to falter in the middle of the meditation because you discover that the light of one candle is not enough for you to make out the words. Try reading and drumming at the same time. This takes a lot of practice. Make sure you have room to spread out the pages where you can see all of them, or have someone turn the pages for you. Make sure there's enough light for you to see them all.

Warding: Working on the Edge

When a group journeys together, it's very useful to have cabin personnel to keep an eye on the travelers. In my tradition, we call these people warders, and their work can make the difference between a productive experience and a painful one. Since I am usually the one driving the tour bus, I have less experience with this part of the job than some of the others on my team. I am grateful to Lorrie Wood for providing much of the following advice on what a warder does.

When you interact with other people, you must be careful in ways that are different from when you are working alone. The more people involved, the more care you must take. A pilot and copilot can watch out for each other, but they need cabin attendants to take care of the rest of the passengers. The same is true in trance work. When you work alone, you can ward yourself; partners can ward each other. But when you lead a trance journey for a roomful of people, you cannot stop "flying the plane" to help one person without disrupting the process for all the others. Thus, large-group trance work requires a team.

Warding can be broken down into three broad categories: self, place, and other people. As in so much of life, however, the key to success is preparation.

Warding Yourself

Until and unless you feel confident enough in yourself, it is difficult to achieve and maintain control over various non-ordinary states. While achieving this on a large scale is one of the most important goals of this work—*as well as one of its desired results*—all warding rightly starts with establishing your own personal safeguards. Remember the watchword chiseled in the forecourt of the temple at Delphi: "Know thyself!"

The same is true for a group when you are working with a team. If those who will be running the ritual take the time to ground and center together and link their energies, they can become the kind of unified team that Ken Kesey describes: their rapport will allow them to sense each others' needs and work symbiotically, even when they are stationed in different parts of the room.

Warding Your Space

Safeguard the space where your work will be done whenever circumstances warrant and permit it. Good manners dictate that you allow the owners or primary tenants of the place to set the rules and take primary responsibility for protecting everyone within, although they may be willing to delegate the job. In the case of a festival or a rented space, you can tacitly assume this permission is given when your group is granted physical access to the space. When possible, respect the rules of your host and his or her tradition regarding how sacred space should be established. Don't cast a Wiccan circle when a Voodoo *mambo* has already made prayers and offerings to Papa Legba, or when a Slavic Reconstructionist has already had a word with a *domovoi* (household spirit). This is considered poor form and can cause conflict within the ritual. When possible, ask whether or not your host wants to or is able to ward the space. Then proceed in whatever way your conscience and the circumstances deem wisest. Sometimes, this means that you must perform a discreet supplemental warding in your own idiom to support an inadequate existing structure.

If you are working in a festival situation, find out what presentations will be in that space in the time slots around yours and consider whether their energy will be incompatible with your own. Also consider the events scheduled in the spaces to either side of yours that will be occurring at the same time. Your quiet contemplation of the sea goddesses of seven different cultures will probably not benefit from the leftovers of the Kali *puja* that just cleared out, or from a Discordian Ritual going on next door. Pay attention to the schedule, and determine if further banishing, cleansing, and/or reinforcements are indicated *before* your group enters the room.

Some problems may not become apparent until you move in to set up. If a previous ritual featured an incense or used herbs to which someone on your team is allergic, sweep or air it out. Check the space for concentrations of energy that, if not negative, may be, at the least, distracting. Break them up and expel them. Smaller venues generally call for less preparation. Simply alert your allied personal and/or house spirits to keep an eye on the group just as they would your personal work.

Once a ritual has begun, the person running it should delegate the job of dealing with the space and how it interacts with the outside world. If circumstances permit and warrant, you can deploy an "outfield" of warders on the perimeter of the group space.

If you are the warder, first determine whether the energies of the place are appropriate. Then deal with people (corporeal or otherwise) who may try to enter from the outside once the work begins. Do not make snap judgments: a latecomer may have good reason to attend; the hotel staff may need to know when the ritual will end so the space can be reset for tomorrow morning's breakfast; an interloping spirit may be there to test *you*!

You may also have to process people who want to leave early. This can mean anything from giving them a drink of water to grounding them, to murmuring a lengthy guided meditation to bring them back to consensual reality, to three hours at a picnic table in the dead of night doing ad hoc counseling. Use your judgment. If that fails, seek advice from those you trust. If no one is available to help . . . congratulations, the Universe has obviously awarded you Yet Another Learning Experience.

Warding Others

In your role as warder, you may have to deal with spirits, humans, or even group members who are disrupting the work. Dealing with uninvited spiritual guests is the job of the warders in the "outfield," to make sure that those stationed in the "infield" know what may reasonably be expected of any invited guest and who those guests may, within reason, invite. An experienced warder will be familiar enough with the cultural context in which a ritual takes place to know this. An inexperienced warder should ask as far in advance as is practical.

For instance, at a possessory event, warders act as servitors to seated deities, which puts them in an excellent position to observe the work and defuse potentially ill-advised situations. It takes experience, however, to know how and when to intervene. What do you do if someone in trance rests the point of an unsheathed spear on the chest of a non-tranced attendee? Do you simply watch? Do you grab the non-tranced person out of the way? Do you have words with the possessing deity? Do you distract the deity with a tray of food? Any one of these may be the right action in a given situation. Knowledge is the best tool you can have.

While it's possible and even desirable to enter a number of states on your own, once another person is involved, try to have a third to chaperone. Practitioners often find it easier to go further from consensual reality if there is someone back home "minding the store"!

In rituals in which only one person is in trance at a time, both the person in trance and the person the trance subject is contacting are vulnerable. The primary concern of the warders stationed among the participants in the "infield" should be the states of both these participants.

We all develop our own sets of conditioned cues for entering and leaving different trance states. Not everyone can articulate them, but we all have them. If you are acting as a warder whose primary concern in a ritual is those who are in trance, try to learn each subject's cues. If you cannot do so, try the ones usually used in that group, or take other logical steps like providing or removing props or speaking certain names. If the goal is removal from trance, try using strong flavors and smells. As always, however, pay attention to context. Keep two containers at hand: one to hold large-grained salt (like kosher or rock salt), and one for some other strong-flavored powder (citric acid, cinnamon, or cocoa). Offering a drink of clear, still water can often help someone regain ordinary consciousness.

An infield warder's next concern is the people who are interacting directly with the person in trance. They may be in a light trance state themselves without knowing it, and may be thrown without warning into deep emotional waters. At the very least, an infield warder should carry tissues and be able to offer emotional support to someone in tears or other obvious distress. You are well-advised, however, to limit your support to that, and allow tears to flow as long as the ritual is not disturbed. Not all tears are evil. Trance events, because they involve direct contact with the numinous, do much to comfort the disturbed and disturb the comfortable. Expect *anything*.

Infield warders are also expected to process people who are not intended trance subjects out of the ritual space. As a warder, you will often be required to act as bouncer. If it becomes apparent after the ritual has begun that someone is going to be a problem—like the gentleman who brought a bottle of beer to an oracular ritual and kept drinking, or someone who is overcome by the energy and breaks into wild weeping—you may have to ease them out gently but firmly. If necessary, try to alert the ritual leader so that he or she can distract everyone from the disturbance by narration, or chanting, or drumming.

As a rule, it is not a good idea to allow animals or young children into group rites involving trance work, unless you know they are familiar with the protocols. In particular, do not trust the parents' assertions in this regard. That said, this can also vary by ritual. If you are honoring a god known to associate with dogs, wolves, or cats, or who finds special joy in children, it may be a dishonor to ask them to leave the event. Just make sure owners and parents take responsibility for any animals or children present. Children are notorious scene-stealers, and a dog that decides to sing along with the trance induction or paw for attention can jerk someone out of trance with painful suddenness.

Working without a Net

What if you don't have all these people to throw at your ritual? In that case, do what you can. Remember that the minimum number for a trance event is either one or three, not two.

For a larger number, try to have at least three people: one as trance subject, one as attendant or guide, and one to handle the audience and the outside world. If your ritual is intended for a medium-sized group (twenty to sixty people), try to have one head warder (who may or may not also be the chief officiant of the rite), and one infield warder for every twenty attendees, with one or two working the outfield. Groups over sixty people can be hard to manage in the best of circumstances, and are beyond the scope of this discussion.

If you are the only one on hand when someone you've just met enters the throes of a spiritual emergency, congratulations. You'll have a great war story.

Debriefing and Grounding

After any ritual involving trance work, it's a good idea to eat a moderate-sized meal. From a warder's point of view, this is also a good time to make sure that all your charges have come back to themselves completely. Don't miss any opportunities—and don't forget to get some food yourself! Being a good warder takes energy—even if all you do is wander around with a plate of snacks.

A meeting over food also provides a good opportunity for the ritual team to share information and impressions. Multiple points of view provide more "coverage" of the event. Things that took place on one side of the room may not have been noticed by those on the other. One warder's solution to a problem may be useful to another the next time around. Note things that worked well and incorporate them into the script. Analyze the things that didn't work so you can avoid or correct them.

The job of a warder is to be aware of him/herself, the ritual, and its surroundings. Those who think this unnecessary are usually those who've never needed a warder's help. Although warders are primarily responsible for their own stations, don't hesitate to step in to help someone outside of your assigned zone if the situation warrants.

Even if you usually have other ritual responsibilities, you should ward from time to time. This is true especially if you are usually the one doing trance work for others. You will improve your own performance by knowing what things look like from the other side of the circle. We usually start anyone interested in learning techniques from our group on "the warding track," followed by intense mentoring with one of our more experienced members.

Besides . . . those who care enough about others to ward their well-being in a ritual may just feel called upon to act more responsibly toward their fellows in the rest of their lives—and this can hardly be a bad thing.

Appendix III

Journeys to Find Allies

These exercises give you three examples of what is essentially the same pathworking, cast in the mythic context of Norse, Celtic, and Greek cultures. Their original purpose was to connect with an ally in animal form, but they can also serve as models for adapting trance inductions for use in different traditions. I give you basic directions in italics and instructions specific to the cultural context in regular type. Breaks between sections indicate a pause.

Exercise 33. Journey to Midgard

In the Norse tradition, *Midgard* (Middle Earth) is the name for the world in which humans live. It is therefore the world of ordinary consciousness. There is another Midgard, however, through whose center the great tree Yggdrasil, which is the axis of all worlds, rises. This place lies "within." It is to this place that you will journey here.

Sink down now and be at ease.
Let the solid earth support you, each muscle relaxes.
Breathe in . . . (4-5 beats), and out . . . (4-5 beats). . . .

In . . . and out again. . . .
Here in our circle/this place, you are secure.
All the sounds you hear outside
make it easier to look within.

See now in your mind's eye a place outdoors (or your base camp) that you know well.
Look at the ground beneath your feet,
feel its texture, observe the plants that grow there,
note their feel and smell.
Feel the air on your skin,
listen to all the night sounds.
Now, as you look around, you see a path leading away–
follow it.

To either side grow shrubs that brush against your clothing.
As you move onward, they become taller.
Now they are fir trees, growing ever closer together and higher
until they arch overhead.
Make your way downward through the tunnel of trees,
pass beneath green-scented shadow,
fallen needles a soft carpet beneath your feet.

At last you see a circle of brightness.
As you draw closer, you glimpse a broad plain,
varied with meadow and stream and woodland,
the Plain of Midgard that lies within.
A great Tree rises in its center.
This is Yggdrasil, axis of all the worlds,
so high its branches brush the heavens,
glimmering with the light that shines from Asgard,
so wide you can scarcely see around it.
Three great roots plunge through the soil,
and a dark opening leads to greater mysteries.
To the north the dim gray mists of Niflheim obscure the horizon;

the southern air shimmers with the heat of Muspelheim.
To the east, mountains rise from the depths to the skies,
shining with ice and snow.
To the west, you can glimpse the blue gleam of the sea.
From the great Tree lead a multitude of pathways–
Field and forest, marsh and desert, mountain and seashore,
for every terrain there is a path.
Stand by the Tree for a moment, centering yourself,
then move forward along whatever pathway draws you. . . .

Note the landmarks so that you will know how to return.
But as you gaze around you,
look also for movement.
Once you begin to pay attention,
you see everywhere the hidden movements
that show you are not alone. . . .
Now you can hear birdsong, and soft rustlings,
a scent of some beast passing.

Find a place that feels welcoming and stand still.
Extend your awareness to every side
and sharpen your perception.
Wait for a creature to appear.
You perceive first one, then another.
Allow them to come and go.
Wait for one to appear to you several times. . . .

Then ask if it will be your ally and helper in walking in the Otherworld.
If it agrees, ask what you should call it. . . .
What would it like you to do for it?
What will it do for you?
Wander together, enjoy each other's company. . . .

It is time now for you and your new friend to part.
You must return to the world of humankind.

Say good-bye, knowing that you will meet again.
Now turn, seeking the sacred center. . . .

The Tree grows larger as you approach it,
it is your center, the center of all worlds.
From here you can see the path
that leads to the Wood Between the Worlds.
Follow that path,
let the green shadows enfold you.
Swiftly and easily, move up the trail
through the tunnel of trees.
Now the trees are farther apart,
you can see the sky above you.
Soon they dwindle to bushes that brush your garments.
(If you are drumming, beat four times quickly and then very rapidly to signal return.)

The gate to the Place You Know is before you.
Pass through and sink down upon the familiar ground.
Now the earth becomes the floor,
the chair supports you.
The air of this room brushes your skin.
Breathe in and out, and in and out again,
sigh and stretch, come into your body again.
Open your eyes.
You have returned.

Exercise 34. Journey to Faerie

Faerie is the best-known term for the Celtic Otherworld and its inhabitants. It may be said to lie across the world we know like a crumpled blanket; where the folds touch, it is very near. According to tradition, we can enter Faerie through places of power like mounds and caverns, from stone circles and the tops of hallowed hills, and from enchanted forests. Sometimes its creatures come through these doorways in the other direction and invade the fields we know. The Celtic clans, like those of the Germanic peoples, originally had their own totems, and the names of animals are often elements in human names. All of the animals of Northern Europe can be found in Faerie, along with a few imports from other worlds—lions and creatures native to the Otherworld like dragons and unicorns.

To learn more about the Celtic Otherworld, read widely in the old literature—Irish and Welsh mythology, especially the stories about Tuan and Taliesin, the *Mabinogion*, and Arthurian romances. I highly recommend any of the books written by Caitlin and John Matthews. R. J. Stewart's books on this tradition are also extremely valuable.

Now let's journey to Faerie.

Sink down now and be at ease.
Let the solid earth support you, each muscle relaxes.
Breathe in . . . (4-5 beats), and out . . . (4-5 beats). . . .
In . . . and out again. . . .
Here in our circle/this place, you are secure.
All the sounds you hear outside
make it easier to look within.

See now in your mind's eye a place outdoors that you know well.
Look at the ground beneath your feet,
feel its texture, observe the plants that grow there,
note their feel and smell.
Feel the air on your skin,
listen to all the night sounds.

Now, as you look around, you see a path leading away—
follow it.

The path leads through a tangle of leaf and branch.
The leaves are shiny, with brown nuts that you recognize as those of the hazel.
You hear the sound of running water,
from beneath the roots of the hazel a spring is welling,
spilling over in a small stream that trickles merrily downhill.

As you follow it, the forest grows more dense.
Rustlings in the undergrowth and fluttering in the branches
tell you that you are not alone.
But you can see nothing.
You move carefully through the green shadow
until you come to a grassy clearing in the center of the forest.

In the center of the clearing stands a mighty figure,
in form like a man, but a very strange one,
for as you draw closer you can see that the giant
has only one leg to stand on, as thick and gnarled as a tree trunk,
and in the middle of his forehead, a single eye.
His hair is dark and shaggy, his face obscured by a black bush of beard,
and dark hair furs most of his body as well.
He has two arms though, and in his strong hands he holds a club of iron.

"I am the Warden of the Wood," he says.
"The Carl who keeps all creatures.
Power over all the animals of the forest is mine. . . .
Who are you, and what are you seeking?
Why are you seeking an animal ally?"
Choose your words carefully,
for only truth may be spoken here.

When you have given your answer, the giant nods.
Then he strikes the green turf with his club–
the blades of grass bend and leaves whisper in the trees.
"I grant you the freedom of the forest," the Warden tells you.
"One of my beasts will choose you for its own."

You salute the Giant and move off in whatever direction attracts you.

Note the landmarks so that you will know how to return.
But as you gaze around you,

look also for movement.
Once you begin to pay attention,
you see everywhere the hidden movements
that show you are not alone.
Now you can hear birdsong, and soft rustlings,
a scent of some beast passing.

Find a place that feels welcoming and stand still.
Extend your awareness to every side
and sharpen your perception.
Wait for a creature to appear.
You perceive first one, then another.
Allow them to come and go.
Wait for one to appear to you several times. . . .

Then ask if it will be your ally and helper.
If it agrees, ask what you should call it. . . .
What would it like you to do for it?
What will it do for you?
Wander together, enjoy each other's company. . . .

It is time now for you and your new friend to part.
You must return to the world of humankind.
Say good-bye, knowing that you will meet again.
Now turn, seeking the sacred center. . . .

Your steps lead you back to the clearing in the center of the forest.
The Warden is still there, but now he is guarded
by a boar, a bull, a bear, and a lion.
They look up as you pass, and you bow in homage once more.

Before you the shining stream is flowing.
Follow it upward through the forest,
remembering all that you need to know.
Follow it to the hazel thicket and push through the branches.

The gate to the Place You Know is before you.
Pass through and sink down upon the familiar ground.
Now the earth becomes the floor,
the chair supports you.
The air of this room brushes your skin.
Breathe in and out, and in and out again,
sigh and stretch, come into your body again.
Open your eyes.
You have returned.

Exercise 35. Journey to Arcadia

The district in Greece called Arcadia was believed to be the favorite haunt of Artemis and her maidens, who bathed in its springs and hunted its forests. Over time, it became mythologized as the essence of the unspoiled natural world, where nymphs and shepherds lived in innocent harmony. The pastoral poetry of the Classical period paints a refined and sometimes sentimental picture of the natural world, but traces of an older and more robust tradition are found in the epics and the tragedies. When Pan played his pipes or the Bacchantes roamed, the wilderness could be a place of terror as well as of magic.

Today, Artemis is best known as a Moon goddess, but her original identity was as a goddess of nature. She is probably identified with the archetypal figure of the Lady of the Beasts. Thus, her realm is a logical place in which to seek an ally. The animals found in Arcadia are those of the Mediterranean world, including some imported from Africa, as well as the magical creatures of Classical mythology. Let's begin.

Sink down now and be at ease.
Let the solid earth support you, each muscle relaxes.
Breathe in . . . (4–5 beats), and out . . . (4–5 beats). . . .
In . . . and out again. . . .
Here in our circle/this place, you are secure.
All the sounds you hear outside
make it easier to look within.

See now in your mind's eye a place outdoors that you know well.
Look at the ground beneath your feet,
feel its texture, observe the plants that grow there,
note their feel and smell.
Feel the air on your skin,
listen to all the night sounds.

Now, as you look around, you see a path leading away–
follow it.

You move along through bushes that cluster thickly.
The scent of artemisia, released by the warm sunshine,
lies heavy on the air.
The path leads downward, worn into sandy stone.
Through the brush you glimpse slopes and meadows
and the blue gleam of the sea.
You can hear the hum of bees, and as you continue, something else–
a thin and distant piping–
it makes you shiver, and yet it draws you.

Now the ground grows more level.
You find yourself wandering through meadows
where crimson poppies nod in the grass.
Occasional oak trees grow, shading the ground,
and scattered groves of laurel, or cyprus, or southern pine
fill the air with spicy fragrance.
The piping has gotten louder.
You pass a slope where the dark leaves of the acanthus curl thickly,
shining in the sun,
and suddenly the piper is before you,
crouched on an outcrop of stone.

You stop, staring at the stubby horns that jut through his brown curls,

at the goat-feet, and the shaggy pelt that covers his thighs.
His yellow goat-eyes gleam as he smiles.

"Aren't you afraid?" he asks. "I am the Great God Pan. . . ."

Think about that–perhaps you should be–
mortals cannot wander without protection in the Otherworld.
Tell Pan that you need a guide and ally–
ask if he will help you to find one. . . .

If you speak boldly, he will laugh.
"Go where you will," he says then.
"But if you hear the splash of water and women laughing,
stay well away, lest you see what you should not!" He laughs once more.

Salute him and choose a direction.
As you move away, the piping grows fainter.

Note the landmarks so that you will know how to return.
But as you gaze around you,
look also for movement.
Once you begin to pay attention,
you see everywhere the hidden movements
that show you are not alone.
Now you can hear birdsong, and soft rustlings,
a scent of some beast passing.

Find a place that feels welcoming and stand still.
Extend your awareness to every side
and sharpen your perception.
Wait for a creature to appear.
You perceive first one, then another.
Allow them to come and go.
Wait for one to appear to you several times. . . .

Then ask if it will be your ally and helper in walking in the Otherworld.
If it agrees, ask what you should call it. . . .

What would it like you to do for it?
What will it do for you?
Wander together, enjoy each other's company. . . .

It is time now for you and your new friend to part.
You must return to the world of humankind.
Say good-bye, knowing that you will meet again.
Now turn, seeking the sacred center. . . .

Listen for the sound of Pan's piping–
it will guide you to the meadowland
and the path that winds upward across the hill.
Pass the oak trees and the pine groves,
follow the scent of artemisia.
Make your way through the bushes,
heading home.

The gate to the Place You Know is before you.
Pass through and sink down upon the familiar ground.
Now the earth becomes the floor,
the chair supports you.
The air of this room brushes your skin.
Breathe in and out, and in and out again,
sigh and stretch, come into your body again.
Open your eyes.
You have returned.

Bibliography

American Psychiatric Association. *Diagnostic and Statistical Manual of Mental Disorders IV* (4th edition). Arlington, VA: American Psychiatric Publishing, 1994.

Bandler, Richard, and John Grinder. *Frogs into Princes.* Boulder, CO: Real People Press, 1979.

Becker, Robert, and Gary Selden. *The Body Electric: Electromagnetism and the Foundation of Life.* New York: Harper, 1998.

Bharati, Agehananda. *The Light at the Center.* Santa Barbara, CA: Ross-Erickson, 1982.

Biello, David. "Searching for God in the Brain." *Scientific American Mind*, October/November 2007.

Blake, William. "Auguries of Innocence." In *The Oxford Book of English Mystical Verse*, #60, edited by Nicholson & Lee. Oxford: The Clarendon Press, 1917.

Block, Ned. "Philosophical Issues about Consciousness." In *The Encyclopedia of Cognitive Science.* Basingstoke, Hampshire, UK: Nature Publishing Group, 2003.

Bonewits, Isaac. *www.neopagan.net/Pagan_Glossary.html*

Booss, Claire, ed. *Scandinavian Folk & Fairy Tales.* New York: Avenel Books, 1984.

Brown, Joseph Epes. *Animals of the Soul.* New York: Elements Books, 1997.

Brown, Tom Jr. *The Tracker.* New York: Berkley Books, 1979.

Budapest, Zsuzsanna E. *The Grandmother of Time.* San Francisco: Harper & Row, 1989.

Bunyan, John. *Pilgrim's Progress. www.iclnet.org/pub/resources/text/*

Butler, W. E. *Apprenticed to Magic.* London: Aquarian Press, 1962.

——. *Magic, Its Ritual, Power and Purpose.* London: Aquarian Press, 1952.

——. *The Magician, His Training and Work.* London: Aquarian Press, 1959.

Byock, Jesse, trans. *The Saga of Hrolf Kraki.* New York: Penguin, 1999.

Campbell, Joseph. *Masks of God IV: Creative Mythology.* New York: Peguin, 1991.

——. *The Way of the Animal Powers.* New York: Harper & Row, 1988.

Campbell, Terence. *Beware the Talking Cure.* El Segundo, CA: Upton Books, 1994.

Chan, Wing-Tsit. *The Way of Lao Tzu.* Indianapolis, IN: Bobbs-Merrill, 1963.

Chaucer, Geoffrey. *Chaucer's Canterbury Tales.* N.Y.: Bantam, 1964.

Crowley, Aleister. *Magick in Theory and Practice.* New York: Castle Books, undated.

Daniélou, Alain. *The Gods of India.* New York: Inner Traditions International, 1985.

Dante Alighieri. *La Divina Commedia, Purgatorio.* Translated by Henry Wadsworth Longfellow. *The Divine Comedy Text Online, http://italian.about.com/library/anthology/dante/blpurgatorio030.htm*

Deren, Maya. *Divine Horsemen.* Kingston, N.Y.: Documentext, McPherson & Co., 1953, 1970.

Dilts, Robert. "Fourth Position." Article of the Month Page, 1998, *www.nlpu.com/Articles/artic21.htm.*

Elgin, Suzette Haden. *The Science Fiction Poetry Handbook*. Carbondale, IL: Science Fiction Poetry Association (also available online via *www.sfpoetry.com/sfpoetryhandbook.html*).
Eliade, Mircea. *Shamanism*. Bollingen Series LXXVI, New York: Bollingen Foundation, 1964.
Fielding, Charles, and Carr Collins. *The Story of Dion Fortune*. York Beach, ME: Star & Cross (Samuel Weiser, Inc.), 1985.
Fortune, Dion. *Applied Magic*. London: Aquarian Press, 1962.
——. *Aspects of Occultism*. London: Aquarian Press, 1962.
——. *The Esoteric Orders and their Work*. St. Paul: Llewellyn Publications, 1962.
——. *Sane Occultism*. Wellingborough, Northamptonshire, UK: Aquarian Press, 1967.
——. *Spiritualism in the Light of Occult Science*. London: Paternoster House, 1931.
Fries, Jan. *Seidways*. Oxford: Mandrake of Oxford, 1996.
Gardner, Howard. *Frames of Mind: The Theory of Multiple Intelligences*. New York: Basic Books, 1983; 1993.
Garrett, Eileen. *Telepathy: In Search of a Lost Faculty*. New York: Creative Age Press, 1945.
Godwin, Joscelyn. *Music, Mysticism, and Magic*. New York: Arkana, 1986.
Greeley, Andrew. *Patience of a Saint*. New York: Warner Books, 1987.
Greer, John Michael. *A World Full of Gods*. Tucson: ADF Publishing, 2005.
Grof, Stanislav and Christina, eds. *Spiritual Emergency: When Personal Transformation Becomes a Crisis*. Los Angeles: Tarcher, 1989.
Harner, Michael. *The Way of the Shaman*. New York: Harper, 1990.
Harrow, Judy. *Spiritual Mentoring*. Toronto, CA: ECW Press, 2002.
Heinrich, Bernd. *The Mind of the Raven*. New York: Harper Perennial, 2000.
——. *Ravens in Winter*. New York: Vintage, 1991.
Hoyt, Sarah F. "Etymology of Religion." *Journal of the American Oriental Society*, vol. 32:2, 1912.

Ingerman, Sandra. *Soul Retrieval.* San Francisco: HarperSanFrancisco, 1991.

Iwa-pele, Awo Fá'lokun Fatunmbi. *Ifá Quest.* N.Y.: Original Publications, 1991.

James, William. *The Varieties of Religious Experience.* New York: New American Library, 1958.

Jung, Carl J. *The Archetypes and the Collective Unconscious.* Princeton: Princeton University Press, 1959.

Karlsdottir, Alice. "Ritual, Religion and Theater." In *Our Troth II.* Charleston, SC: Booksurge, 2007.

Kesey, Ken. *Sometimes A Great Notion.* New York: Bantam Books, 1965.

King, Francis, ed. *Astral Projection, Ritual Magic, and Alchemy.* Rochester, VT: Destiny Books, 1987.

Kipling, Rudyard, *Kim. www.bibliomania.com*, ch. 9.

Kornfield, Jack. *After the Ecstasy, the Laundry.* New York: Bantam, 2000.

Kvideland, Reimund, and Henning K. Sehmsdorff. *Scandinavian Folk Belief and Legend.* Minneapolis, MN: University of Minnesota Press, 1988.

Laing, R. D. *The Politics of Experience and the Bird of Paradise.* New York: Penguin Books, 1990.

Landau, Diana, ed. *Wolf: Spirit of the Wild.* New York: Sterling, 1993.

Lau, D.C. *Tao Te Ching.* New York: Penguin Books, 1963, rev. ed. (with Mawang Dui texts).

Laurie, Erynn. *Ogam, Weaving Word Wisdom.* Stafford, UK: Megalithica Books, 2007.

LeGuin, Ursula K. *A Wizard of Earthsea.* New York: Parnassus Press, 1968.

Lessing, Doris. *A Briefing for a Descent into Hell.* New York: Vintage, 1981.

Lewis, C. S. *The Complete Chronicles of Narnia.* New York: HarperCollins, 1998.

——. *The Four Loves.* New York: Harcourt Brace, 1960.

——. "On Stories." In *Of Other Worlds.* New York: Harcourt, 1966.

Lohr, Bethany A., and Forrest Scogin. "Effects of Self-Administered Visuo-Motor Behavioral Rehearsal on Sport Performance of Collegiate Athletes." *Journal of Sport Behavior*, vol. 21, 1998.

Lopez, Barry. *Of Wolves and Men*. New York: Scribner, 1979.

McKinnell, John, trans. *Viga-Glum's Saga, with the Tales of Ogmund Bash and Thorvald Chatterbox*. Canongate, Edinburgh: Williams and Norgate, 1972.

Mech, L. David. *The Wolf: Ecology and Behavior of an Endangered Species*. Minneapolis, MN: University of Minnesota Press, 1981.

Mitchell, Stephen. "Einstein, Albert." In *The Enlightened Mind*. New York: Harper Collins, 1991.

Moore, Sonia. *The Stanislavski System: The Professional Training of an Actor Digested from the teachings of Konstantin S. Stanislavsky*. New York: Viking Press, 1965.

Nelson, Richard K. *Make Prayers to the Raven*. Chicago: University of Chicago Press, 1986.

Netter, Frank. *Atlas of Human Anatomy*. New York: Saunders, 2006.

Norris, Patricia, Ph.D. "Dynamics of Visualization and Imagery in Therapy." In *Why Me? Learning to Harness the Healing Power of the Human Spirit*. Walpole, NH: Stillpoint Publishing 1985. Excerpted on: *www.healthy.net/scr/Article.asp?Id=392&xcntr=2*.

Palsson, Hermann, and Paul Edwards, trans. *Eyrbyggja Saga*. London: Penguin Books, 1989.

Perrine, Laurence, and Thomas R. Arp. *Sound and Sense*. New York: Harcourt, 1991.

Post, J. B. *An Atlas of Fantasy*. Baltimore, MD: Mirage Press, 1973.

Raine, Kathleen, and George Mills Harper, eds. *Thomas Taylor the Platonist*. Princeton: Princeton University Press, 1969.

Sacks, Oliver. *Musicophilia, Tales of Music and the Brain*. New York: Alfred A. Knopf, 2007.

Silliker, Bill. *Giants of the Northern Forest*. Somerville, MA: Firefly Press, 2005.

Simonton, Carl, and Stephanie. *Getting Well Again: A Step-by-Step Self-Help Guide to Overcoming Cancer for Patients and their Families*. New York: Bantam Books, 1992.

Stevenson, Robert Louis. "El Dorado." In *Virginibus Puerisque.* In the *Random House Dictionary of Popular Proverbs & Sayings.* (1996) by Gregory Titelman. New York: Random House, 1996.

Storms, G. *Anglo Saxon Magic.* New York: Gordon Press, (1948), 1974.

Sturlason, Snorre. *Heimskringla (The Lives of the Norse Kings).* New York: Dover, 1990. (Includes "Ynglingasaga" and the "Olaf Trygvason saga.")

Tart, Charles T., ed. *Altered States of Consciousness*, 3rd edition. San Francisco: Harper, 1990.

——. *Body, Mind, Spirit.* Charlottesville, VA: Hampton Roads, 1997.

Thorsson, Edred. *Futhark.* York Beach, ME: Weiser Books, 1984.

Tolkien, J. R. R. *The Fellowship of the Ring.* New York: Houghton-Mifflin, 1956.

——. "On Fairy Stories." In *The Tolkien Reader.* New York: Del Rey, 1986.

Underhill, Evelyn. *Mysticism.* New York: E. P.Dutton, (1911) 1961.

Vinge, Vernor. *True Names: And the Opening of the Cyberspace Frontier.* New York: Tor, 2001.

Williams, Charles. *Descent into Hell.* London: Faber & Faber, 1961.

——. *Outlines of Romantic Theology.* Berkeley, CA: Apocryphile Press, 2005.

Zimmer, Paul Edwin. "The Womb in the Head." In *Wine of Kvasir.* Privately printed, 1979.

About the Author

Photo by Shirine Morton © 2007

Diana L. Paxson is the author of twenty-seven novels, including the bestselling Avalon series and several works of spiritual nonfiction, including *Taking Up the Runes*. She has been a practicing priestess for more than twenty-five years and is well known as a spiritual leader and teacher who has served as leader of the Covenant of the Goddess and the Troth. She lectures and conducts workshops in North America and Europe. She lives in Berkeley, CA.

To Our Readers

Weiser Books, an imprint of Red Wheel/Weiser, publishes books across the entire spectrum of occult and esoteric subjects. Our mission is to publish quality books that will make a difference in people's lives without advocating any one particular path or field of study. We value the integrity, originality, and depth of knowledge of our authors.

Our readers are our most important resource, and we appreciate your input, suggestions, and ideas about what you would like to see published. Please feel free to contact us, to request our latest book catalog, or to be added to our mailing list.

Red Wheel/Weiser, LLC
665 Third Street, Suite 400
San Francisco, CA 94107
www.redwheelweiser.com